Empire, Racism and Genocide

Robert Fantina

Empire, Racism and Genocide

A HISTORY OF U.S. FOREIGN POLICY

2013

Red Pill Press

Contents

For Edwina and Travis.

Introduction

Despite what is taught in public schools across the nation, the U.S. is not unique in the road it took to become a world power. The happy thought of the Founding Fathers, finding themselves in an unpopulated land, rich in natural resources, and only needing to shed the oppression of Britain in order to fulfill the Manifest Destiny of the United States, is similar to the myths of Santa Claus and the tooth fairy. Pleasant, whimsical, but void of any truth.

Yet unlike other fairy tales, this one hides the horrendous crimes of murder, land theft and blatant and shocking disregard for human rights, all in the greedy pursuit of wealth and power. From the extermination of the 'Indians,' natives who'd lived on the North American continent since time immemorial, through the barbaric murders of Filipinos defending their nation from U.S. invasion, to the killing of 'insurgents' (Iraqi freedom fighters), the U.S., often under the guise of freeing an oppressed people, has caused those very people far more suffering than the governments they were supposedly being freed from.

The irony of an imperial U.S.A. is striking:

> [H]ere is a government created in the fires of bourgeois-democratic revolution against colonialism, and a government whose success in revolution served as an inspiration for scores of similar efforts in many parts of the world in subsequent years; at the same time, this very government, as the U.S. economy became monopoly capitalist – towards the close of the 19th century – itself entered upon a career of colonialism and in our own day stands as the main bastion of what still remains of colonialism.

> The anti-colonialist nature of U.S. beginnings and the inspirational character of the American Revolution have been among the elements helping the American ruling class obscure the pro-colonial and therefore anti-popular essence of its foreign policy.[1]

In the early part of the twenty-first century, the myth of a freedom-loving people, spreading American-style democracy everywhere, began to be cracked. The U.S. invaded the sovereign nation of Iraq in March of 2003, in order, the world was told by U.S. President George W. Bush, to protect the U.S. from the imminent threat that Iraq posed to the U.S. With these lofty and frightening ideas, Congress, always wanting to appear strong against whatever current bugaboo 'threatened' the U.S. (e.g. communism in the 1950s; terrorism in the early 2000s), granted the president broad powers to wage war, powers he wasted no time in exercising. Although the war ravaged Iraq; killed hundreds of thousands of its citizens and thousands of U.S. soldiers; displaced millions of Iraqis and left at least hundreds of thousands of them homeless, many languishing in refugee camps in neighboring countries, no weapons of mass destruction, believed by many Americans, based on the statements of Mr. Bush and his cohorts, to be aimed at the living rooms of middle America, were found. In his memoir, published in 2008, Republican economist Alan Greenspan, who'd served as chairman of the U.S. Federal Reserve for nearly 20 years, said this about the Iraq war: "I am saddened that it is politically inconvenient to acknowledge what everyone knows: the Iraq war is largely about oil."[2]

Like that war, most, if not all, of the U.S.'s wars have had more to do with the accumulation of wealth and the increase of power than forcing U.S.-style democracy on foreign nations, whether they wanted it or not. Even during World War II, which established the U.S. as an undisputed world power, and defeated the horrific Hitler

---

[1] Aptheker 1962, p. 97.
[2] Greenspan 2008, p. 463.

regime, the U.S. granted special permission for some U.S. companies to deal with the Nazi regime. Despite Hitler's savagely cruel trek across Europe, the idea of making a buck from his activities was too enticing for the U.S. to avoid.

An investigation of the nation's past wars shows stark similarities to those it currently wages. Certainly, the means of invading a nation, overthrowing its government and killing its citizens has been made far more effective with modern weaponry. President James Madison may have been happy to have had heat-seeking missiles when he invaded Canada, but he had to manage with horses. But the reasons for the wars have changed little, and the lies that are used to convince either the populace or Congress, or both, to invade sovereign nations, are alarmingly similar.

From the War of 1812, where Canada was the target, through World War I, the 'war to make the world safe for democracy,' all the way to Iraq, the war to rid that nation of weapons of mass destruction that it did not have, the underlying goal has always been empire. In some ways it is subtle: the U.S. fought in Korea ostensibly to prevent a takeover of that nation by Chinese Communists, but 60 years later the U.S. maintains a strong military presence in that nation, again ostensibly for its own protection. U.S. military bases span the globe, 'protecting' those nations from their enemies, real or imagined, and also 'protecting' the U.S. from its self-defined enemies. This defining of enemies is vital for the government to gain the support of the citizens to fight its wars, thus fueling the continuation and expansion of what President Dwight D. Eisenhower called the military-industrial complex. And once a nation is invaded, the disillusionment of the citizens of the U.S. does nothing to bring about the war's end; starting a war is far easier for the U.S. than ending one.

The country that proudly proclaims its own success in shedding the yoke of imperialism does not hesitate to exploit, or even create, opportunities to build empire. In the early nineteenth century, when Britain and France were embroiled in war, the U.S. found it convenient to invade Canada. Nearly 200 years later, after the terrorist attacks on the U.S. of September 11, 2001, the nation's leaders fanned the fears of a frightened populace to inflame hatred for, and justify an invasion of, an oil-rich nation that was in no way associated with those attacks.

Like most nations, the U.S. writes its own history to serve its own purposes. How willing, one might ask, would young men and women be to go to Iraq to fight and die for the benefit of U.S. oil company profits? How willing, generations ago, would they have been to leave their homes to fight in the Philippines, to help ensure profitable trade routes between the U.S. and China? Will they be willing, in the near future, to fight in Iran, so that U.S. politicians' reelection campaigns can continue to receive the generous largess of AIPAC (American Israel Public Affairs Committee)?

It is beyond the scope of this work to study over 200 years of foreign policy in great detail; such a work would require volumes. But there have been similar, over-arching policies that are manifested in very different foreign-policy decisions. All of them have as their foundation either increased wealth, increased power, or both.

This book is divided into three distinct sections (shown below), although there is much overlap between them. Events and policies from one section do not cease with the start of the one following. The divisions are created simply to show the general, imperialist evolution of the U.S.; there has been little if any significant change in motives, although increasing power has brought increased suffering at the hands of the U.S. There may be information from one section included in one following it, when those policies accompany ones reflecting the new period.

Each chapter includes information about the U.S. economic considerations for the war; the conditions in the U.S. that enabled the government to wage war; the reasons each war was, at least initially, favored by the citizenry, and the blatant disregard for the freedom, dignity and basic human rights of the U.S.'s self-identified 'enemies' and, in many cases, its own citizens.

- Period 1: 1750–1898. Manifest Destiny

- Period 2: 1899–1953. A New World Power

- Period 3: 1954–Present. Fighting Invented Enemies

The author recognizes that the material in this book brings into question some of the United States' most cherished principles, and sheds a less-than-flattering light on them. Yet the facts speak for themselves: the U.S. is, and always has been, an imperial nation, far less concerned about human rights than corporate profits; less interested in peace than in power.

Part I.

1750–1898: Manifest Destiny

Chapter 1.

Native Americans

While the treatment of Native Americans is not generally viewed as U.S. 'foreign policy,' it must be remembered that the many tribes living in what eventually became the United States were independent nations when the first explorers reached the North American continent, and remained so until conquered by the U.S.

A complete study of U.S. genocidal practices against the Native Americans would require volumes; no effort is made in this book to accomplish that task. Oppression of the peoples once known as 'Indians' began centuries before the American Revolution and has continued to the present day. This chapter provides an overview of the unspeakable cruelties and policies against Native Americans that were perpetrated by the U.S. government in order to expand its territories into Native lands. For information regarding continued racism and oppression against these peoples, please refer to any of the many writings easily available on this topic.

When Christopher Columbus, attempting to find a new route to India, stumbled upon the North American Continent, he found a population of people that "were numerous and magnificently diverse,"[1] and most importantly, significantly different from the Europeans.

Prior to the explorations of Columbus in 1492, the concept of ownership of private property did not exist among Native peoples: "'The earth is like fire and water that cannot be sold' said the Omahas.

---

[1]Prucha 1986, p. 1.

..."[2] The Shawnee chief Tecumseh said it this way: "Sell land! As well sell air and water. The Great Spirit gave them in common to all."[3] This concept, though deeply embedded in Native culture, was completely alien to white settlers.

For centuries, the Natives had lived in mutual peace and understanding. They protected their territories, expelling and even killing those who threatened tribal lands, but within individual tribes, no one 'owned' the land. It was there for anyone for hunting, fishing or whatever purposes were required for subsistence. "Anyone in the tribe, for example, could borrow without permission the belongings of another – and return them without thanks. There were no debtors or creditors where private property and money were absent. William Penn wrote: 'Give them a fine gun, coat or any other thing, it may pass twenty hands before it sticks. ... Wealth circulateth like the blood, all parts partake, and ... none shall want what another hath."[4]

Columbus's exploration was followed by explorers of other European nations, all of whom marveled at the Natives of this New World. Each of these groups carefully studied every aspect of Native life. The facts that they assembled, however, were heavily influenced by their one prejudices and deeply held beliefs. Gradually, two very contradictory impressions were somewhat firmly established:

> The first was that of the 'noble savage,' natural man living without technology and elaborate societal structures. Naked without shame, unconcerned about private ownership and the accumulation of material wealth but sharing all things unselfishly, and free from the problems of government, the Indian represented an idyllic state from which the European had strayed or fallen. Dwelling in an earthly paradise, the

---

[2]http://www.marxists.org/archive/lafargue/1890/property/2-prim-comm.html. Accessed on January 22, 2013.

[3]Warde 1949 [January].

[4]Oplinger and Halma 2006, p. 234.

Indians were a living example of a golden age, long past in European history but now suddenly thrust again upon the world's consciousness. This good Indian welcomed the European invaders and treated them courteously and generously. He was handsome in appearance, dignified in manner, and brave in combat, and in all he exhibited a primitivism that had great appeal to many Europeans.

The second pattern was that of the 'ignoble savage,' treacherous, cruel, perverse, and in many ways approaching the brute beasts with whom he shared the wilderness. In this view, incessant warfare and cruelty to captives marked the Indians. Ritual cannibalism and human sacrifice were the ultimate abominations; but countless descriptions of Indian life noted the squalor, the filth, the indolence, the lack of discipline, the thievery, and the hard lot accorded Indian women. Not a few Englishmen saw the Indians with their superstitions and inhuman practices as literally children of the Devil.[5]

Note that each impression still regulated the Native Americans to 'savage' status.

Sadly, the concept of the 'noble savage' soon gave way to a hybrid of 'ignoble' and simply 'backward.' With the lush forests and rich lands promising seemingly unlimited natural resources, the white settlers simply had no patience for such Native beliefs as shared ownership and use of land. This New World represented the opportunity for greatly increased commerce, and the 'bottom line,' then as now, was king.

Starting with Columbus's first foray into the New World, Native culture was threatened. There was some peace as the Natives assisted the pilgrims in cultivating small areas of land, but they were never seen as better than savages. With the birth of the U.S., these 'savages' became far more tragic victims than ever before.

---

[5]Prucha 1986, p. 2.

Despite the efforts of some to convert the Natives to Christianity, a program of removal from lands, rather than conversion and assimilation, was enacted. The diseases that Europeans brought, for which the Natives had no immunity, devastated populations, and the white settlers were only too happy to take over the cleared fields that now had no Native peoples to farm them. In a strange twist, they often considered this 'good fortune' to be a blessing from God.

Not all the future revolutionaries held the 'Indians' in such disdain. Benjamin Franklin was one exception.

> Beginning in 1736, Franklin published Indian treaty accounts on a regular basis until the early 1760s, when his defense of Indians under assault by frontier settlers at Lancaster cost him his seat in the Pennsylvania Assembly. In 'Narrative of the Late Massacres in Lancaster County' (1763), Franklin condemned the massacre of Christianized Conestoga Indians by a mob from Paxton, Pennsylvania. He called these vigilantes 'Christian white savages.' He also argued that liquor and disease, brought on by increasing contact with non-Indians, would cause the Indians' decline in North America. When the Paxton Boys marched on Philadelphia to exterminate the city's Indians in February 1764, Franklin led a delegation to the Indian camp and counseled peace.[6]

The massacre of the Conestoga Indians herein referred to occurred over a two-day period, when over 50 men, referred to as 'The Paxton boys,' attacked and killed more than 20 Conestoga Indians, who had been living for years in peaceful coexistence with the settlers. On the first night they killed six people and burned their cabins; on the second, they killed and scalped six adults and eight children.

In 1775, the Continental Congress established the first federal 'Indian' policy. Some highlights of this are as follows:

> Whereas by the ninth of the Articles of Confederation, it is among other things declared, that 'the United States in

---

[6] Johansen 1998, p. 102.

Congress assembled have the sole and exclusive right and power of regulating the trade, and managing all affairs with the Indians, not members of any of the states, provided that the legislative right of any State, within its own limits, be not infringed or violated.'

The Federal government, not states, would 'manage all affairs' with the Indians.

That it is represented, and the committee believe with truth, that although the hostile tribes of Indians in the northern and middle departments, are seriously disposed to a pacification, yet they are not in a temper to relinquish their territorial claims, without further struggles."

There is an assumption that the 'territorial claims' of the Indians are to be surrendered. If that involves 'further struggles,' so be it.

Even if all the northern and western tribes of Indians inhabiting the territories of the United States could be totally expelled, the policy of reducing them to such an extremity is deemed to be questionable; for in such an event it is obvious that they would find a welcome reception from the British government in Canada, which by so great an accession of strength would become formidable in case of any future rupture, and in peace, by keeping alive the resentment of the Indians for the loss of their country, would secure to its own subjects the entire benefit of the fur trade.

The writers recognized that the Indians have lost their country, but the idea of total expulsion is only considered in the light of how it might compromise the U.S.'s foreign policy goals, i.e. hostilities with Britain in Canada and, notably, the profitable fur trade.

That although motives of policy as well as clemency ought to incline Congress to listen to the prayers of the hostile Indians for peace, yet in the opinion of the committee it is just and necessary that lines of property should be ascertained and established between the United States and them, which will be convenient to the respective tribes, and commensurate to the public wants, because the faith of the United States stands pledged to grant portions of the uncultivated lands as a bounty to their army, and in reward of their courage and fidelity, and the public finances do not admit of any considerable expenditure to extinguish the Indian claims upon such lands; because it is become necessary, by the increase of domestic population and emigrations from abroad, to make speedy provision for extending the settlement of the territories of the United States.[7]

The 'uncultivated lands' herein referred to include both lands the Natives used for farming, and wooded land used for hunting. The government had promised lands to members of the army, and stealing that land from the Indians was viewed as completely acceptable.

With the success of the American Revolution, things became worse for the Native Americans, and the downward spiral of their civilization, which began when the first white settlers set foot on the continent, accelerated. Following the end of the war, treaties were created, designating areas of land for the Native Americans, who were treated as a conquered people.

Yet regardless of treaties, more and more hostile settlers streamed into Native territory, taking their land, introducing an agricultural economy that altered the environment on which the Natives relied. Forests were cut to make farms, destroying the homes of the wild game, the major food source for the Natives. The environment the Natives had lived within for generations untold was quickly disappearing.

Possibly because of this constant violation of treaties, Congress reaffirmed the treaties in the Northwest Ordinance of July 13, 1787:

---

[7]Prucha 1975, p. 4.

The utmost good faith shall always be observed towards the Indians, their lands and property shall never be taken from them without their consent; and in their property, rights and liberty, they shall never be invaded or disturbed, unless in just and lawful wars authorised by Congress; but laws founded in justice and humanity shall from time to time be made, for preventing wrongs being done to them, and for preserving peace and friendship with them.[8]

But these statements had little effect.

General Henry Knox, secretary of war under the Confederation, reported to Congress in July 1788 the unprovoked and direct outrages against Cherokee Indians by inhabitants on the frontier of North Carolina in open violation of the Treaty of Hopewell. The outrages were of such extent, Knox declared, 'as to amount to an actual although informal war of the said white inhabitants against the said Cherokees.' The action he blamed on the 'avaricious desire of obtaining the fertile lands possessed by said Indians of which and particularly of their ancient town of Chota they are exceedingly tenacious,' and he urged Congress to take action to uphold the treaty provisions and thus the reputation and dignity of the Union.[9]

Continual skirmishes and tensions between the Native Americans and white settlers did not lessen. Thomas Jefferson wanted to assimilate them into white society, but this was not happening; the government apparently did not understand why separate nations and cultures were not willing to give up their sacred, ancient traditions to fit into a mold that had no attraction for them.

Several tribes formed a confederacy in an attempt to maintain their homelands. In 1791, when they were victorious in the battle of the Wabash, they may have believed that they had struck a blow for

---

[8]Prucha 1986, p. 8.
[9]Ibid., p. 8.

their homeland. But in the battle of Fallen Timbers, in 1794, they were decisively defeated, and the following year surrendered most of what is now Ohio to the U.S. In return they were promised that the new boundary would enable them to live independently. This commitment lasted no time; as soon as it was established it was violated, as more explorers moved into the area, with at least tacit government approval.

In 1804, the U.S. established a treaty with the Sac and Foxes, allied tribes holding lands along the Mississippi. This treaty was interpreted by the U.S. to mean that that the Indians surrendered their agricultural land in the Rock River basin and would move to the west side of the Mississippi River. The War Department claimed that chiefs from the two tribes in question were authorized to make this deal. Chief Blackhawk saw it quite differently:

> According to the version of Blackhawk, a white man had been killed by a Fox Indian and the slayer had been arrested and was imprisoned at St. Louis. The Indians had a custom by which blood guilt could be compounded by heavy payments. ... Certain chiefs went to St. Louis, sought the American commandant, and offered their remission payments for the offense of their friend. The commandant told them that what he wanted was land. They agreed to give him tracts on both sides of the Mississippi. On this composition the Indian slayer was released – and then shot dead as he left his prison.[10]

On September 30, 1809, the Treaty of Fort Wayne was signed, in which several tribal leaders sold 3,000,000 acres to the U.S. government. Tecumseh, who was not part of the treaty, demanded that it be nullified, claiming that all land was owned in common by all tribes, and therefore all tribes needed to agree to any land disposal. The governor of the Indian Territory, William Henry Harrison, who had overseen the treaty as part of U.S. territorial expansion, and

---

[10]Russell 2001, pp. 13, 14.

who had a desire to attract sufficient white settlers to qualify for statehood, was not impressed. He met with Tecumseh in the late summer of 1811, but there was no resolution from the meeting. In November, the battle of Tippecanoe occurred, causing the deaths of 62 of Harrison's forces and about 50 Natives. Harrison then ordered the Native village of Prophetstown burned, and all cooking utensils destroyed, thus depriving the Natives of the means to subsist over the winter.

Following this 'victory,' cries for war increased. The conquest of Canada, it was said, was necessary to keep any additional foreign aid from the Natives. The oppression of the Native peoples was necessary to curtail their opposition to U.S. expansionist desires. The length of an entire continent awaited; it could only be acquired by the conquest of British-owned Canada and the oppression of the Natives allied with Britain. This would have the added benefit of expanding the U.S. not only westward, but northward as well. For a nation filled with its own belief as a divinely led country, the stakes were high, and Canada and Native territory were only the beginning.

Into this mix was added the British government's alliance with most of the Native American tribes. These alliances had been established, or at least strengthened, during the American Revolution. The British wanted to establish a Native homeland within western Canada, which would be mutually beneficial: the tribes would be able to continue living as they had for generations, and the area would be easier to defend from a U.S. attack. During this time, British fur traders moved freely through Native territories, and this further helped to strengthen these alliances.

The government and people of the U.S., however, were convinced that British alliances with Native peoples were simply one more evidence of a British plot against them; they were still too close to their old colonial status to see anything but offense in the British associations with the Natives.

President James Monroe established the policy of 'Indian' removal firmly, through Andrew Jackson. In 1817, Monroe wrote Jackson, saying that "the hunter or savage state requires a greater extent of territory to sustain it, than is compatible with the progress and just claims of civilized life, and must yield to it."[11] How Mr. Monroe defined 'just claims' was not clarified.

While little was done during his term of office, or during that of his successor, John Quincy Adams, tensions remained high. With the inauguration of Andrew Jackson as president, oppression of the Native Americans greatly increased. When first addressing Congress as the new president, Mr. Jackson said, which was true, that some Native Americans had "lately attempted to erect an independent government within the limits of Georgia and Alabama."[12] He pointed out that this was in direct contradiction to the U.S. Constitution, ignoring, apparently, any consideration of the rights of the Native Americans who had lived on 'American' soil for centuries prior to the writing of that document.

In response, Congress passed legislation offering aid to the Native Americans in relocating and guaranteeing them possession of new lands. The Native Americans had no interest in relocating; they were more than content to hunt and farm on the same lands where their ancestors had done so from time immemorial. If they were to move, it would be by force.

Unfortunately, this land that was sacred to the Native Americans was coveted by the white expansionists. With the invention of the cotton gin, countless thousands of acres of land were being cultivated to grow cotton, and the land possessed by the Cherokees in Georgia was considered prime cotton-growing land. They had no choice but to surrender it.

Things were no better in other areas for the Native Americans. In 1830, President Jackson took possession of all the lands owned by the Choctaws in the state of Mississippi, providing land allotments to tribal leaders. In surrendering their land east of the Mississippi,

---

[11]Prucha 1986, p. 65.
[12]Konkle 2004, p. 73.

the Choctaws received "'in fee simple to them and their descendants, to inure to them while they shall exist as a nation and live on it' the territory that had already been marked out in the treaty of 1825."[13]

In 1831 the Chief Justice of the Supreme Court, John Marshall, attempted to further define the status of Native Americans. He took a less cruel, but certainly paternalistic view. "He declared that Indian tribes were 'domestic dependent nations' whose 'relation to the United States resembles that of a ward to his guardian'."[14]

This 'guardian–ward' relationship unfortunately resembled something Charles Dickens may have described: cruelty, abuse, betrayal and exploitation were the characteristics the 'guardian' demonstrated toward its unwilling 'ward.'

Treaties and agreements between the United States and anyone else, even its own citizens, are only viable when they suit the United States. By the 1830s, it appeared that Native American removal had come to an end, with most tribes now secure in what is now the midwestern United States, from the Red River, bordering Arkansas, north and northeast to Lake Superior. But this was not to be. Between 1845 and 1848, U.S. imperial goals added Texas, the Oregon territory and California, wherein resided more nomadic Natives, more warlike than their eastern counterparts. The Sioux, Cheyennes, Arapahos, Crows, Kiowas, Comanches and Pawnees were even less interested than the Choctaws and the Iroquois in becoming gentlemen farmers. The U.S. foresaw trains going as far west as the ocean, with farmlands opening up in unprecedented amounts. The Commissioner of Indian affairs noted this 'problem' in 1856:

> When that time arrives, and it is at our very doors, ten years, if our country is favored with peace and prosperity, will witness the most of it; where will be the habitation and what the condition of the rapidly wasting Indian tribes of the plains, the prairies, and of our new States and Territories?

---

[13]Ibid., p. 73.
[14]Boxer 2009.

> As sure as these great physical changes are impending, so
> sure will these poor denizens of the forest be blotted out
> of existence, and their dust be trampled under the foot of
> rapidly advancing civilization, unless our great nation shall
> generously determine that the necessary provision shall at
> once be made, and appropriate steps be taken to designate
> suitable tracts or reservations of land, in proper localities,
> for permanent homes for, and provide the means to colonize,
> them thereon.[15]

It was following this statement that that 'great nation' first established the policy of moving Native Americans to reservations,
generally small tracts of land carved out of the vast areas on which
these Natives and their ancestors had lived for generations.

Today, these once-proud people, descendants of men and women
who, from time immemorial, lived on and worked the land that
is now the United States, live in poverty and suffer astronomical
rates of alcoholism, drug addiction, depression and suicide. The
U.S. Bureau of Indian Affairs still regulates much of their lives,
keeping them in these conditions. Many tribes no longer exist. But
the U.S. accomplished its goal: it found and coveted a land rich in
natural resources, inhabited by other people, and so it simply lied
to, cheated and killed those people until their land was no longer
their own, but was possessed by their white conquerors. This pattern,
so successful for the U.S. in terms of Native Americans, has been
replicated repeatedly, with untold amounts of blood being spilled so
global capitalist expansion could succeed.

---

[15]Prucha 1986, p. 110.

Chapter 2.

The War of 1812

Relations between the United States and Great Britain had not improved much following the American Revolution. There was some trade between the two nations, but the U.S. felt restricted in expanding its trade routes due to Britain's war with France. This, despite the fact that U.S. trade grew dramatically in the years prior to the outbreak of the War of 1812, partly as a result of the hostilities between France and Britain.

During the years leading up to the War of 1812, the British, French and the United States passed, but usually did not enforce, a variety of laws restricting trade either with each other, or with each other's enemies. None of these laws did anything to help matters, and many of them made things worse. For example, "To strengthen the British provinces further at the expense of the United States, the British government issued an Order-in-Council in 1811 excluding American salted fish from the West Indian colonies and imposing heavy duties on other U.S. imports. This was a blow to President Madison, who had assumed that the West Indies simply could not be fed without American fish, and thus it demonstrated the weakness of his trade policies as vehicles of coercion."[1]

This may have contributed to President James Madison's fear of losing reelection. Already perceived as weak in domestic policy, but more especially in foreign affairs, the Order-in-Council only high-

---

[1] Benn 2003, p. 16.

lighted his vulnerability. What better way, one might have thought, to assert his strength in foreign affairs than by waging war?

In addition to feeling that Britain and France somehow constrained U.S. opportunities in the world market, and President Madison's need to appear strong on foreign policy, there were many other factors that contributed to the hostilities that eventually led to war. The British Royal Navy needed more manpower to staff its ships than it was able to provide; it therefore began or increased a policy of 'impressment,' by which ships from other nations were boarded and crew members from those ships forced to serve in the Royal Navy. Some men so 'impressed' served for years; authentic proof of citizenship was sufficient to get them released, but obtaining that often took years.

This issue was not quite as simple as some in the U.S. at the time may have attempted to portray it. British sailors sometimes deserted the Royal Navy and found work on U.S. ships. When British ships encountered U.S. sailing vessels, they were within their rights to board them, search for, and remove, any British deserters.

One incident that caused much anger in the U.S. concerned the U.S. frigate Chesapeake. The captain of Her Majesty's Ship Leonard demanded permission to board the Chesapeake to search for British deserters. When the captain of the Chesapeake refused, the Leonard fired on it, killing or wounding 21 U.S. soldiers. The Chesapeake quickly surrendered; the captain then boarded and found and removed four deserters from the Royal Navy.

This incident, and the policy of impressments or enforced slavery, enraged many Americans; whether the anger would have been the same had it been any other nation that kidnapped U.S. sailors, or retrieved their own, can only be speculated. The wounds from the American Revolution, less than 30 years ended, were still fresh, and the British were still seen as monsters.

Yet trade and impressment were not the only issues about which the Americans were angry.

Since before the American Revolution, the British had maintained positive relations with the Native Americans within its colonies and nurtured those relationships during the time leading up to, during and after that war. Britain felt it needed the Native Americans to assist in the defense of Canada, should the U.S. decide to invade. As a result, every problem the U.S. had with Native Americans was seen as at least supported by Britain, and at worst, spawned by that nation. From prior to the American Revolution, Native Americans had watched as their lands were stolen, the environment that they relied on for their very existence altered unrecognizably and the game animals they ate chased away. These aboriginal people were slowly and cruelly driven out of the Old Northwest (consisting today of Ohio, Michigan and Indiana), and from the late 1780s through the next decade, they battled with the U.S. settlers.

Since the British had formed alliances with many Native tribes and had provided them with weapons and other supplies during their struggles to keep their lands, U.S. citizens saw Britain as complicit in their troubles with the Natives. The 'evil' British, it seemed, were determined to crush the new nation.

America had already been forcibly removing people from lands they'd owned for generations in order to take possession of it themselves. That this removal meant the murder of men, women and children did not seem to matter much as long as those men, women and children were 'savages,' and not the refined population that came to slaughter them. The expansionist fever, quickly and firmly rooted in the national consciousness, flowered as the U.S. prepared for war with Britain.

Mr. Madison believed that the Great Lakes and the St. Lawrence system might be a lucrative trade route for American goods going to Europe. The president decided that the adjacent provinces had to be conquered. This, he felt, would enable the U.S. to dictate exactly under what terms Britain could trade in all of North America.

This expansionist philosophy, which caught the imagination of so many Americans in the early nineteenth century (and continues to seduce far too many people today), was perhaps best articulated by Congressman John Harper. Said he: "'[T]he Author of Nature' himself had 'marked our limits in the south, by the Gulf of Mexico; and on the north, by the regions of eternal frost.'"[2] It must be remembered that those southern border areas were Spanish-owned; the desired conquest of Canada to the north was only to be the beginning.

Another motivation for expansion of the U.S. remains popular in 2012: personal profit. Prominent businessman Peter B. Porter was a vocal proponent of the war and sought the conquest of Canada. Mr. Porter felt that Britain could be a trade competitor in Canada; if Canada were annexed by the U.S., that threat would be removed.

> 'Free trade and sailor's rights' was not the simple cry of justice that popular history would have us believe. It was fraught with its own ambiguities and, perhaps more importantly, it was a cry co-opted to promote belligerency by annexationists who drove much of the government's thinking.[3]

Overriding any anger about impressments or Native American hostility was the desire for territorial expansion.

> By 1800, Kentucky had a population of 221,000. By 1810 Ohio contained 230,760 people, and settlers were thrusting onward into what are now Indiana and Illinois. America was rapidly conquering the land between the Ohio and the Mississippi. So-called 'permanent' boundaries were established, separating the United States from Native lands, following Anthony Wayne's defeat of the Indians at Fallen Timbers. Yet "the 'permanent' boundaries between American and Indian that had been established at Greenville meant nothing to settlers eager for land.[4]

---

[2] G. R. Taylor 1963, p. 53.
[3] Benn 2003, p. 19.
[4] Horsman 1962, p. 158.

In November of 1811, President James Madison told Congress to prepare for war with Canada. "Much of the ensuing debate was led by the War Hawks – mainly younger men from frontier regions who saw expansion, and destruction of native resistance, as "fundamental objectives for war."[5]

Although these two specific objectives – the conquest of Canada and the neutralizing of the Native American 'threat' – were the main motivations for war, they played into other expansionist dreams. The defeat of the Native Americans and the conquest of Canada, it was believed, would help pave the way for the annexation of the Creek nation within the Mississippi Territory. Tensions at this time between the Natives and the colonists were high, and the defeat of the Natives to the north was seen as instrumental in their defeat there.

Additionally, the Spanish Territories consisting of east and west Florida were also coveted by the colonists. Already occupied by colonists, they saw the distraction of Spain's ally, Britain, by a war with the United States, as helping to achieve their expansionist goals there.

President Madison, as has been mentioned, found himself in a precarious political position. He was seen as a weak, incompetent president and felt that the decisiveness of a war would help to bolster his standing among the electorate. He was up for re-election in the fall of 1812, and there was talk within his own party, the Democratic-Republicans, of finding a challenger to him. Therefore he made the decision to convene Congress for an early session in late 1811, to begin preparations for war.

"James Madison's choice became almost a necessity. The pressure of frontier imperialism was not the only nor the most efficient cause of the War of 1812: it was, rather, the most immediate and obvious one."[6] And it appears to have served Mr. Madison's purposes: he

---

[5]Benn 2003, p. 26.
[6]Dangerfield 2008, pp. 45, 46.

was re-elected in 1812.

The War of 1812 was perhaps the first of the United States' ill-conceived wars, fought for dubious reasons, none of which can be classified as the reason for a 'just war.' And like so many of the country's later wars, the citizenry soon became disenchanted with this imperial misadventure.

The war between Britain and France ended, so Britain was then able to concentrate its military efforts against its former colony, the United States. When victory is not seen as a quick accomplishment, those who must provide the manpower and other resources soon become disillusioned. By 1814, this was becoming more and more apparent. In reference to the war, the Secretary of the Navy, William Jones, said that "our affairs are as gloomy as can well be." Yet the clarion call of freedom was still heard. One Republican newspaper encouragingly said this: "We are contending with an exasperated foe whose might and power will soon be leveled at our liberties."[7] Yet Secretary Jones's assessment may have been more accurate.

Economically, the country was also faltering: the government defaulted on the national debt in late November, 1814. The deteriorating economic conditions served to erode the country's tax base, adding to a general feeling of discontent among the populace. By this time, too, Washington, D.C., had been burned, and any visitors to the nation's capital, often visiting members of Congress, were overwhelmed at the destruction they saw.

With the war and the country in both economic and political crisis, there was agreement by the Administration and the president's party that forceful measures were required. However, they were unable to agree on what those measures should be. Instituting a draft and starting a national bank were both proposed and discussed, but there was as much argument as agreement about both, so neither became law at that time.

James Monroe, the new Secretary of War, brought it back to its

---

[7]Hickey 1990, p. 221.

basics with an address to Congress in February of 1815: "The great object to be attained is to carry the war into Canada, and to break the British power there, to the utmost practicable extent."[8] An unidentified New Englander agreed, saying that "the character of the war [had] not changed," and that the administration was still "eager for conquest and aggrandizement." Governor Morris concluded the following: "The Notion of some Federalists that this War had become defensive ... must vanish with Mr. Monroe's late Declaration that their Object is to conquer Canada."[9]

Despite all the reasons for this war – impressments, the 'evil' British and, most of all, expansion – the War of 1812 was arguably the U.S.'s most unpopular war. That may seem to be an extreme statement, considering the long, vocal and sometimes violent opposition to the Vietnam War generations later. Yet one scholar noted,

> It generated more intense opposition than any other war in the nation's history, including the war in Vietnam. Although most scholars have focused on New England's opposition, Federalists in the middle and southern states opposed the conflict, too. Except for two brief periods – one in the summer of 1812 and the other in the fall of 1814 – the party presented a united front against the war.[10]

The War of 1812 has one other significant component in common with the Vietnam War: each was a war that the U.S. lost. While the United States took some major advantages on the bargaining table when the war ended, and could be viewed as victorious there, the main reason for the war – the conquest of Canada to thwart and punish the British and provide the U.S. with more land and reduced competition for trade – did not occur. Indeed, the British made so many advances that they were actually able to burn down the White House.

---

[8]Ibid., pp. 237–238.
[9]Ibid., p. 238.
[10]Ibid., p. 255.

But this did not deter the U.S. government. Still firmly convinced that it was divinely mandated to expand as a beacon of freedom and opportunity to anyone and everyone that it deemed worthy, the country's long trek on the road of expansion, coupled with racism and genocide, did not slow.

Chapter 3.

Mexican–American War

By the time the United States decided it wanted the Mexican territory of Texas, the concept of Manifest Destiny was deeply imbued in the American psyche. The term is believed to have been coined by one John O'Sullivan, the co-founder and editor of *The United States Magazine and Democratic Review* (generally called the *Democratic Review*). The term signified "the mission of the United States 'to overspread the continent allotted by Providence for the free development of our yearly multiplying millions.'" Mr. O'Sullivan further told his readers: "Until every acre of the North American continent is occupied by citizens of the United States, the foundation of the future empire will not have been laid."[1] Manifest Destiny became a catchphrase for what many considered to be a divinely authorized continental expansion.

There were many reasons why the U.S. wanted to expand. Following its victory in its war for independence, the new government knew that France, Spain and Britain had not lost interest in the American continent. Enlarging the physical size of the nation seemed to be one way of mitigating the perceived European threat. As early as 1801, "Thomas Jefferson described his vision of a nation vast enough to hold 'our descendants to the thousandth and thousandth generation.'"[2] His purchase of the Louisiana territory doubled the

---

[1]Christensen and Christensen 1998, p. 41.
[2]Ibid., pp. 8–9.

size of the United States.

Additionally, the controversy over slavery continued to roil the nation, and the addition of a huge territory in the south would strengthen the position of the slave-favoring southern states and politicians: "it needed no foresight to teach any man, when the foreign territory of Texas was acquired, that it was done expressly and avowedly in order to enlarge the area of slavery and to fortify the political power which rested upon it. ..."[3] While that may be a simplistic view, it was certainly one of the many factors that encouraged the nation to take possession of Texas.

Any resistance to this desired expansion was effectively thwarted during the War of 1812, during which the British attacked the capital and burned the White House. From this point on, voices of reason in terms of territorial expansion were mainly silent.

The Monroe Doctrine served to tell the world that the Americas were no longer open for colonization; however, that mandate did nothing to restrict the U.S. from continuing its own empire building.[4]

Mexico's Internal Problems

In the early part of the nineteenth century, Mexico was plagued with internal problems, which the U.S. was only too happy to exploit. In 1810, Mexico was still a Spanish colony. Miguel Hidalgo, a Catholic priest, led a revolt that started Mexico's long struggle for independence and drew attention to the class divisions in the country. Although Mr. Hidalgo was executed, the independence movement he spearheaded finally united the poor and the upper classes, and Mexico became an independent country in 1821. At that time, Agustin de Iturbide became emperor of Mexico. After his overthrow in March of 1823, a republican constitution was created. However, promises for

---

[3]Curtis 2012, p. 255.
[4]Acuña 2010, p. 14.

free elections were not quickly fulfilled, as a series of revolts ended one administration after another.

The area of Texas was not of great interest to the people of Mexico; few of the 6,000,000 people living in Mexico resided in, or had any desire to relocate to, Texas. Immigrants from the U.S. however, with a population at that time of 11,000,000, saw in Texas a land of economic opportunity. Their arrival was considered illegal, but was difficult to stop.

With so few Mexicans interested in moving to Texas, and with Mexico fully aware that the U.S. had its imperial eye on it, Mexico invited Europeans to take up residence there, giving them incentives, such as land and exemption from taxation to do so. Europeans came in droves; however, they had no loyalty to Mexico. When a small group rebelled in 1827, in what was called the Fredonian Rebellion, Mexico quickly defeated it. The U.S. press seized upon this opportunity to rally around these 'freedom fighters.' This resonated with U.S. citizens, still not that distant from their own revolution.

Because this revolt followed U.S. offers to purchase Texas, Mexican suspicion of the U.S. increased. By 1835, Antonio Lopez de Santa Anna, a popular and controversial military and political leader, was president. Under his rule, power was centralized in Mexico City, and the military and the Church grew in authority. The following year, the constitution was rewritten.

Since its uneasy independence more than a decade earlier, the Mexican states had been basically autonomous. They did not readily accept Santa Anna's new centralism. By 1835, Mexico was struggling to hold onto its territory, as its own citizens continued to rebel. The Yucatan became an independent state for a while, California expelled its Mexican governor, and New Mexico, at that time a very large part of Mexico, had a long list of grievances. Santa Anna managed to suppress a revolt in Zacatecas, but throughout the country problems continued to plague the government.

The U.S. popular press, then as now, also fanned the flames of jingoism that have always been a precursor to war.

In February of 1836, Santa Anna attacked the Alamo and killed 200 soldiers. General Sam Houston, hearing of this, ordered his troops at Goliad to retreat. Santa Anna pursued them, they surrendered, but, instead of being treated humanely, Santa Anna ordered their execution, and 340 Texans were killed.

On April 21, 1836, as Santa Anna and his troops camped by the San Jacinto River, Mr. Houston's army attacked. "A three-hour massacre followed, making San Jacinto a war atrocity in its own right."[5] Six hundred thirty Mexicans were killed. Santa Anna was captured, but his life spared in exchange for promising to remove Mexican troops from Texas and advocate for Mexico to recognize Texas as an independent republic. However, when he returned to Mexico City, he denied ever making such an agreement.

During that time in this same year, 1836, when Santa Anna was busy putting down another revolt in Texas, Mexican conservatives returned former president Anastasio Bustamante to power. This was not a major defeat for Santa Anna; he served 11 times, non-consecutively, as president of Mexico, over a 22-year period.

While political turmoil roiled the Mexican government, conditions were ripe within the U.S. citizenry for war. Native Americans were viewed suspiciously, some tribes having fought against settlers in the French and Indian War, the American Revolution and the War of 1812. The British had long had far better relations with the Native Americans than the colonists; any antagonism against the U.S. by the Native Americans is easily understood (see Chapter 2: 'War of 1812'). But U.S. citizens' hostility toward the Natives helped fan the flames of war.

Mexico continued having difficulties with Texas, resulting in the Texas Convention of 1836. In March, delegates at the Convention voted to become an independent nation and named an acting president and vice president of the new Lone Star Republic. Later that same year, the new nation petitioned the U.S. for statehood.

---

[5]Christensen and Christensen 1998, p. 26.

The government of Mexico was in too much disarray to do much about this latest development and viewed Texas as a province in revolt. U.S. President Andrew Jackson, who had tried to purchase Texas for years, exercised an uncharacteristic restraint, telling Congress: "Beware of a too early movement. ... Prudence ... seems to dictate that we should still stand aloof."[6] Apparently not wanting to allow the world to perceive that the Texas revolt was U.S.-spawned, he decided to recognize the independent nation of Texas and ignore, for the time being, the question of statehood.

The U.S. debated the issue on and off for the next several years. Texas's constitution made slavery legal, which the northern states opposed. The southern states were, of course, in favor of slavery and were strong proponents of national expansion to the south.

In 1840, Whig presidential candidate William Henry Harrison was elected. His running mate, John Tyler, had been designated at least partly because he was from a southern state (Virginia), and it was thought he would add appeal to the southern voters. When President Harrison died 30 days after taking office, Mr. Tyler became president. Soon after, he was expelled from the Whig party and was left with no constituency. Partly hoping to create an independent power base, he aggressively pursued the annexation of Texas. By April of 1844, the treaty of annexation was submitted to the Senate for ratification.

The question of Texas became a major political issue in the presidential election of 1844. When James K. Polk defeated Henry Clay for president, the annexation of Texas was assured.

Annexation

In March of 1845, the U.S. formally offered Texas statehood. Mexico immediately severed diplomatic relations with the U.S. That country had long said that the annexation of Texas by the United States would be considered an act of war.

---

[6]Ibid., p. 31.

The situation changed with the administration of President James K. Polk, and not for the better. The U.S. and Mexico had a number of disputes. Among them was Mexico's dissatisfaction with the U.S. recognition of Texas as a separate nation and not a province of Mexico. Mr. Polk "held the niceties of diplomacy in contempt."[7] He believed in a unique diplomatic style, in which the use of force was an ongoing companion of negotiations, rather than a last resort after negotiations fail. With Mexico considering the annexation of Texas by the U.S. an act of war, and with Mr. Polk wanting to further the expansion of the U.S. and not interested in diplomacy, war was inevitable.

In the spring of 1846, President Polk ordered General Zachary Taylor to occupy disputed territory along the Texas–Mexico border. Following a clash between Mexican and American forces, Mr. Polk claimed that Mexico, "after a long-continued series of menaces [has] at last invaded our territory and shed the blood of our fellow-citizens on our own soil."[8]

Whether or not it was 'our own soil' is debatable. One might ask if Texas ceased to be a province of Mexico simply because the U.S. said it had done so. One might further ask if the outright theft of the province was sufficient to call it 'American soil.'

Mr. Polk further said that, due to this particular incident, a state of war existed.

As has been the tragic case many times since then, voices of reason were unheard over the jingoistic din. During House debate, Representative Isaac E. Holmes of South Carolina said this: "We know nothing more than that the two armies have come into collision within the disputed territory, and I deny that war is absolutely, necessarily, the result of it. Suppose the Mexican Congress should not recognize the conduct of their general, and condemn it, and send

---

[7]Christensen and Christensen 1998, p. 49.
[8]Fisher 2010.

here a remonstrance, or rather an apology – is it war?"[9]

The United States was undergoing remarkable transitions at this time. There was unprecedented commercial and industrial expansion, along with a new grasping for material advancement. There were also many sectional divisions: southern, agricultural slave states; northern, slave-free industrial states; westward expansion, etc. These all served to dilute the feelings of nationalism that had been so prevalent following the Revolutionary War and the War of 1812. "A lot of people felt that the war was an opportunity to go back to the ideals on which the nation had been founded, to bring back the notion of service and sacrifice ... a new age of heroism on behalf of the republic."[10] The war with Mexico, it was believed, offered a fresh sense of national unity.

Additionally, the U.S. population was skyrocketing: between 1820 and 1860, the population grew from about 10,000,000 to about 31,000,000. Coal mining and copper development contributed to a greater consumer society, along with increased feelings of the special beneficence of divine providence upon the U.S. The bulldozer known as the United States was now prepared to plow across the continent, even if its attempt to colonize Canada, just 30 years earlier, had failed.

Atrocities

As in its later wars, the U.S. did not see the Mexicans as people, equal to themselves. "The propaganda surrounding the war effort was nakedly opportunistic and expressly promised plunder as the right of the [military] volunteer."[11] During the Mexican–American War, the concept of Manifest Destiny added to this feeling of entitlement. This was true more for the volunteer soldiers than the regular militia,

---

[9]Ibid.

[10]Christensen and Christensen 1998, p. 71.

[11]Foos 2002, p. 113.

but both were willing participants, although to somewhat different degrees. For the volunteers, "their proclivity for racist, religious or nationalist rationales for their crimes took up the language of manifest destiny, suffusing their criminal activity with the heroism and comradeship implicit in that cause."[12] Crimes committed by members of the regular militia might have been caused, in part, by the pressures of severe discipline; this was not so for the volunteers.

The atrocities committed by U.S. forces had many reasons, racism certainly not the least of them. In 1850, author Abiel Abbot Livermore wrote this: "The Anglo-Saxons have been apparently persuaded to think themselves the chosen people, anointed race of the Lord, commissioned to drive out the heathen, and plant their religion and institutions in every Canaan they could subjugate. . . . Our treatment both of the red man and the black man has habituated us to feel our power and forget right . . . The passion for land, also, is a leading characteristic of the American people."[13]

The soldiers, both regulars in the militia and volunteers, expected little, if any, resistance from the Mexicans, who they expected to be servile, and easy victims of their conquest. One soldier, Luther Giddings, described the alleged laziness of the Mexicans in this way: they were "vagrant herdsmen shepherds while others would reap the wealth of their land."[14] Yet even facing the reality of the Mexicans' resistance did nothing to sway these soldiers from the belief that the Mexicans were undeserving of their own land.

Evidence of these atrocities are mainly found in the letters and diaries of some of the soldiers themselves who, while perhaps not participating in them, did not often condemn their activities. One newspaper, The Mercury of Charleston, South Carolina, published letters from soldiers. One, from a private to his father, said this: "The majority of the volunteers sent here, are a disgrace to the nation;

---

[12]Foos 2002, p. 113.
[13]Livermore 2011, pp. 8, 11, 12.
[14]Foos 2002, p. 114.

think of one of them shooting a woman while washing on the bank of a river – merely to test his rifle; another taking forcibly from a Mexican woman the rings from her ears. Their officers take no notice of these outrages, and the offenders escape. If these things are sent to the papers, they are afraid to publish, and so it happens."[15]

This and similar reports arrived in letters to family members and newspapers. But far more unspeakable atrocities were regularly occurring.

In October of 1846, the Mexicans fought bravely to protect and maintain the city of Monterrey. After the U.S. defeated the Mexicans and took control of the city, military patrols of the city were soon suspended. As a result, at least 100 inhabitants were murdered, and the thatched huts of the peasants were burned (many other buildings in the city were fire-proof).

In February of the following year, an Arkansas cavalryman was murdered by the Mexicans, possibly in retaliation for a murderous raid on the Agua Nueva rancho on Christmas Day, 1846. Samuel Chamberlain, the regular army dragoon, described that raid as an orgy of rape and robbery by the volunteers.

Yet the Americans were determined to avenge the death of the cavalryman. The Arkansas cavalry rode into Buena Vista, where the remaining inhabitants of Agua Nuevo rancho had fled, and quickly executed between 25 and 30 Mexican civilians, while their families watched in horror.

In March of 1847, a U.S. wagon train was ambushed outside of Cerralvo, north of Monterrey. Twelve teamsters were killed and a third of the 120 wagons were either missing or destroyed in the ambush. Several Texas Rangers left the company, ostensibly looking for forage, but in reality seeking revenge. A nearby Mexican village was attacked and 24 men murdered.

This brutality was performed under the direction of General Mabby B. (Mustang) Gray. His regiment is described thusly: "Texas

---

[15]Ibid., p. 116.

Rangers ... were mostly made up of adventurers and vagabonds. ... The gang of miscreants under the leadership of Mustang Gray were of this description. This party, in cold-blood, murdered almost the entire male population of the rancho of Guadalupe, where not a single weapon, offensive or defensive could be found! Their only object was plunder!"[16]

The Catholic Church in Mexico, like the Mexican people themselves, was also seen as somehow inferior to the Catholic Church in the U.S. and as being in need of reformation from the U.S. Church. This view was held not only by Protestant soldiers, but by many Catholic soldiers as well. Clergymen were robbed and churches looted. Near Saltillo, Texas Rangers tore a crucifix from a church altar and dragged it through the streets; they then trampled the parish priest. Following a counter-attack by the enraged inhabitants, the Rangers responded, "sparing neither age or sex in their terrible fury"[17] as they inflicted severe casualties upon the residents of the town.

One young man who enlisted at the age of 17 documented his observations. He described one massacre:

> The cave was full of our volunteers yelling like fiends, while on the rocky floor lay over twenty Mexicans, dead and dying in pools of blood. Women and children were clinging to the knees of the murderers shrieking for mercy. Most of the butchered Mexicans had been scalped; only three men were found unharmed. A rough crucifix was fastened to a rock, and some irreverent wretch had crowned the image with a blood scalp. ... No one was punished for this outrage.[18]

Once U.S. forces occupied Mexico City, things didn't improve. In early 1848, a Texas Cavalryman known as Cutthroat was killed by the Mexicans. The following night, Texans assembled in the quarter where

---

[16]S. C. Smith 2012, p. 294.
[17]Foos 2002, p. 131.
[18]Spickard 2007, p. 148.

the killing had taken place and began random shooting, continuing for at least two hours. Regular army patrols who heard the shooting joined in. The following day, 80 bodies lay unclaimed by friends or relatives.

A summary of the general atrocities is provided by an unnamed officer, after the conclusion of the war.

> We have often heard of deeds of extreme cruelty perpetrated by [Mexicans] on the Rio Grande; but it remains to be seen how far they were acts of retaliation, provoked, (but not justified) by the outrages they have endured. From Saltillo to Mier, with the exception of the large towns, all is a desert, and there is scarcely a solitary house (if there be one) inhabited. The smiling villages which welcomed our troops on their upward march are now black and smoldering ruins, the gardens and orange groves destroyed, and the inhabitants, who administered to their necessities, have sought refuge in the mountains. The march of Attila was not more withering and destructive.[19]

The U.S. coveted the entire continent, and Mexico was not going to stand in its way. In a landmark work entitled *untes para la historia de la guerra entre Mexico y los Estatud Unidos* (Notes for a History of the War between Mexico and the United States), a comprehensive history of the war written by Mexican intellectuals, soldiers and politicians, the following conclusion is reached: "The insatiable ambition of the United States, favored by our weakness, caused the war."[20] Ulysses S. Grant, who served as quartermaster and officer in the Texas and Mexico campaigns, also grew disillusioned with the war. In his memoirs, he describes it as "the most unjust war ever waged by a stronger against a weaker nation."[21]

---

[19]Foos 2002, pp. 119–120.
[20]Christensen and Christensen 1998, p. 4.
[21]Waldrep and Bellesiles 2006, p. 216.

The two-year war began in 1846. As a result, 1.2 million square miles of territory were added to the U.S.

In 1880, the Republican Congressional Committee produced an extensive 'campaign textbook,' that described the Mexican–American War as follows: a "Feculent, reeking Corruption" and "one of the darkest scenes in our history – a war forced upon our and the Mexican people by the high-handed usurpations of Pres't Polk in pursuit of territorial aggrandizement of the slave oligarchy."[22]

Regardless of this later evaluation of the war, at the time the new territory acquired was seen as proof that the United States had a God-given right to the continent.

That the Mexican–American war was fought solely to expand U.S. territory, and in doing so, the U.S. cared little if anything for the loss of innocent life the war would cause, can hardly be disputed. Yet this does not preclude the attempt by some historians to do so. One study of the Mexican–American War, conducted in 1920, "entitled *The War with Mexico*, used analyses such as the following to support its thesis that the Mexicans were at fault for the war":

> At the beginning of her independent existence, our people felt earnestly and enthusiastically anxious to maintain cordial relations with our sister republic and many crossed the line of absurd sentimentality in the cause. Friction was inevitable, however. The Americans were direct, positive, brusque, angular and pushing; and they would not understand their neighbors in the south. The Mexicans were equally unable to fathom our goodwill, sincerity, patriotism, resoluteness and courage; and certain features of their character and national condition made it far from easy to get on with them.[23]

This one-sided, biased and completely inaccurate view was for years considered a milestone study on the war. It assuaged the

---

[22]The Republican National Committee 1884, p. 97.
[23]Acuña 2010, p. 14.

consciences of U.S. citizens (if such assuaging was even necessary), by implying that the Mexicans in the conquered territory should have been grateful for all the glorious benefits of democracy bestowed upon them by the U.S. Any clashes between the Mexicans and their imperial occupiers must certainly, this theory holds, be due to the Mexicans' lack of understanding of, and appreciation for, a free society.

The fact that the war caused the death of at least 12,000 people and reduced the size of the nation of Mexico by half should not, according to this theory, have caused any anger or resentment among the Mexican people.

This myopic view of the U.S.'s goals, and of the attitudes of the innocent victims of those goals, has been a mainstay of U.S. foreign policy since the nation's birth.

Abraham Lincoln, then a rising star on the political horizon, disapproved strongly of the war and the way it was started by the United States. In 1848, he wrote a letter to a friend criticizing President Polk's entrance into the war and presaging similar abuses by future presidents. He wrote, in part:

> Allow the President to invade a neighboring nation, whenever *he* shall deem it necessary to repel an invasion, and you allow him to do so, *whenever he may choose to say* he deems it necessary for such purpose—and you allow him to make war at pleasure. Study to see if you can fix *any limit* to his power in this respect, after you have given him so much as you propose. ... You may say to him, 'I see no probability of the British invading us' but he will say to you, 'be silent; I see it, if you don't.'
>
> The provision of the Constitution giving the war-making power to Congress, was dictated, as I understand it, by the following reasons. Kings had always been involving and impoverishing their people in wars, pretending generally, if not always, that the good of the people was the object. This, our Convention [of 1787] understood to be the most oppres-

sive of all Kingly oppressions; and they resolved to so frame the Constitution that *no one* man should hold the power of bringing this oppression upon us.[24]

At the start of the twenty-first century, this important lesson remained unlearned.

---

[24]LaFeber 1994, p. 125.

Chapter 4.

The Spanish–American War and the Philippine–American War

As Spain gradually lost control of its North American colonies, the U.S. was only too happy to acquire them. But it had to be done subtly. Like most of the United States' imperial wars, this one started with cries of freedom and liberty for the people perceived to be oppressed by Spain.

Yet, as has been the case throughout the nation's history, the desire to free oppressed people was only a convenient cover for the quest for power, profit and international expansion.

In 1895, the Cuban War of Independence began. Newspapers in the U.S., most notably the *New York World* and the *New York Journal*, were filled with sensational stories, many of which had little or no truth behind them. "Stories of atrocities, injustices and suffering, which were often exaggerated, sowed the seeds of anger and indignation among a great many U.S. Citizens."[1] They were not alone in calling for the 'liberation' of the downtrodden people of Cuba, people who certainly had difficult situations with their imperial masters, but not nearly as difficult as the jingoistic press claimed. Influential men, including Captain Alfred Mahan, described

---

[1] Keenan 2001, p. 372.

as 'the most important American strategist of the nineteenth century,' Assistant Secretary of the Navy Theodore Roosevelt, and U.S. Senator Henry Cabot Lodge, lusted for expansion and military grandeur. Mahan believed that sea power was the gateway to world power, and Roosevelt and Lodge were willing to follow any plan that would result in increasing the ever-growing U.S. empire.[2]

It would be reasonable to believe that the U.S., which had adopted a policy of neutrality in Spain's conflicts with its own colonies, would stay out of any conflict involving them. However, with more than $50 million invested in Cuba – in plantations, transportation and other business enterprises – the U.S. was experiencing significant losses because the conflicts between Cuba and Spain had devastated trade between the U.S. and Cuba. Then, as now, human rights abuses were insufficient to motivate the U.S. to step in, but the almighty dollar was not. "Big business urged McKinley to lead America into war. American properties were quickly being destroyed in Cuba. ..."[3]

President William McKinley, however, was not interested in going to war. While it is not now, nor was it then, politically expedient for a U.S. president to avoid war, President McKinley knew that a war with Cuba at this time would be an economic disaster for the U.S.

But the reasons to go to war continued to pile up: Japan had defeated China in 1895 and was looking for further expansion in the Pacific. With the Philippines rebelling against Spain and the U.S. coveting Hawaii, it seemed that quickly resolving the problem in Cuba was becoming a good idea. Continually, "Of major concern to the U.S. government was the danger posed to American business investments in Cuba. ..."[4]

So with the political winds blowing towards war, President McKinley was hard pressed to avoid it. He was beginning to believe that war was necessary to protect American business interests in Cuba

---

[2]Rosenfeld 2000, p. 3.
[3]Ibid., p. 4.
[4]Feuer 1993, p. 1.

and also to prevent the Cuban revolution from moving too far to the left, causing the Cuban people to resent subservience to the Americans. It would also serve to silence accusations of weakness, or worse, from the Democratic Party. And, by having a successful war, the Japanese would realize the need to tread carefully before challenging the U.S. in the Pacific. Despite all this, the president still hesitated.

Theodore Roosevelt, Assistant Secretary of the Navy, was desperate to establish the U.S. as a world power. He and Senator Lodge also wanted to send a strong message to Europe that the U.S. was now a global power: challenge it at your own risk.

All doubt about going to war ended on February 15, 1898. The U.S. had sent the battleship Maine into Havana Harbor as a show of strength and to intimidate the Spanish. On that day, the Maine exploded, killing 266 men. Its cause was quickly, if inaccurately, determined. Initially, it was thought to be an accident. "Lieutenant Frank F. Fletcher, on duty at the Bureau of Ordnance, wrote in a personal letter to [Lieutenant Albert] Gleaves: 'The disaster to the Maine is the one topic here now. Everybody is gradually settling down to the belief that the disaster was due to the position of the magazine next to the coal bunkers in which there must have been spontaneous combustion.'"[5]

An inquiry was immediately launched to determine the cause, and within a month it was determined that an underwater mine had detonated, igniting parts of the forward magazines of the ship. This, for the American citizenry, was the last straw, and on April 25, 1898, the U.S. declared war on Spain. The battle cry, 'Remember the Maine,' helped rally the troops.

Even a cursory look at the investigation in 1898 casts doubt on its legitimacy. Two experts who were qualified, willing and able, were not called to assist in it. "Professor Philip Alger, whose abilities had won him an outstanding reputation in ordnance, was available.

---

[5]Rickover 1976, p. 46.

Professor Charles E. Munroe, president of the American Chemical Society, an authority on explosives, had promptly offered his services. Munroe was familiar with naval procedures, having taken part in an earlier investigation of a paint explosion on the cruiser Atlanta. He received an acknowledgment but no request for assistance. At least one newspaper called attention to the absence of technically qualified members on the court."[6]

Professor Alger had greatly displeased Secretary Roosevelt on February 18, immediately after the sinking of the Maine when, in an interview published in the *Washington Evening Star*, he said this:

> As to the question of the cause of the Maine's explosion, we know that no torpedo such as is known to modern warfare, can of itself cause an explosion of the character of that on board the Maine. We know of no instances where the explosion of a torpedo or mine under a ship's bottom has exploded the magazine within. It has simply torn a great hole in the side or bottom, through which water entered, and in consequence of which the ship sunk. Magazine explosions, on the contrary, produce effects exactly similar to the effects of the explosion on board the Maine. When it comes to seeking the cause of the explosion of the Maine's magazine, we should naturally look not for the improbable or unusual causes, but those against which we have had to guard in the past.[7]

Mr. Roosevelt, an avid proponent of establishing the U.S. Navy as the strongest in the world, was not anxious to hear opinions contrary to his own, despite the expertise of the person expressing the opinion: "his own views were hardening toward the conviction that there had been no accident."[8]

However, the inquiry at the time focused the pent-up anger of the U.S., anger stoked by the expansionist newspapers of the day, on

---

[6]Rickover 1976, pp. 46–47.
[7]Ibid., pp. 64–65.
[8]Ibid., p. 47.

the evil Spaniards and their dastardly act of sinking the Maine. The U.S. was once again at war.

It is interesting to note that in 1974, a thorough analysis of all available documentation available from the earlier investigations regarding the sinking of the Maine strongly indicated that an internal explosion, possibly caused by the ship's design and an alteration in the kind of coal used to fuel the ship, destroyed the Maine. There was no evidence found of any penetration of the ship from the outside. The initial investigation, the one that led to war, indicated that the Navy "made little use of its technically trained officers during its investigation of the tragedy."[9]

Mr. McKinley's reasons for finally going to war are instructive. There were four points, which included, in part, the following:

> First: In the cause of humanity and to put an end to the barbarities, bloodshed, starvation, and horrible miseries now existing there. ...
>
> Second: We owe it to our citizens in Cuba to afford them that protection and indemnity for life and property which no government there can or will afford. ...
>
> Third: The right to intervene may be justified by the very serious injury to commerce, trade, and business of our people, and by the wanton destruction of property and devastation of the island.
>
> Fourth: The present condition of affairs in Cuba is a constant menace to our peace, and entails upon this government an enormous expense.[10]

Note especially the first point, wherein Mr. McKinley wishes to end the 'barbarities, bloodshed, starvation, and horrible miseries' of the people. Yet in this war, and the Phillipine–American War that

---

[9] Compare to Bush's selective information in going to war with Iraq; see Chapter 15.

[10] Gambone 2002, p. 119.

was spawned by it and immediately followed it, the U.S. perpetrated unspeakable horrors on the people it was ostensibly protecting.

See also Mr. McKinley's third point. '[S]erious injury to commerce, trade, and business' must not be allowed. So while the intervention did nothing to prevent barbarities and bloodshed, and there may have been no real threat to the U.S. from Cuba's internal problems, war was necessary to prevent any major disruption of commerce.

The Spanish–American War had fewer reported atrocities than other U.S. wars. The fact that it lasted less than four months may have much to do with that fact. One incident will suffice:

> Suddenly, about 200 Spaniards approached our position. They were a disorderly mob, and we poured a terrible fire down upon the unsuspecting enemy. A few minutes later, a Spanish officer frantically waved a white cloth at the end of his sword. At the sign of surrender, we clambered down the hill to take our first prisoners. Less than 50 enemy soldiers survived the massacre.[11]

When the U.S. defeated Spain in the Caribbean, it demanded possession of Guam, Puerto Rico and the Philippines. Spain had little choice and, although anxious to keep the Philippines, which was already occupied by the U.S., was forced to surrender it. Why did the U.S. want the Philippines? "The Philippine–American War was a colonial war, fought for the purpose of retaining a Pacific archipelago ceded to the United States by Spain."[12]

Some historians postulate that the decision to take the Philippines was made prior to the invasion of Cuba, which started the three-month Spanish–American War.

Once the treaty was signed, giving the U.S. exactly what it demanded, President McKinley said that the U.S. possession of the Philippines would be "benevolent assimilation."[13] In that same

---

[11]Feuer 1993, p. 80.
[12]Welch 1987, p. xiii.
[13]Bautista 2002.

proclamation, he named General Elwell Otis as commander of U.S ground forces in the Philippines and said he was to "extend by force American sovereignty over this country." General Otis and the other leading soldiers in the Philippines took this charge seriously. 'Benevolence' and 'force' seem incompatible, but as will be seen, any thoughts of benevolence quickly gave way to force.

William Howard Taft, later president of the U.S., was appointed the civil governor general of the Philippines. He referred to the Filipinos as his "little brown brothers"[14] Under his supervision, some of the most horrendous atrocities possible were committed against his 'brothers'.

Mr. Taft wrote, about a month after arriving in the Philippines, that the islands were inhabited by "a vast mass of ignorant, superstitious people, well intentioned, light-hearted, temperate, somewhat cruel, domestic and fond of their families, and deeply wedded to the Catholic Church."[15] This did not bode well for the future of the Filipino people at the hands of the American conquerors.

Maud Huntley Jenks, the wife of a government anthropologist, said this: "It looks to me as though it will take fifty generations of 'line upon line' and 'precept upon precept' before these natives will know enough to govern themselves. [M]any of them seem to be very stupid. The men here in the house, who teach in Manila schools, say the natives can't reason."[16]

Major General Adna R. Chaffee described the Filipino people thusly: "We are dealing with a class of people whose character is deceitful, who are absolutely hostile to the white race and who regard life as of little value and, finally who will not submit to our control until absolutely defeated and whipped into such condition."[17]

The concept of Taft's 'little brown brothers,' 'incapable of reason,' 'superstitious,' 'ignorant' and needing to be 'whipped' into submis-

---

[14]Roosevelt 1926, p. 185.

[15]Kramer 2006, p. 197.

[16]Ibid., p. 197.

[17]Luzyiminda 1973, p. 15.

sion, did nothing to help the soldiers serving in the Philippines to see the Filipino people as people. During a time when international travel was extremely limited, when the memory of enslaved African-Americans was not too distant, and anyone not white, Anglo-Saxon Protestant was viewed with suspicion, U.S. soldiers let loose in the Philippines to subdue their 'little brown brothers' could only have a disastrous result.

In 1898, Indiana State Senator Albert J. Beveridge visited the Philippines, and his observations about American soldiers were reported in *The Saturday Evening Post*. They read, in part, as follows:

> Everywhere the pale blue or gray eye, everywhere the fair skin, everywhere the tawny hair and beard. ... Here thoroughbred soldiers from the plantations of the South, from the plains and valleys and farms of the west, look the thoroughbred, physically considered. The fine line is everywhere. The nose is straight, the mouth is sensitive and delicate. ... The whole face and figure is the face and figure of the thoroughbred fighter who has always been the fine-featured, delicate-nostriled, thin-eared and generally clean-cut featured man.[18]

One can only wonder what Senator Beveridge thought of "the dark skinned native who might lack delicate nostrils and who surely could not exhibit a tawny beard."[19] Emilio Aquinaldo, a Philippine general and the nation's first president, was depicted in cartoons in U.S. newspapers as a 'monkey-man' or a cannibal, as all other Filipinos were also depicted. Even the very fact that the Filipinos fought against the conquering U.S. soldiers was seen as an indication of their inferiority.

Although it took some time for reports of atrocities committed by U.S. soldiers to leak into the U.S. press, it took little time for those atrocities to occur.

---

[18]Welch 1987, p. 101.
[19]Ibid., p. 101.

Captain Elliot of the Kansas Regiment described the massacre at Caloocan in the spring of 1899: "Caloocan was supposed to contain seventeen thousand inhabitants. The Twentieth Kansas swept through it, and now Calloocan contains not one living native. Of the buildings, the battered walls of the great church and dismal prison alone remain."

This same soldier wrote about the village of Maypaja: "The village of Maypaja, where our first fight occurred on the night of the fourth, had five thousand people on that day – now not one stone remains upon top of another. You can only faintly imagine this terrible scene of desolation."[20]

The report about Caloocan was first mentioned in *The Saturday Evening Post,* but following a hurried investigation by the War Department, the *Post* printed a retraction: "H.L. Wells, correspondent for several New York papers, concurrently reported that 'it was a source of great satisfaction to know that earlier reports of the misconduct of our soldiers are disproved,' although undoubtedly, 'our men do shoot niggers somewhat in the sporting spirit.'"[21] The following year, the *Press-Knickerbocker*, in Albany, reported on the hanging of several 'insurgents' by Colonel Frederick Funston, without benefit of trial. Later that same year came the first reports of the 'water cure torture' being used against Filipinos.

In 1901, about three years into the war, the Balangiga massacre occurred during the Samar campaign. In the town of Balangiga, on the island of Samar, the Filipinos surprised the Americans in an attack that killed 40 U.S. soldiers. In retribution, Brigadier General Jacob H. Smith ordered the execution of everyone in the town over the age of ten. Said he: "Kill and burn, kill and burn; the more you kill and the more you burn, the more you please me."[22] Between 2,000 and 3,000 Filipinos, one third of the entire population of Samar,

---

[20]Bautista 2002, p. 67.

[21]Welch 1987, p. 34.

[22]Schirmer et al. 1999, p. 32.

died in this massacre.

General Smith was court-martialed for this horrendous crime, but his sentence was later reduced by President Theodore Roosevelt. His punishment resulted in only a reprimand and his forced retirement from the military. Smith's second in command, Major Littleton W. T. Waller, was charged with murder, but was acquitted.

This was not an isolated incident. There exist various records of soldiers who witnessed or participated in atrocities.

"Anthony Michea of the Third Artiller wrote: We bombarded a place called Malabon, and then we went in and killed every native we met, men, women and children. It was a dreadful sight, the killing of the poor creatures."[23]

A soldier by the name of Burr Ellis, from Frazier Valley, California, described his actions in Cavite: "the first one I found, he was in a house, down on his knees fanning a fire, trying to burn the house, and I pulled my old Long Tom to my shoulder and left him to burn with the fire." "I killed seven that I know of, and one more, I am almost sure of. ... I had lots of fun that morning."[24]

Fred D. Sweet, of the Utah Light Battery, reported this: "The scene reminded me of the shooting of jack-rabbits in Utah, only the rabbits sometimes got away, but the insurgents did not."[25]

There was, however, some very vocal opposition to the war. Mark Twain was a vociferous opponent. In October of 1900, the year after the start of the war, he wrote this in the *New York Herald*:

> I left these shores, at Vancouver, a red-hot imperialist. I wanted the American eagle to go screaming into the Pacific. It seemed tiresome and tame for it to content itself within the Rockies. Why not spread its wings over the Phillippines, I asked myself? And I thought it would be a real good thing to do.

---

[23]Bautista 2002, p. 67.
[24]Ibid., p. 68.
[25]Ibid., p. 68.

I said to myself, here are a people who have suffered for three centuries. We can make them as free as ourselves, give them a government and country of their own, put a miniature of the American constitution afloat in the Pacific, start a brand new republic to take its place among the free nations of the world. It seemed to me a great task to which had addressed ourselves.

But I have thought some more, since then, and I have read carefully the treaty of Paris, and I have seen that we do not intend to free, but to subjugate the people of the Phillippines. We have gone there to conquer, not to redeem ...

It should, it seems to me, be our pleasure and duty to make those people free, and let them deal with their own domestic questions in their own way. And so I am an anti-imperialist. I am opposed to having the eagle put its talons on any other land.[26]

Four months later, he wrote this: "And as for a flag for the Philippine Province, it is easily managed. We can have a special one – our States do it: we can have just our usual flag, with the white stripes painted black and the stars replaced by the skull and cross-bones."[27]

He continued to battle U.S. imperialism. *The War Prayer*, written around 1904 or 1905, rejected by his publisher, discovered after his death and published in 1932, further demonstrates his opposition to war.

O Lord our Father, our young patriots, idols of our hearts, go forth to battle – be Thou near them! With them – in spirit – we also go forth from the sweet peace of our beloved firesides to smite the foe. O Lord our God, help us to tear their soldiers to bloody shreds with our shells; help us to cover their smiling fields with the pale forms of their patriot

---

[26]http://www.loc.gov/rr/hispanic/1898/twain.html. Accessed on January 19, 2013.
[27]Ibid.

dead; help us to drown the thunder of the guns with the shrieks of their wounded, writhing in pain; help us to lay waste their humble homes with a hurricane of fire; help us to wring the hearts of their unoffending widows with unavailing grief; help us to turn them out roofless with little children to wander unfriended the wastes of their desolated land in rags and hunger and thirst, sports of the sun flames of summer and the icy winds of winter, broken in spirit, worn with travail, imploring Thee for the refuge of the grave and denied it – for our sakes who adore Thee, Lord, blast their hopes, blight their lives, protract their bitter pilgrimage, make heavy their steps, water their way with their tears, stain the white snow with the blood of their wounded feet! We ask it, in the spirit of love, of Him Who is the Source of Love, and Who is the ever-faithful refuge and friend of all that are sore beset and seek His aid with humble and contrite hearts. Amen." [28]

Like the voices of so many others, Mr. Twain's opposition to war was unheeded.

So once again the U.S. invaded a foreign nation, a former colony of its vanquished opponent, Spain, and with a complete disdain for anything even approaching basic human rights slaughtered the citizens in its perennial quest for expansion and economic gain.

---

[28] http://www.midwinter.com/lurk/making/warprayer.html. Accessed on August 27, 2012.

Chapter 5.

Other Foreign Policy Activities of this Period: 1812–1858

Between the War of 1812 and the Mexican–American War (1846–1848), which added greatly to the U.S. territory, a number of factors were in play that either encouraged, or were spawned, by U.S. imperialism. The Louisiana Purchase of 1803, which added 828,000 square miles to the United States (comprising all or part of 15 current states), protected passage to the port of New Orleans and enabled traders to move freely along the Mississippi River. This helped to spur greater industry. The nation grew again, following the Mexican–American War (see Chapter 3). By the 1848 Treaty of Guadalupe Hidalgo, along with the 1851 Gadsden Purchase from the Mexican government, which historian Elliott West described as "an after-dinner mint following the expansionist gorging,"[1] another 1,200,000 square miles were added to the United States, comprising the present boundaries of Arizona, California, Nevada, New Mexico, Utah and portions of Colorado and Texas. And while the Industrial Revolution is generally considered to have occurred between 1877 and 1901, in the U.S., its roots were in the development of textile mills in New England in the early part of the nineteenth century.

---

[1]Wrobel 2006 [Fall].

That, and the new opportunities afforded by the Louisiana Purchase, greatly increased industry and trade. By 1830, canals, which had been a principle means of transporting goods, were being replaced by railroads. Farm machinery was a major product of the U.S.

The concept of Manifest Destiny was still strong; a belief in U.S. exceptionalism stemmed from it, yet U.S. imperial goals sometimes conflicted with the lofty belief "of benign national distinctiveness, of republican purity and innocence."[2] During the years when the nation simply moved westward, bulldozing anyone standing in its way, it was easy for the citizenry to avoid any comparisons to other imperial nations that had risen and eventually fallen. From sea to shining sea seemed a reasonable goal for the nation; one could, theoretically, walk from one end to the other.

> The notion of a nation growing into its foreordained bound-
> aries has such power that we can forget the foreign policy
> context of nineteenth-century western history. The myth of
> a manifest destiny has endured so well because it provides
> such incredible comfort to the national psyche. Better for
> the national mental health to believe that the world's great-
> est democracy had grown naturally, providentially, into its
> God-given skin than to consider that it, like so many other
> nations, has a history of empire building.[3]

Benjamin Franklin, Thomas Jefferson and others had long considered the area beyond the then current western boundaries of the U.S. as the future heart of the nation, areas unpolluted by the European thought that was, they felt, so much a part of the eastern seaboard. America would discover and expand westward, growing into itself. "But, of course, this new nation was not discovering itself or expanding into itself so much as constituting itself incrementally (in quite large chunks to be sure) on a world stage and displacing those residents

---

[2] Wrobel 2006 [Fall].
[3] Ibid.

who were already there – primarily Indians, Californians, Mexicans, and Tejanos."[4]

For many, though, the often brutal displacement of these peoples, including at times their savage murders, was not even considered; they simply either didn't know about it, or chose not to pay attention. "Anthropologists have grossly underestimated ... the length of time this hemisphere has been occupied – promoting the myth of an empty continent, ready for settlement."[5] Causing the nation's citizens to see the 'enemy' as somehow less than human (see Chapter 4: 'Spanish–American War and Philippine–American War') is certainly only a second choice to somehow convincing them that they simply don't exist. The myth of the North American continent as a vast, uninhabited land, rich in natural resources and provided by divine providence to the new nation of the United States still resonates with many people today, possibly because the truth of the matter is almost too barbaric to even be considered.

In 1823, the Monroe Doctrine was introduced. This doctrine served to advise the rest of the world that any incursions by European countries to colonize or otherwise interfere with countries in North or South America would be seen as acts of aggression, requiring intervention from the U.S. This doctrine was introduced by President James Monroe during his seventh State of the Union address.

> [C]ouched in the language of idealism and high principle, such affirmations of presidential purpose often purported to advance the cause of humankind, or at least a substantial portion thereof, by upholding values such as freedom, democracy, and peace. Such language sometimes served as a cover for less ennobling purposes connected with the defense of strategic and economic interests, and usually contained some kind of threat to take countermeasures if other nations went beyond what the United States regarded as appropriate bounds.[6]

---

[4]Ibid.

[5]"Winds of Change" 1998 [Summer].

[6]Gilderhus 2006 [March].

As indicated by the above quotation, the Monroe Doctrine was typical. The document states that the nations of North and South America are free and must remain so. It further states that "With the existing colonies or dependencies of any European power we have not interfered and shall not interfere."[7] Yet, quite pointedly, it says nothing to prevent the U.S. from interfering with the same independent nations that are now untouchable, under threat of U.S. retaliation, by Europe. The U.S. increasingly exploited that loophole throughout the twentieth century (see Chapters 6 through 17).

Events happened in quick succession to help the U.S. achieve its dreams of global dominance. In 1846, the U.S. minister to New Granada, Benjamin Bidlack, signed a treaty giving the United States transit rights across Panama. "The Bidlack pact enabled Americans to build the first transcontinental railway (of 48 miles) in Panama during the 1850s and provided the excuse, in 1903, for Theodore Roosevelt's seizure of Panama to build the present canal."[8]

In 1848, gold was discovered in California, and the population of that area increased greatly, as fortune hunters from around the world flocked there in the hope of striking it rich. The U.S. now had significant populations across the continent, but its imperial dreams were not sated. In 1850, the Senate passed the Clayton–Bulwer Treaty, which approved a canal in Nicaragua, connecting the Atlantic and Pacific Oceans. Great Britain, at this time, dominated trade in Central America, and the U.S. had no intention of letting those lucrative markets remain in British hands.

Great Britain also controlled much of the Chinese market. The U.S. had no formal agreements with China and worked through Great Britain, "even to the point of working with English traders to develop the highly profitable opium traffic."[9] This changed in response to the U.S.'s economic depression of 1837–1841. President John Tyler,

---

[7]Gambone 2002, p. 157.
[8]LaFeber 1994, p. 124.
[9]Ibid., p. 102.

recognizing that there was insufficient domestic demand for the goods being produced by the United States, appointed Secretary of State Daniel Webster as the first U.S. minister to China. Secretary Webster arranged for the Treaty of Wangxia, which provided the U.S. with most-favored-nation status in China's trade, meaning that the U.S. automatically received any trade rights that China provided to any other nation. The U.S. was also granted extraterritorial rights, which provided that U.S. citizens were free from Chinese law and would be regulated and protected by U.S. officials and U.S. law. Although this was apparently, and unbeknownst to the Americans ratifying the treaty, "a practice [that] had begun with medieval China's decision to let foreign 'barbarians' and their queer ways stay to themselves so that they would not disturb the superior Chinese civilization,"[10] the U.S. saw it as a great victory.

The Clayton–Bulwer Treaty resulted in another, somewhat minor international conflict for the U.S. Britain at this time maintained a protectorate over the territory of the Miskito Indians. Britain no longer wanted to maintain the protectorate, but wanted to leave it honorably, meaning with some consideration afforded to the Miskito Indians. Nicaragua wanted to assert sovereignty over the protectorate, situated along its coast.

Additionally, there was some question about the status of the Bay Islands. First settled by the British in the mid-eighteenth century, they were abandoned under a 1786 convention with Spain, but reoccupied in the early nineteenth century. In 1852, Britain made the Bay Islands a British colony, partly, at least, to prevent U.S. expansionism, and partly to prevent the loss of isthmian transit routes.

The U.S., however, believed that the Bay Islands were part of Honduras, and therefore were subject to the Clayton–Bulwer Treaty. Based on this belief, it was expected that the British would withdraw. Additionally, the naming of the Bay Islands as a British colony

---

[10]Ibid., p. 103.

appeared to some to be a violation of the Monroe Doctrine. This could not be allowed to happen.

In 1852, British Minister to the U.S. John F. Crampton entered into an agreement ceding Greytown, a Nicaraguan port city that was the Caribbean terminus of the transit route, to Nicaragua, and providing relocation to the Indians. Nicaragua was to pay for obtaining Greytown.

The agreement never passed, because "The Nicaraguan government flatly rejected it, asserting that Nicaragua should not be compelled to pay for reacquisition of territory that had always been rightfully Nicaraguan. Since British acceptance of the agreement was conditional upon Nicaraguan consent, Nicaragua's refusal to do so torpedoed the whole scheme."[11]

The situation took another turn in typical U.S. fashion. By 1852, the U.S. minister to Nicaragua was Solon Borland,

> ... an arrogant individual who disliked Nicaraguans, the British and the Clayton–Bulwer Treaty, not necessarily in that order. In early 1854 Borland was a passenger on an American-owned steamer cruising on the San Juan River when the captain shot to death a black man in a trivial dispute. When town authorities moved to arrest the captain, Borland protected him, denying that Greytown police had jurisdiction over an American citizen. In a melee that occurred in front of the U.S. consul's residence, where Borland was staying, someone in a crowd threw a bottle which slightly injured the minister.
>
> Deciding that U.S. citizens and property were no longer safe in Greytown, Borland went to the United States and convinced the government that naval protection was needed. Accordingly, the U.S.S. *Cyane*, commanded by Capt. George A. Hollins, was dispatched to serve as a threatening presence in Greytown harbor. The ship arrived in June, and Hollins and the local American consular agent, J.W. Fabens, determined

---

[11] Jones 1974, pp. 104–105.

to extract reparations from Greytown officials. After their initial demands were ignored, Hollins issued an ultimatum in July 11, giving the town twenty-four hours to respond to the American demands. When still no answer came, the *Cyane* bombarded the town on July 13, and Hollins then sent a landing party to burn any building that had escaped the naval artillery. The town was totally destroyed, but because of Hollins' warning, the towns people had evacuated and there was no loss of life.[12]

The British, of course, were outraged, but due to their preoccupation with the Crimean War, could do little about it. The foreign secretary, Lord Clarendon, "called it an 'outrage without parallel in the annals of modern times' and declared that the Pierce administration was 'unprincipled and ready for any foreign outrage to give a turn to opinion at home.'" The British requested that the Pierce administration disavow the actions of Capt. Hollins, but the U.S. refused even this gesture.

Negotiations concerning the Bay Islands and the protectorate continued. The British remained concerned about potential U.S. expansion in Central America, but also recognized the need to maintain good trade relations with the U.S. Lord Palmerston, the British foreign secretary, commented on these two conflicting needs: "These Yankees are most disagreeable fellows to have to do with any American Questions; they are on the Spot, strong, deeply interested in the matter, totally unscrupulous and dishonest. ... We are far away, weak from Distance, controlled ... by our strong commercial interest in maintaining peace with the United States. The result of this State of things has been that we have given away Step by Step to the North Americans."[13]

The situation was resolved through the efforts of the British charge in Guatemala, Charles Lennox Wyke. In November, 1859, he arranged

---

[12]Finding 1987, pp. 21–22.
[13]Ibid., p. 25.

a treaty with Honduras, which ceded the Bay Islands to Honduras and settled the Miskito question in a manner favorable to them. "In January 1860, Wyke signed the treaty of Managua with Nicaragua, effectively ending both the Miskito protectorate and, except for Belize, now called British Honduras, the British presence in Central America. With the exception of the Clayton-Bulwer provision for mutual control of any future canal, the British had left Central America open for the Americans to do with as they pleased."[14]

As the U.S. grew in size, this imperialist foray was not without its opponents, including Henry David Thoreau and an up-and-coming politician named Abraham Lincoln.

Thoreau's landmark work, *Resistance to Civil Government*, generally published as *Civil Disobedience*, was written during the Mexican War, but published shortly after it ended.

"Thoreau left in the references to imperialism because, for him, they represent a type of misgoverning that calls for resistance. He recommends disobeying unjust laws, and then drawing attention to the injustice by accepting the punishment. Honest citizens, seeing someone punished unjustly, would then be motivated to change the laws."[15]

Mr. Lincoln, for his part, took more than a little flack for his opposition to the war against Mexico during his campaign for the presidency. On June 25, 1858, he wrote a letter to Joseph Medill, the publisher of the *Chicago Tribune*. He wrote, in part: "I was in Congress but a single term. I was a candidate when the Mexican war broke out – and I then took the ground, which I never varied from, that the Administration had done wrong in getting us into the war, but that the Officers and soldiers who went to the field must be supplied and sustained at all events."[16] This support for the soldiers while opposing the war they fought, a theme that occurred again in

---

[14]Finding 1987, p. 26.

[15]Chevalier 1997, p. 840.

[16]Basler 1946, p. 382.

the U.S. in the early part of the twenty-first century, was addressed during Mr. Lincoln's debate with his presidential-election opponent, Stephen Douglas. His reply to Mr. Douglas in the Ottawa Debate reads, in part, as follows:

> And so I think my friend, the Judge [Douglas], is equally at fault when he charges me at the time when I was in Congress of having opposed our soldiers who were fighting in the Mexican war. The Judge did not make his charge very distinctly, but I can tell you what he can prove, by referring to the record. You remember I was an old Whig, and whenever the Democratic Party tried to get me to vote that the war had been righteously begun by the President, I would not do it. But whenever they asked for any money, or land-warrants, or anything to pay the soldiers there, during all that time, I gave the same vote that Judge Douglas did.[17]

As president, Mr. Lincoln's foreign policy work was limited; he was soon preoccupied with the Civil War (1861–1865). His main foreign policy initiatives during this time were preventing British aid to the Confederacy, and working to minimize French influence in Mexico, fearing that the French, too, sympathized with the Confederate States. The Emancipation Proclamation was a major, and successful, tool in this effort; Mr. Lincoln knew that Britain and France couldn't assist the Confederacy without appearing to favor slavery. The president also rebuffed all efforts by the Confederacy for any kind of official recognition of its leaders.

The U.S., by the end of the nineteenth century, had fully established itself as a global bully, using force whenever it deemed it necessary to achieve whatever goals it set for itself.

---

[17]Ibid., p. 445.

Part II.

1899–1953: A New World Power

Chapter 6.

The Early Twentieth Century

Since its birth in 1776, the U.S. had, by the end of the nineteenth century, expanded in size nearly tenfold. It had bought or stolen land from Britain, Spain, France, Russia and, most notably, Native Americans. It was "'commercially, industrially and financially ... invading every part of the globe [and] acquiring an economic stranglehold, which is gradually tightening and squeezing out all competitors'. ... the United States might be regarded as 'the best example of modern economic imperialism serving, for the present at any rate, purely economic ends' ..."[1]

The annexation of Hawaii demonstrates the bold lengths to which the U.S. will go to achieve its imperial ends. The island nation was a stopping point for U.S. ships trading in China. In Hawaii, these ships picked up supplies and cargo before proceeding to China. Throughout the middle of the nineteenth century, U.S. influence grew, as many U.S. citizens moved to Hawaii for employment. "So many Yankees had settled in Hawaii by 1840 that Honolulu had the atmosphere of a New England town."[2]

In 1890, President McKinley placed a tariff, making sugar grown in Hawaii, virtually all of which was sold to the U.S., now without a major market. Sugar planters felt that annexation to the U.S. would save this industry.

---

[1]Richardson, Stone, and Stone 1994, p. 194.
[2]Morris, Greenleaf, and Ferrell 1971, p. 475.

Three years earlier, King Kalakaua had been forced by the U.S. to accept a new constitution, one which deprived most of the natives of any voice in the government. When he died in 1891, his sister became queen. No fan of the white rule of Hawaii, in January 14, 1893, Queen Liliuokalani attempted to force the acceptance of a new constitution by royal decree. Panicked, the white population fostered a revolution. John L. Stevens, the U.S. minister in Honolulu, ordered 160 sailors and marines ashore. On February 1, 1893, the U.S. flag was raised in Honolulu. On that day he sent the following message to the State Department: "The Hawaiian pear is now fully ripe, and this is the golden hour for the United States to pluck it."[3]

There were, it seemed, no further frontiers to conquer on the North American continent. With the end of Reconstruction following the Civil War, a heightened sense of patriotism seemed to expand. "A sense of prestige in a world where great powers had already taken the path of imperialism made it seem necessary for the nation to become an imperial power."[4] This sentiment seems to be captured exceptionally well in an article in the 1878 issue of *Overland Monthly*:

> The subjugation of a continent was sufficient to keep the American people busy at home for a century. ... But now that the continent is subdued, we are looking for fresh worlds to conquer; and whether our conservative stay-at-homes like it or not, the colonizing instinct which has led our race in successive waves of emigration ... is the instinct which is now pushing us out and on to ... the isles of the sea, – and beyond.[5]

Additionally, as the century drew to a close there was a growing sense that agricultural exports, the overwhelming bulk of what the U.S. sold to other countries, were causing the nation to fall behind

---

[3]Morris, Greenleaf, and Ferrell 1971, p. 475.

[4]Ibid., p. 470.

[5]Ibid., p. 471.

the progress being made abroad, most notably in Europe and South America. This, too, was a concern.

With its newly acquired size and might, and the wounds of the Civil War beginning to heal, the nation was ready to further exert itself on the world stage.

One man who would play a major role in the U.S.'s imperial adventures during the first part of the twentieth century was Theodore Roosevelt. In June of 1897, the Assistant Secretary of the Navy, and future Governor of New York, vice president and president, addressed the Naval War College. He warned the assembled audience against the dangers of a wealthy nation becoming lazy or timid. Such a nation, he advised, "... is an easy prey for any people which still retains the most valuable of all qualities, the soldierly virtues. Peace is a goddess only when she comes with a sword girt on hip."[6] The diplomat, he told them, is the servant, and not the master, of the soldier.

More and more, politicians, evangelical clergymen and others began publically voicing racist ideas, all somehow tied to the resurrected, albeit never fully discarded, idea of Manifest Destiny. In 1885, John Fiske lectured that the Anglo-Saxon people had survived and thrived, thus fulfilling the logic of the survival of the fittest. They were, therefore, "destined to rule over less gifted races, and bring civilization and peace to the entire globe."[7] John W. Burgess, in 1890, then Dean of the faculty of political science at Columbia University, wrote that "if need be the superior nations must use force to impose civilization upon backward peoples."[8] Prominent Congregational minister Josiah Strong wrote that "America had a mission to regenerate the world with the ideals of civil liberty and pure spiritual Christianity."[9] It has been shown how these ideas were not new; they had been put in practice prior to this time period. In the forthcoming chapters, it

---

[6]Ibid., p. 473.
[7]Ibid., p. 472.
[8]Ibid., p. 472.
[9]Ibid., p. 472.

will be shown how some of these ideas again came to fruition, with devastating results for their victims.

For the world, the U.S. began the century as a menace to be watched. "In 1899 John Bassett Moore, then serving as assistant secretary of state, wrote that the United States, during the preceding ten years, had moved "from a position of comparative freedom from entanglements into the position of what is commonly called a world-power."[10] "Where formerly we had only commercial interests," he explained, "we now have territorial and political interests as well."[11] "The annexation of the Philippines, Hawaii and Puerto Rico and the temporary occupation of Cuba appeared to have thrust the United States into the vortex of international politics."[12]

The economic greed of the nation and the lust for imperial power, long engaged, consummated their relationship by the turn of the new century. "There can be no empirical resolution of the question whether American policy after 1900 should be explained in terms of strategic objectives (excluding European influence from the Caribbean) or economic ones (protecting American investors), because American expansion coincided with both growing military and economic power."[13]

The presidential campaign of 1900 included attempts, at least, to raise foreign policy as an issue. Democrat William Jennings Bryan was determined to make it an issue, although he was unsuccessful in those efforts. His denunciation of the U.S. occupation of the Philippines and the country's brutal suppression of the Philippine people, did not arouse any interest in a populace more concerned with domestic policies. The Republicans tried to play both sides of the foreign policy coin. "Vice-presidential nominee [Theodore] Roosevelt and Wisconsin gubernatorial candidate [Robert M.] La Follette, waved the flag frenetically and scorned calls to pull out of the

---

[10]LaFeber 1994, p. 194.
[11]Ibid., p. 194.
[12]Braeman, Bremner, and Brody 1971, p. 207.
[13]Krasner 1978, p. 163.

Philippines as cowardly and unpatriotic. Still, even they denied that Republican policies contemplated any departure from the nation's traditional avoidance of international alliances and overseas power politics."[14] The William McKinley–Theodore Roosevelt ticket was victorious and, with President McKinley's assassination in 1901, the globally aggressive Mr. Roosevelt became president.

Mr. Roosevelt "frequently proclaimed himself an unabashed, unapologetic imperialist. In an address to Congress in December, 1904, he said this:

> Chronic wrong-doing, or an impotence which results in the general loosening of the ties of civilized society may in [North and South] America, as elsewhere, ultimately require intervention by some civilized nation, and in the western hemisphere the adherence of the United States to the Monroe Doctrine may force the United States, however reluctantly, in flagrant cases of such wrong-doing or impotence, to the exercise of an international police power.[15]

Yet it wasn't just in 'flagrant cases of wrong-doing or impotence' that the United States chose to exercise international police power.

Mr. Roosevelt repeatedly said that the best guide to foreign policy was the motto of a West African tribe: 'Speak softly and carry a big stick and you will go far.'

Mr. Roosevelt watched with concern as Russia acquired huge blocks of territory and was soon to complete the trans-Siberian railroad. He now had concerns about present Russian industrial strength, due mainly to severe government mismanagement. Said he: "Undoubtedly the future is hers, unless she mars it from within. But it is the future, not the present."[16] He was content at the time to let a rising Japan alone, but put a 'check' on Russia, and felt that

---

[14]Cooper 1990, p. 28.
[15]Ibid., p. 50.
[16]Stueck 2004, p. 17.

that check would be even more effective with Japan's acquisition of Korea. This power conflict contributed to the Korean War later in the century.

One of the challenges Mr. Roosevelt faced and sought to resolve was the long delay transporting goods by ship from the eastern U.S. to the west. There had long been talk of a canal across either Panama or Nicaragua. As early as 1846, the U.S. signed a treaty with Columbia, agreeing to offer all nations equal terms for the use of any canal or railroad constructed across the isthmus. Four years later, with the signing of the Clayton–Bulwer Treaty, the U.S. and Britain agreed to guarantee the neutrality of any canal built there.

During the Spanish–American War, the need for some better and faster means of transport was underscored. In 1902, Congress voted to approve a canal through Panama. This was not done without considerable political posturing.

In 1850, the Clayton–Bulwar Treaty was signed by the U.S. and Great Britain. The main provision is as follows:

> The Governments of Great Britain and the United States hereby declare, that neither the one nor the other will ever obtain or maintain for itself any exclusive control over the said Ship-Canal; agree, that neither will ever erect or maintain any fortifications commanding the same, or in the vicinity thereof, or occupy or fortify, or colonize, or assume, or exercise any dominion over Nicaragua, Costa Rica, the Mosquito Coast, or any part of Central America; nor will either make use of any protection which either affords or may afford, or any alliance which either has or may have, to or with any State or People for the purpose of erecting or maintaining any such fortifications, or of occupying, fortifying or colonizing Nicagarua, Costa Rica, the Mosquito Coast or any part of Central America, or of assuming or exercising dominion over the same.[17]

---

[17]Humphreys 1961, pp. 52–53.

Wildly unpopular in the U.S., since for some, it seemed that it violated the Monroe Doctrine, and it certainly impeded the U.S.'s imperial goals, it was eventually superseded by Hay–Pauncefote Treaties,[18] ratified in 1901.This agreement was more in keeping with what the U.S. populace, and certainly the government, expected from an up-and-coming world power. It allowed the U.S. to build a canal and have complete control of both its management and its regulation. It still mentioned neutrality, but under the sole guarantee of the United States. And while it provided for ships of all nations to use it under equal terms, any discussion forbidding fortifications was pointedly omitted.

The Clayton–Bulwar Treaty would have prevented the U.S. from building the canal, but Secretary of State John Jay was able to secure its abrogation by way of the Hay–Pauncefote Treaties. The U.S. then attempted a new treaty, called the Hay–Herran treaty, which would have granted the U.S. a lease in perpetuity across the Isthmus of Panama, which was then part of Columbia, for which Columbia would be paid $10,000,000, with a yearly rental of $250,000. Columbia rejected the offer. The U.S., apparently, then used a method it would come to employ many times in the future.

> On November 3, 1903, 'a quiet uprising' occurred in Panama, and the Columbian authorities were politely expelled. A week later, Bunau-Varilla, the representative of the new republic, was in Washington, and on November 18, 1903, the Hay–Bunau–Varilla Treaty, practically the same as the Hay–Herran Treaty, except that [the U.S.] bought the ten mile strip outright, was negotiated. Enemies of the administration called [the U.S.] part in the transactions an '... ineffaceable blot of dishonor.' Official Washington knew of the negotiations and the development, for gunboats were there and Acting Secretary of State Loomis sent a dispatch to Panama

---

[18] "Unfulfilled Hope: The Joint Board and the Panama Canal, 1903-1919" 2006 [July].

asking how the revolt was progressing several hours before it began.[19]

Columbia demanded that the U.S. make reparation for the events of the 1903 'revolution.' It wasn't until April of 1914, four months before the opening of the Panama Canal, that the U.S., through the American minister at Bogota, expressed "sincere regret that anything should have occurred to interrupt or mar the relations of cordial friendship that had so long subsisted between the two nations."[20] That, $25,000,000 and the right for Columbia to use the canal for military purposes, mollified Columbia. Yet the treaty was not signed by the U.S. Congress until 1921. Congress didn't like Columbia's tone and didn't want the president to have to apologize for anything the U.S. had done. This innocuous statement was seen as somehow too demeaning, although it was eventually accepted.

Always with an eye on the bottom line, the U.S. purchased the Virgin Islands in 1917 for $25,000,000. This provided the U.S. with a direct route with European ports and an excellent harbor with access to oil distribution for oil-burning steamers.

Roosevelt, a shameless imperialist, worried during his first term about public repudiation of his imperialist goals, "due to the time, money and lives invested in the Philippine War."[21] After the war, people "questioned the wisdom and justice of imperialism when it involved the suppression of freedom-seeking people in the Philippines, although those critics tended to wait until retirement to voice such sentiments."[22]

As the U.S. continued to grow in size, economic and military power, a variety of viewpoints arose on how best to proceed.

[T]here emerged the view among many congressmen, journalists, and some business representatives that the capacity to

---

[19] Jennings 1926, p. 564.
[20] Longley 2002, p. 121.
[21] Oyos 2000 [June].
[22] Ibid.

produce goods was outrunning the economic demand of the home market. All were agreed that foreign markets were of increasing importance because of the danger of an industrial surplus. Some set forth a reciprocal trade program as the best answer to this problem. Others adhered to the traditional protective tariff policies and thought the solution to the surplus lay in a policy of opening up foreign markets by aggressive pursuit of colonies, or by strong pressure on governments to open the door to American goods.[23]

With the opening of the new century, U.S. foreign policy continued to focus on further enriching the nation. "[T]arrif laws gave protection to our manufacturers, and so a sort of guarantee of return led to the continued investment of capital in industry. With the leading nations of Europe locked in a death struggle, some neutral country had to produce the commodities which they could not provide for themselves."[24] The U.S. didn't hesitate to continue providing those commodities after any talk of neutrality had long since ended. And the nation had a variety of reasons for going to war, not the least of which is indicated by the following: "War stimulated the demand for explosives, iron, steel, automobile parts, copper, brass, bronze, zinc, boots and shoes, meat, canned goods, dairy products, etc. ... Practically every class in the country had its purchasing power temporarily increased. That big profits were an incentive to development is proved by the sudden crop of millionaires. ... "[25]

With Europe 'locked in a death struggle,' the U.S. watched, at first from the sidelines. British writer Norman Agnell, in a widely translated and widely read book, argued in 1909 "that even a victorious warring power would suffer extraordinary economic and financial loss as a result of war."[26] Woodrow Wilson, who became president

---

[23]Spanier and Hook 2009, p. 209.

[24]Jennings 1926, pp. 593–594.

[25]Ibid., p. 594.

[26]Keegan 2000, p. 12.

in 1913, never seemed anxious to go to war, but was not hard to push into it.

Chapter 7.

World War I

The sinking of the British passenger ship, the *Lusitania*, in 1915, enraged Americans. Germany was already at war with England, and had warned the U.S. that British ships would be targeted and that U.S. citizens should not board them. The anger of the U.S. towards Germany was unabated, even when Germany claimed that the ship was carrying munitions to Britain, a claim that was later substantiated.[1] Newspapers darkly warned about the dangers of the U.S. German-American immigrant community, speculating about their possible behavior should the U.S. enter the war.

In early 1917, at least six ships either owned by U.S. citizens, or carrying U.S. citizens or U.S. goods, were sunk. President Wilson still proclaimed: "We stand fast on armed neutrality."[2] That same year, President Wilson said this: "this country does not intend to become involved in this war. We are the only one of the great white nations that is free from war to-day and it would be a crime against civilization for us to go in."[3]

Yet the business community was getting nervous, and war was inevitable.

> U.S. entry into World War I was closely bound up with this global ambition and moral renditions of it. Never before had

---

[1] Jaher 1974, p. 89.
[2] Ibid., p. 314.
[3] Keegan 2000, p. 306.

the United States intervened in a European war, although there had been several military forays into Asia, and when Woodrow Wilson finally made the decision to intervene in April 1917, the immediate justification was a series of German naval attacks on U. S. trading ships. Commerce on the high seas, he argued, was a global and inviolable right. But U. S. neutrality had been merely formal. The sunken ships were hauling part of the U. S. surplus – war materiel and related goods – to the European Allies, and by 1917 U. S. financiers had lent the Allies a staggering $2.3 billion, almost a hundred times what they had released to Germany. These bankers had so much at stake in an Allied success that the Treasury Department and the Federal Reserve Board were 'alarmed.' The success of U. S. economic expansion had become inextricably bound up with the necessity of an Allied victory, and the possible effects of a German victory raised geopolitical fears concerning Latin America. Moral authority to design the resulting peace would belong to those who had fought on the battlefield, and these very practical considerations were recycled into a moral rationale for war against a militaristic and autocratic aggressor. Heightened nationalism at home targeted socialists and pacifists who broadcast the less noble economic grounds for U. S. involvement.[4]

The U.S., if its own public relations program is to be believed, has always been a beacon of peace and freedom. Its long history of war-making and oppression of individual freedoms in the country with which it is at war, as well as within the U.S., along with its countenance of horrific human rights abuses globally, certainly belie that reputation. As the country prepared to enter World War I, Congress passed the Espionage Act of 1917. This law included punishments for "anyone intentionally making false reports that interfered with military operations, willfully obstructing the draft, or willfully causing, or attempting to cause, 'insubordination, disloyalty, mutiny, or

---

[4]N. Smith 2004, pp. 115–116.

refusal of duty, in the military or naval forces of the United States.'"[5] It was amended in 1918 with the Sedition Act, which expanded the scope of the Espionage Act and included "'any disloyal, profane, scurrilous, or abusive language' about the form of government of the United States, the Constitution, the flag, or the military. ... '"[6] For the U.S., freedom and human rights have always taken a back seat to the pursuit of power and monetary gain.

In its quest to protect commercial routes, U.S. involvement in World War I cost the lives of nearly 117,000 Americans. Over 16,500,000 people were killed around the world in the most horrific conflict the world had ever seen up to that time.

Back home, although the U.S. didn't experience the unspeakable horrors being inflicted on the European nations, ugly aspects of the war were felt. "Fear of 'enemy aliens' and sweeping, often unwarranted, government programs of investigation, incarceration and deportation have been recurrent in U.S. history during times of war or confrontation with a foreign enemy. Federal and state administrations have in the past targeted national origin groups during times of crisis as scapegoats."[7] The Alien Enemies Act, passed in 1798, which authorized the president to apprehend and deport any resident aliens whose home countries were at war with the United States of America, was brought into use. At least 6,300 German-Americans were arrested under this act. German males over the age of 14 were forbidden from owning guns or radios, and a quarter of a million German-Americans were required to register and to carry their government-issued identification cards with them at all times. German immigrants, who had assimilated remarkably well into U.S. society, were now viewed with suspicion, and were harassed on many fronts. German-American organizations were attacked; many Lutheran churches switched from using German in their services to using English. As former President

---

[5] J. A. Smith 1999, p. 39.
[6] Ibid., p. 39.
[7] Barkan 2007, p. 247.

Theodore Roosevelt put it: "We are convinced today that our most dangerous foe is the foreign-language press and every similar agency, such as the German-American Alliance, which holds the alien to his former associations and through them to his former allegiance. We call upon all loyal and unadulterated Americans to man the trenches against the enemy within our gates."[8]

African-Americans, too, felt the sharp sting of racism, even when valiantly defending the nation that deprived them of basic freedoms. At least 200,000 African-Americans served in the American Expeditionary Forces (AEF) in France and England. Another 170,000 served in the United States. Frequently they felt that fighting to provide freedoms to others might result in the improvement in their treatment at home.

Yet willingness to fight the nation's battle was not universally felt by all African-Americans. On August 23, 1917, white police raided the quarters of African-American enlisted men, resulting in a riot in which 15 people died, and after which 41 African-American soldiers were given life sentences. Another 13 were hanged less than two months later. In response, the *San Antonio Inquirer*, an African-American newspaper, published this: "We would rather see you shot by the highest tribunal of the United States Army because you dared protect a Negro woman from the insult of a southern brute in the form of a policeman, than to have you forced to go to Europe to fight for a liberty you cannot enjoy."[9] The editor, G. W. Bouldin, was charged with "attempting to cause insubordination, disloyalty, mutiny, and refusal of duty."[10] He was sentenced to two years in jail.

White soldiers often did nothing to hide their disdain for these men who were risking their lives the same as they themselves. Chaplain Samuel Arthur Devan of the 58th Field Artillery Regiment said this: "There are lots and lots of darkeys in the big camp where I am now

---

[8]Reimers 1999, pp. 18–19.
[9]Mead 2000, p. 372.
[10]Ibid., p. 372.

located. They are the most interesting soldiers you could ever hope to find – always cheerful and respectful. A darkey soldier will never fail to salute if he can possibly disengage a hand to do it without encurring [sic] serious consequences. One lost his mess kit today in his eagerness to salute me as he passed." [11]

Although African-Americans were anxious to join the Army, they still faced discrimination. Some recruiters overlooked conditions that made whites ineligible. "One Georgia county exemption board discharged forty-four percent of white registrants on physical grounds and exempted only three percent of black registrants based on the same requirements." [12] Other areas intentionally caused problems for African-Americans. "It was fairly common for southern postal workers to deliberately withhold the registration cards of eligible black men and have them arrested for being draft dodgers. African American men who owned their own farms and had families were often drafted before single white employees of large planters." [13] While African-Americans at the time comprised ten percent of the U.S. population, they accounted for 13 percent of draftees. At the start of the war, African-Americans could only serve in the Army, Navy and Coast Guard, but only in menial roles in the latter two. They could not serve in the Marines.

Despite this discrimination, tens of thousands of African-Americans served bravely and valiantly. Additionally, "[t]he African-American experience in the Great War served as a crucible that sparked the Civil Rights movement and the Harlem renaissance. Black veterans returned to a country that spurned them, even after having bled for it. The Great War experience revolutionized Black culture, re-shaped the country, and paved the way for future movements." [14]

---

[11] Ibid., p. 373.

[12] http://www.militaryhistoryonline.com/wwi/articles/fightingforrespect.aspx. Accessed on October 2, 2012.

[13] Ibid.

[14] "World War I and the Politics of Race." http://wsu.academia.edu/Kevin Belting/Papers/1392 432/World_War_I_and_the_Politics_of_Race. Accessed

Yet the war was hardly the great equalizer that many African-Americans, both soldiers and political leaders, hoped it would be. There was a belief that, standing side-by-side with their white compatriots, serving the country they both lived in, a new racial equality would be born. And while the birth process may have started then, it was not an easy transition. During World War I, the government was only interested in them as cannon fodder.

The first African-American troops to serve overseas were part of service units, responsible for work that was vital to the war effort. Commanding officers promised special privileges to be awarded based on high-yield results. Initially responsible for unloading ships and transporting men and supplies to and from different bases, railroad depots and ports, they later were "responsible for digging trenches, removing unexploded shells from fields, clearing disabled equipment and barbed wire, and burying soldiers killed in action. Despite all the hard and essential work they provided, African American stevedores received the worst treatment of all black troops serving in World War I."[15]

German propaganda efforts were directed, in part, to African-American soldiers.

> Hello, boys, what are you doing over here? Fighting the Germans? Why? Do you enjoy the same rights as the white people do in America, the land of freedom and Democracy, or are you not rather treated over there as second class citizens?
>
> Can you get into a restaurant where white people dine? Can you get a seat in a theatre where white people sit? Can you get a seat or berth in a railroad car, or can you even ride in the South in the same street car with white people?
>
> And how about the law? Is lynching and the most horrible crimes connected therewith a lawful proceeding in a

---

on October 2, 2012.

[15]http://www.militaryhistoryonline.com/wwi/articles/fightingforrespect.aspx. Accessed on October 2, 2012. Article originally appeared in *On Point*, an Army Historical Foundation publication.

Democratic country? Now all this is entirely different in Germany.[16]

The points Germany raised in this propaganda document must have resonated with at least some African-Americans fighting the war.

Germany, it must be noted, was not universally sympathetic to the African-Americans. They issued other propaganda that included false information about the rape of white women by these soldiers.

But it wasn't only the Germans who were producing propaganda concerning African-Americans fighting for the U.S. The United States itself, while willing to throw African-Americans into the trenches, wasn't particularly interested in elevating their status back home.

> Throughout the war, the U.S. government and the military feared the ramifications of African American soldiers participating freely in French culture. They warned the French not to associate with African Americans and disseminated racist propaganda. African Americans' experience of equal rights in France directly challenged the segregationists in the U.S. armed forces who were also stationed in France. French society was far more open than U.S. society, despite its own colonial racism in relation to Africa.[17]

U.S. propaganda, like that of the Germans, also falsely accused African-American soldiers of raping white women.

The French, however, didn't seem impressed with U.S. propaganda efforts against African-Americans. Unlike the U.S., which awarded no medals to any African-American soldier who served in World War I until years after the war, and then only posthumously, the French awarded hundreds of its most important and prestigious

---

[16]http://historymatters.gmu.edu/d/5330/. Accessed October 10, 2012.
[17]Batkar 2000, p. 61.

medal, the crois de guerre, to African-American soldiers due to their exceptionally heroic efforts.[18]

It wasn't just African-Americans, of course, who experienced the wrath of the government and its citizen-followers. During World War I, as today, any disagreement with the government's war plans is viewed with traitorous suspicion. During The Great War,

> enemy aliens, conscientious objectors, free speech advocates, socialists and other political and labor radicals, and urban, working-class African-Americans all came to be painted with the same brush as the collective 'enemy within.' This simple-minded conceptualization of patriot and enemy facilitated the prosecution of the war, but it also proved difficult to dislodge after hostilities ceased. Historian John Higham, among others, has noted that the overwrought patriotic emotionalism of the war era spawned a nativist torrent of vituperation and violence against enemy aliens. An omnipresent, unreasonable abhorrence of dissent from any source overlapped dramatically with the antiradical, anti-labor spirit that sprang up immediately following the war.[19]

As the war drew to a close, even President Wilson – who, while reluctant to declare war, did so anyway – disillusioned and demoralized, recognized the true reason for the war. Said he: "Why, my fellow-citizens, is there any man here, or any woman – let me say, is there any child here – who does not know that the seed of war in the modern world is industrial and commercial rivalry? This war, in its inception, was a commercial and industrial war."[20]

In order for the United States to continue its imperial march across the globe, its stated intentions, long used as an excuse and a method for exciting the citizenry to hop on its bandwagon, were finally

---

[18]http://www.bookrags.com/research/african-americans-world-war-i-aaw-03/. Accessed on October 2, 2012

[19]Early 1997, pp. 157–158.

[20]Allen 1972, p. 158.

crystallized. "Usually, moves toward involvement had to be clothed in terms of duty and national obligation or described as necessary to protect the helpless against the imperialism of others."[21] This had been demonstrated successfully in the Spanish–American War, wherein the nation had been enraged by what it saw as the barbarous oppression of the Spanish government toward its Cuban colony, and earlier, in the Mexican–American War when it was reported that Mexico had violated U.S. sovereignty by attacking soldiers on U.S. soil. The fact that that 'U.S. soil' was at best disputed, and at worst, stolen, was not much discussed. In those conflicts, the U.S. government framed the situation in the light best able to motivate the citizens into throwing their wholehearted support behind a new, imperial war. In order to enter World War I, the sinking of several ships and the deaths of U.S. passengers whipped the nation into a jingoistic frenzy of war.

---

[21]Spanier and Hook 2009, p. 210.

Chapter 8.

Between World War I and World War II

Towards the close of World War I, the 'war to end all wars,' President Wilson, who had reluctantly given way to the economic interests of the U.S. as superior to peace, presented to Congress 14 points for 'a new world order.' The introduction to this document shows how brazen the U.S. can be. Mr. Wilson presented his reasons for establishing these points. The reasons read, in part, as follows: "It is that the world be made fit and safe to live in, and particularly that it be made safe for every peace-loving nation which, like our own, wishes to live its own life, determine its own institutions, be assured of justice and fair dealing by the other peoples of the world as against force and selfish aggression."[1]

The preceding chapters in this book show that the U.S. has had no wish to 'be assured of justice and fair dealing,' or to be free of 'force and selfish aggression,' except for itself. It has seldom been just and fair in dealing with other nations, and has often used 'force and selfish aggression' against them. Its dealings with any country that stood in the way of its imperial goals have lacked any semblance of justice, and have nearly always used force and aggression to achieve its imperial goals.

World War I had given the U.S. economy a tremendous lift; Mr.

---

[1] Valone 1995, p. 56.

Wilson was not mistaken in his evaluation of it as a commercial and industrial war. By 1929, the U.S. was producing 46 percent of the entire world's industrial goods. This was more than the next 23 countries combined. U.S. exports doubled during the period of the 1920s, to a total of $5.4 billion, the highest of any nation on earth.[2]

Because the U.S. rejected joining the League of Nations, strongly supported by President Wilson, the nation was referred to by some commentators as 'isolationist.' However, by this time the U.S. had a far-flung empire that included Alaska, Hawaii, Midway, Wake Island, Guam, Samoa, the Philippines, Puerto Rico and the Virgin Islands. "America also exercised protectorates (a large measure of military and financial control) over Cuba, Panama, the Dominican Republic, Nicaragua, and Haiti. This empire was protected by a navy that ranked second or third in the world."[3]

Yet the conquests that the U.S. had made to obtain this empire didn't stop it from paying lip-service to a desire for peace. In 1928 the U.S. was a signatory to the Kellogg-Briand Pact. Named after U.S. Secretary of State Frank Kellogg and French Foreign Minister Astiride Briand, it was eventually signed by 62 nations, and it renounced war "as an instrument of national policy in their relations with one another."[4] The two articles of the pact read as follows:

> *Article I*
> The High Contracting Parties solemnly declare in the names of their respective peoples that they condemn recourse to war for the solution of international controversies, and renounce it as an instrument of national policy in their relations with one another.
> *Article II*
> The High Contracting Parties agree that the settlement or solution of all disputes or conflicts of whatever nature or of

---

[2]Bagby 1999, p. 52.
[3]Ibid., p. 50.
[4]U.S. Government Printing Office 1942.

> whatever origin they may be, which may arise among them,
> shall never be sought except by pacific means.[5]

It didn't take long for the U.S., and many other countries, to ignore this high-minded pact.

While the U.S. was making noble-sounding efforts at eliminating war, efforts it basically would exempt itself from, the lust for continued and increased economic strength never wavered. Herbert Hoover, who served as president from 1929 to 1933, had worked internationally as a mining engineer. As Secretary of Commerce he enthusiastically promoted U.S. business interests internationally. As president, he said: "'We have no hates; we wish no further possessions; we harbor no military threats' but wish only to 'advance the cause of peace.'"[6]

Oddly, he appointed Henry L. Stimson as his Secretary of State. Mr. Stimson previously served under President William Howard Taft as Secretary of War, had been an artillery colonel in World War I and was a close friend of Theodore Roosevelt. "He spoke of the 'joy of war' and at times, said Hoover, was 'more of a warrior than a diplomat.'"[7]

One incident occurring in Asia underscores the duality of U.S. policy, ostensibly fostering independence and democracy on the one hand, but keeping a close hold on the bottom line with the other. China and Japan had long had serious border disagreements, culminating in what became known as the Manchurian Incident (or Mukden Incident). On September 18, 1931, a minor explosion occurred on the South Manchurian Railway in northeastern China. This railway was Japanese-owned. Japan had had a presence in the area for over 25 years, mainly, at least ostensibly, to protect railway operations. Therefore, Japanese soldiers were on hand to defend the nation's interests. Japanese leadership accused China of planting the explosives, in what they called "only the latest in a series of

---

[5] Valone 1995, p. 68.
[6] Bagby 1999, p. 51.
[7] Ibid., p. 51.

anti-Japanese 'outrages.'"[8] It soon became apparent that Japan, and not China, had set the explosives, in a bid to increase Japan's authority in Manchuria.

The U.S., once again calling on its self-defined moral authority, expressed its displeasure over this increasing conflict. President Herbert Hoover, through his Secretary of State, Henry Stimson, put forth the Stimson Doctrine. This policy states, in part, that the U.S. doesn't recognize, "nor does it intend to recognize any treaty or agreement entered into between those Governments, or agents thereof, which may impair the treaty rights of the United States ... including those which relate to the sovereignty, the independence or the territorial and administrative integrity of the Republic of China. ..."[9]

But while cautiously watching the situation, and condemning Japan for its actions in starting this particular problem, the U.S. continued to expand economic ties with Japan, ceasing only in 1939.[10] Once again, economic interests would not take a back seat to international justice.

In the election of 1932, Franklin Delano Roosevelt was elected president. The Great Depression had taken hold. The Depression reached its worst milestone the month Mr. Roosevelt took office, with production being cut in half from its post-war zenith and unemployment exceeding 25 percent. The new president was anxious to restore foreign markets for U.S. products.[11]

In order to make international trade more attractive for the world community, Mr. Roosevelt reduced tariffs: "instead of unilaterally cutting America's tariff, he employed a technique that enabled him to secure reductions in other nation's tariffs as well. In June 1934, Congress enacted the Reciprocal Trade Agreement Act, which authorized the president to negotiate treaties to cut U.S. tariffs on specific items by as much as 50 percent in return for reciprocal cuts by other

---

[8] Wilson 2001, p. 1.
[9] Valone 1995, p. 69.
[10] Kovalio 2006 [Spring].
[11] Bagby 1999, p. 74.

nations in their tariffs on U.S. products."[12]

While dealing with the devastating effects of the Great Depression, Mr. Roosevelt didn't completely ignore foreign affairs. "Latin Americans were demanding, with growing heat, that the Unites States renounce its practice of invading their countries."[13] The president was willing to accommodate this demand, at least ostensibly. He said that "single-handed intervention by us in the internal affairs of other nations must end; with the cooperation of others we shall have more order in this hemisphere and less dislike."[14] To that end he initiated the 'Good Neighbor Policy,' an expression coined from his inaugural address, wherein he promised to "dedicate this nation to the policy of the good neighbor – the neighbor who resolutely respects himself and, because he does so, respects the rights of others – the neighbor who respects his obligations and respects the sanctity of his agreements in and with a world of neighbors."[15] This policy, like many of the U.S.'s benevolent global initiatives, eventually became a farce, as will be shown in subsequent chapters.

Senator Robert Taft (Republican – Ohio) seemed almost prophetic when urging against rampant U.S. global intervention. In 1939, he said this: "We should be prepared to defend our own shores ... but we should not undertake to defend the ideals of democracy in foreign countries. ... No one has ever suggested before that a single nation should range over the world, like a knight-errant, protect democracy and ideals of good faith, and tilt, like Don Quixote, against the windmills of fascism. ... Such a policy is not only vain, but bound to lead to war."[16] As will be shown, the U.S.'s continued purported efforts to 'protect democracy' has been used as a mask to hide its real agenda of expanding its power and economic might, on multiple occasions. And these efforts have often led to war. Yet during this

---

[12]Ibid., p. 74.
[13]Ibid., p. 75.
[14]Meyer 2004 [April 12].
[15]Greer 1999, p. 158.
[16]Quint and Cantor 1975, p. 235.

period between the two most devastating wars the world has ever known, there were at least some half-hearted attempts to reign in the imperial beast.

Following World War I, international planners considered that Germany and Great Britain were key to the rebuilding of Europe. By 1930, Nazi ideology was ascendant in Germany, and Adolph Hitler rode that wave of popularity to power. But even before he became Chancellor, the U.S. supported the Nazi regime. "Twenty of the leading Fortune 500 U.S. firms had extensive investments in Germany during the 1920s and 1930s. In the 1930s, U.S. capital-intensive investors worked closely with the State Department in developing an appeasement policy toward the Nazi regime of Adolf Hitler. The aim was to steer Hitler away from a series of preferential bilateral trading agreements that had systematically reduced U.S. trade and investment in Germany during the 1930s."[17] Nazism, a form of fascism that includes biological racism with anti-Semitism, in all its ugliness was, to the U.S., worth appeasing, in order to foster greater U.S. trade. Germany was a lucrative trade and investment market for U.S. business.

U.S. business support for fascism began even earlier: during the Spanish Civil War, when Francisco Franco's fascists were aided by Hitler and Benito Mussolini, U.S. corporations including General Motors, Ford, DuPont and Standard Oil were major suppliers of fascist European powers.

These and other U.S. corporations invested heavily in Hitler's Germany. Once the U.S. declared war on Germany, the 'Trading with the Enemy Act' supposedly prevented any further trade between U.S. corporations and countries with which the U.S. was at war. "Despite this, some companies and individuals still maintained a business relationship with the Third Reich. Ford and GM supplied European fascists with trucks and equipment as well as investing money in I.G. Farben plants. Standard Oil supplied the fascists with

---

[17]Cox and Skidmore-Hess 1999, p. 28.

fuel. U.S. Steel and Alcoa supplied them with critically needed metals. American banks gave them billions of dollars worth of loans." [18]

It was only after the German invasion of Poland that the U.S. moved from appeasement to war preparation, and only because that action provided further evidence that Germany was not interested in loosening trade restrictions the U.S. found somewhat stifling.

---

[18] http://www.rationalrevolution.net/war/american_supporters_of_the_europ.htm. Accessed on July 17, 2012.

Chapter 9.

World War II

Germany's invasion of Poland did nothing to deter American business from investing in the Nazi regime. Of course, this could only be done with at least the tacit consent of the U.S. government.

The 'Trading with the Enemy' act had been passed in 1917. This law restricted trade with countries hostile to the United States and gave the president the power to restrict all trade between the U.S. and its enemies in times of war. On December 13, 1941, less than a week after Pearl Harbor was bombed by the Japanese, President Franklin D. Roosevelt signed an amendment to the act. The crux of the amendment is as follows:

> A general license is hereby granted, licensing any transaction or act proscribed by section 3(a) of The Trading with the Enemy Act, as amended, provided, however, that such transaction or act is authorized by the Secretary of the Treasury by means of regulations, rulings, instructions, licenses or otherwise, pursuant to the Executive order No. 8389, as amended.[1]

It appears that the Secretary of the Treasury did not hesitate to issue such rulings and instructions, almost arbitrarily.

The following quotation, from a report of the United States Senate Committee on the Judiciary in 1974, provides some context for the

---

[1]Hingham 2007, p. xv.

behaviors of these global businesses during the time leading up to
World War II, and during the war itself:

> The activities of General Motors, Ford and Chrysler prior
> to and during World War II ... are instructive. At that time,
> these three firms dominated motor vehicle production in both
> the United States and Germany. Due to its mass production
> capabilities, automobile manufacturing is one of the most
> crucial industries with respect to national defense. As a re-
> sult, these firms retained the economic and political power to
> affect the shape of governmental relations both within and
> between these nations in a manner which maximized corpo-
> rate global profits. In short, they were private governments
> unaccountable to the citizens of any country yet possessing
> tremendous influence over the course of war and peace in
> the world. The substantial contribution of these firms to the
> American war effort in terms of tanks, aircraft components,
> and other military equipment is widely acknowledged. Less
> well known are the simultaneous contributions of their for-
> eign subsidiaries to the Axis Powers. In sum, they maximized
> profits by supplying both sides with the materiel needed to
> conduct the war.
>
> During the 1920's and 1930's, the Big Three automakers un-
> dertook an extensive program of multinational expansion ...
> By the mid-1930's, these three American companies owned
> automotive subsidiaries throughout Europe and the Far East;
> many of their largest facilities were located in the politi-
> cally sensitive nations of Germany, Poland, Rumania, Austria,
> Hungary, Latvia, and Japan ... Due to their concentrated
> economic power over motor vehicle production in both Al-
> lied and Axis territories, the Big Three inevitably became
> major factors in the preparations and progress of the war. In
> Germany, for example, General Motors and Ford became an
> integral part of the Nazi war efforts. GM's plants in Germany
> built thousands of bomber and jet fighter propulsion systems
> for the Luftwaffe at the same time that its American plants

produced aircraft engines for the U.S. Army Air Corps. . . .

Ford was also active in Nazi Germany's prewar preparations. In 1938, for instance, it opened a truck assembly plant in Berlin whose 'real purpose,' according to U.S. Army Intelligence, was producing 'troop transport-type' vehicles for the Wehrmacht. That year Ford's chief executive received the Nazi German Eagle (first class). . . .

The outbreak of war in September 1939 resulted inevitably in the full conversion by GM and Ford of their Axis plants to the production of military aircraft and trucks. . . . On the ground, GM and Ford subsidiaries built nearly 90 percent of the armored 'mule' 3-ton half-trucks and more than 70 percent of the Reich's medium and heavy-duty trucks. These vehicles, according to American intelligence reports, served as 'the backbone of the German Army transportation system.' . . .

After the cessation of hostilities, GM and Ford demanded reparations from the U.S. Government for wartime damages sustained by their Axis facilities as a result of Allied bombing . . . Ford received a little less than $1 million, primarily as a result of damages sustained by its military truck complex at Cologne . . .

Due to their multinational dominance of motor vehicle production, GM and Ford became principal suppliers for the forces of fascism as well as for the forces of democracy. It may, of course, be argued that participating in both sides of an international conflict, like the common corporate practice of investing in both political parties before an election, is an appropriate corporate activity. Had the Nazis won, General Motors and Ford would have appeared impeccably Nazi; as Hitler lost, these companies were able to re-emerge impeccably American. In either case, the viability of these corporations and the interests of their respective stockholders would have been preserved.[2]

---

[2]http://www.rationalrevolution.net/war/american_supporters_of_the_eu-

This rather lengthy quotation is worth deeper exploration. Consider the following points:

1. The "firms retained the economic and political power to affect the shape of governmental relations both within and between these nations in a manner which maximized corporate global profits." After stating that the companies acted as governments, accountable to no citizens (except, perhaps, their shareholders), the government report attributes to them great power to influence political and military actions.

2. While these companies are typically seen from a U.S. perspective of doing all in their power to aid in the war effort and are, on some level, considered heroic for doing so, they worked as hard to support the Axis powers as they did the Allied powers. The causes of freedom, liberty, etc., were not important to them; maximizing profits was all that mattered.

3. While General Motors was busy building automotive-related supplies for the U.S., it was not idle in Germany. As stated, "In Germany, for example, General Motors and Ford became an integral part of the Nazi war efforts." These companies were equal opportunity suppliers, building planes for the U.S. Army Air Corps and for the Luftwaffe.

4. Ford and General Motors built vehicles "that were the backbone of the German transportation system." This, while U.S. soldiers were dying fighting the Germans.

5. If it were possible for these companies to further slap U.S. citizens in the face, they successfully sued the U.S. government after the war for damages to their plants in Germany.

rop.htm. Accessed on July 17, 2012.

It could be argued that these were the actions of independent corporate entities and not reflective of U.S. government policy. However, it was certainly within the ability of the U.S. to prevent these companies from continuing their activities, which supplied the U.S.'s enemy with items that were essential in their war against the U.S. And, lacking taking any action to prevent these activities, the managers and leaders of these corporate giants could have been charged with a variety of serious infractions after the war, instead of being compensated for the destruction of industrial plants that were creating products for the enemy. Surely these activities violated the 'Trading with the Enemy' Act.

One might reasonably ask why these companies were able to work both sides of the fence, assuring that, regardless of the outcome of the war, corporate profits would not be adversely affected.

A specific look at just three examples is instructive on how these companies were able to supply provisions to both the Axis and the Allies.

1. Bank for International Settlements

The charter for the Bank for International Settlements stated that the bank would "be immune from seizure, closure or censure, whether or not its owners were at war."[3] This bizarre provision in the charter was approved by all the respective governments involved, which included Germany, Japan, Italy, Great Britain and the United States. The stated purpose of the establishment of the bank (1930) was to be a means of providing reparations to the Allies after the anticipated war. However, before and during the war it was a major means of funneling U.S. and British funds into Germany to assist Hitler in building and maintaining his murderous war machine.

By 1944, this Nazi-controlled bank had an American president, one Thomas Harrington McKittrick. During a meeting in May of

---

[3]Hingham 2007, p. 2.

1944, one of the issues was how to handle gold that the bank had received from the Nazi government after Pearl Harbor, to be used by Nazi leaders after the war. "Gold that had been looted from the national banks of Austria, Holland, Belgium, and Czechoslovakia, or melted down from the Reichbank holding of the teeth fillings, spectacle frames, cigarette cases and lighters, and wedding rings of the murdered Jews."[4]

The Bank for International Settlements was not the only U.S.-based financial institution playing both sides of the war fence. Six months before the outbreak of war, Joseph J. Larkin, Chase National Bank's (later Chase Manhattan) vice president of European affairs, secured $25,000,000 in U.S. funds to assist Germany's expanding war economy.[5]

2. Standard Oil of New Jersey

Perhaps among the most blatant, and possibly traitorous, activities were those of Standard Oil of New Jersey. On October 28, 1941, Secretary of State Cordell Hull sent a letter to Edward H. Foley, Jr., the Secretary of the Treasury, asking if Standard Oil could sell petroleum and related products to persons who were known Nazi collaborators. Foley's response was this: "'Such transactions, irrespective of whether they are provided for by contract, should not be engaged in except as specifically authorized by the Secretary of Treasury under Executive Order 8389.' What Foley was pointing out was that it would be quite possible to trade with Nazi associates with Treasury's specific approval."[6] After the bombing of Pearl Harbor, just over a month after this correspondence was written, Standard Oil and other companies were granted licenses, allowing them to trade with enemy collaborators.

---

[4]Hingham 2007, p. 1.
[5]Ibid., p. 22.
[6]Ibid., p. 41.

3. Ford Motor Company

Another influential American business executive who worked closely with the Nazi regime was Edsel Ford. In 1940 he and his father, Henry Ford, met with German agent Gerhardt Westrick in Dearborn, Michigan. After that meeting, Ford "refused to build aircraft engines for England and instead built supplies of the 5-ton military trucks that were the backbone of German army transportation. They arranged to ship tires to Germany despite the shortages; 30% of the shipments went to Nazi-controlled territories abroad."[7] Westerick also celebrated the Nazi victory over France with a lavish party at his suite at New York's Waldorf-Astoria Hotel; among the guests celebrating this event were James D. Mooney of General Motors; Edsel Ford; William Weiss of Sterling Products, and Torkild Rieber of the Texas Company.

Chase Manhattan Bank, Standard Oil of New Jersey and the Ford Motor Company were only three of the major U.S. companies that provided supplies to both Allied and the Axis forces. Others include the following:

- *Davis Oil Company*, which provided Germany with thousands of tons of Mexican oil;

- *Standard Oil* of California, whose chairman "told *Life* Magazine in 1940, 'If the Germans ever catch [any of my ships] carrying oil to the Allies they will have my hearty permission to fire a torpedo into her.'"[8]

- *ITT*, which worked tirelessly throughout the war to improve Germany's telephones, teleprinters, aircraft intercoms, submarine and ship phones, alarm systems, radio and radar parts, and Fock-Wulf bombers.

- *Sterling Products*, a pharmaceutical company that manufactured such common products as aspirin and Phillips Milk of

---

[7]Ibid., p. 156.
[8]Ibid., p. 77.

Magnesia. "Millions of Americans would have been shocked to learn that by their use of these familiar nostrums they were helping to finance an army of secret agents north and south of Panama who supplemented the Max Ilgner N.W.. spy network in supplying information on every aspect of American military possibilities."[9]

There were others.

Various members of the Rockefeller family, with far-flung business interests, and Aristole Onassis were among those exempted. It's interesting to note that during the war, every Greek merchant ship was sunk, except those belonging to Mr. Onassis. This would indicate close agreements on both sides not to sink particular ships.[10] All this, however, was hardly made public.

What would have happened if millions of American and British people, struggling with coupons and lines at the gas stations, had learned that in 1942 Standard Oil of New Jersey managers shipped the enemy's fuel through neutral Switzerland and that the enemy was shipping Allied fuel? Suppose the public had discovered that the Chase Bank in Nazi-occupied Paris after Pearl Harbor was doing millions of dollars' worth of business with the enemy with the full knowledge of the head office in Manhattan? Or that Ford trucks were being built for the German occupation troops in France with authorization from Dearborn, Michigan? Or that Colonel Sosthenes Behn, the head of the international American telephone conglomerate ITT, flew from New York to Madrid to Berne during the war to help improve Hitler's communications systems and improve the robot bombs that devastated London? Or that ITT built the Focke-Wulfs that dropped bombs on British and American troops? Or that crucial ball bearings were shipped to Nazi-associated customers in Latin

---

[9]Hingham 2007, p. 141.
[10]http://www.whale.to/b/aristotle_onassis.html. Accessed July 18, 2012.

America with the collusion of the vice-chairman of the U. S. War Production Board in partnership with Goring's cousin in Philadelphia when American forces were desperately short of them? Or that such arrangements were known about in Washington and either sanctioned or deliberately ignored?[11]

The U.S. may have been interested in stopping Nazi atrocities, but not at the expense of corporate profits.

Once Pearl Harbor was bombed and the U.S entered the war, all Japanese residents in the U.S., including native born citizens, were under suspicion. "Soon after the attack, martial law was declared and leading members of the Japanese American community were taken into custody. On Feb. 19, President Roosevelt signed Executive Order 9066, authorizing the War Department 'to prescribe military areas in such places and of such extent ... from which any or all persons may be excluded, and with such respect to which, the right of any person to enter, remain in, or leave shall be subject to whatever restrictions the Secretary of War or the appropriate Military commander may impose at his discretion."[12] This policy impacted approximately 110,000 Japanese people, two-thirds of whom were U.S. citizens living on the west coast of the United States.

Their treatment was far from humane.

> When the government decided to relocate Japanese Americans ...
> 'they were not merely driven from their homes and communi-
> ties on the West Coast and rounded up like cattle, but actually
> forced to live in facilities meant for animals for weeks and
> even months before being moved to their final quarters.' Con-
> fined in stockyards, racetracks, cattle stalls at fairgrounds,
> they were even housed for a time in converted pigpens. When
> they finally got to the concentration camps, they might find
> that state medical authorities tried to prevent them from

---

[11]Hingham 2007, p. xv.
[12]Ducat 2009, p. 191.

receiving medical care or, as in Arkansas, refused to permit doctors to issue state birth certificates to children born in the camps, as if to deny the infants' legal existence, not to mention their humanity. Later, when the time came to begin releasing them from the camps, racist attitudes often blocked their resettlement.[13]

The decision to inter Japanese-Americans had many justifications, all based in racism. California Attorney General Earl Warren was, perhaps, most prominent among them. On February 21, 1942, he presented testimony to the Select Committee Investigating National Defense Migration, displaying great hostility to foreign-born and American born Japanese people. The following is part of an exchange between Mr. Warren and Congressman Laurence F. Arnold:

Mr. Arnold: Do you have any way of knowing whether any one of this group that you mention is loyal to this country or loyal to Japan?

Attorney General Warren: Congressman, there is no way that we can establish that fact. We believe that when we are dealing with the Caucasian race we have methods that will test the loyalty of them, and we believe that we can, in dealing with the Germans and the Italians, arrive at some fairly sound conclusions because of our knowledge of the way they live in the community and have lived for many years. But when we deal with the Japanese we are in an entirely different field and we cannot form any opinion that we believe to be sound. Their method of living, their language, make for this difficulty. I had together about 10 days ago about 40 district attorneys and about 40 sheriffs in the State to discuss this alien problem, I asked all of them ... if in their experience any Japanese ... had ever given them any information on subversive activities or any disloyalty to this country. The

---

[13]O'Brien and Parsons 1995, p. 21.

answer was unanimously that no such information had ever been given to them.

Now, that is almost unbelievable. You see, when we deal with the German aliens, when we deal with the Italian aliens, we have many informants who are most anxious to help ... authorities to solve this alien problem.[14]

The Constitutionality of the program to imprison Japanese-Americans was upheld in 1942. Chief Justice Harlan Fiske Stone, writing for the unanimous Court "conceded that racial distinctions in the law were 'odious to a free people' but maintained that the 'racial attachments' of the Japanese Americans to 'the Japanese enemy' provided a reasonable basis for the governments' action."[15] Interestingly, one justice, Frank Murphy, wanted to dissent, but was convinced by Justice Felix Frankfurter to concur, in order to "maintain and enhance the corporate reputation of the Court."[16]

Japanese-American prisoners were not released until 1945 and 1946, and this internment had a devastating economic effect on them.

Women during the war were called upon for the first time (at least in large numbers) to fill non-traditional roles, as the men went to war. In order to fulfill the many needs of the war machine, production could not stop, or even slow. The image of Rosie the Riveter seemed to exemplify how woman stepped in to keep the domestic economy running as their husbands, sons, brothers and fathers served in far-flung corners of the globe. Yet, like African-Americans who expected gains in equality by their military service and were bitterly disappointed to find, when the war ended, that nothing had changed, women too were expected to return to the kitchen once the men came home.

There is a strong "contradiction between our image of Rosie the Riveter, a strong, capable woman in nontraditional work, and her

---

[14]S. T. Joshi 1999, pp. 449–450.
[15]O'Brien and Parsons 1995, p. 21.
[16]Ibid., p. 21.

ultimate replacement by Marilyn Monroe, Lucille Ball, and other stars of the 1950s, who embodied a childlike sexuality and comic naivete that were far removed from the images of competence in wage work so recently highlighted by women's entry into war production. Did the public experience a mass amnesia that eliminated all memory of its reliance on women as home-front amazons? How were women themselves able to accept being stripped of so much power and authority?"[17]

But also like African-Americans, who refused, after their military service to a country that discounted their citizenship, to maintain the brutally cruel and inhumane status quo, it may have been these war time experiences – the learning of their own capabilities and the enjoyment of independence and autonomy – that led to the women's movement two decades later.

As the Allied forces entered and occupied Germany, some U.S. and Russian soldiers abused their position as conquerors and occupiers. An estimated 11,000 women were raped by U.S. soldiers,[18] and while this number pales in comparison to the number raped by Russian soldiers (estimates range from the tens of thousands to two million), it has not been widely reported.

In 1945, as the U.S. army was crossing the Rhine, Major-General Raymond Hufft told "the troops under his command to take no prisoners. After the war, he said that, when he reflected on his instructions, which he recognized as war crimes, 'if the Germans had won, I would have been on trial at Nuremberg instead of them.'"[19]

Historian Stephen Ambrose related this: "I've interviewed well over 1000 combat veterans. Only one of them said he shot a prisoner ... Perhaps as many as one-third of the veterans ... however, related incidents in which they saw other GIs shooting unarmed German prisoners who had their hands up."[20]

---

[17]O'Brien and Parsons 1995, p. 83.
[18]Lilly 2007, p. 85.
[19]Thayer 2009, p. 189.
[20]Ibid., p. 190.

It could reasonably be argued that these were isolated incidents, and pale in comparison to the horrific crimes committed by the soldiers of other nations, mainly the unspeakable genocide of the Germans. Yet, regardless of that, they call into question the U.S. belief in a nation whose only goal is freedom and liberty. As has been mentioned before, the U.S. government tries, with a great deal of success, to sell to its citizens a view of the country as a beacon of freedom and justice, wanting nothing more than to foster democracy around the world in the same model that is practiced at home. It allows no dissent from that view, questioning the loyalty of those who see a very flawed democracy at home, and who recognize that not all the world wants what the U.S. has. Additionally, U.S. soldiers, like those of any nation, are subject to the same dehumanizing horrors experienced in any war, and may react as the soldiers of any other nation react to those horrors.

Only one nation on the planet has ever used nuclear weapons, and that, of course, is the United States. On August 6, 1945, the first atomic bomb was dropped on the Japanese city of Hiroshima, immediately killing an estimated 80,000 people. By the end of the year, radiation and injuries brought the death toll to an estimated 90,000–140,000. Three days later, the U.S. bombed the city of Nagasaki, killing another 70,000 people and leaving approximately 75,000 badly injured. Several hundred thousand more suffered and died from radiation-related diseases.

It is beyond the scope of this work to discuss the atrocities committed by the Japanese, the Germans or any other country. However, it is hypocritical for the U.S. to condemn the horrors committed by other nations, when the U.S. itself has perpetrated what could arguably be seen as two of the most horrific single-day atrocities committed in the history of the world. Referring to the U.S. bombing of Hiroshima and Nagasaki, Nobel Prize winner George Wald said: "If we had lost the war, it might have been our leaders who had to answer for such actions."[21]

The war helped propel the U.S. to a level of unprecedented power. "The war economy greatly stimulated technological innovation. The nuclear power industry was the offspring of the atom bomb. Radar and its industrial applications is another outstanding example of a wartime product with significant industrial futures."[22] Among pharmaceutical and chemical advances are included "penicillin, synthetic quinine, atabrine, sulfa drugs, and the mass dissemination of DDT. Two studies by the Bureau of Labor Statistics of wartime technological developments ... listed over 2,300 items of wartime technical advance, many with postwar applications."[23]

As World War II drew to a close,[24] the U.S. feared the rise of leftist and nationalist groups throughout Europe. Business internationalists, once again at the forefront of U.S. foreign policy, "insisted that the United States must be prepared to defuse politically the threat to the emergence of private enterprise, trade, and investment in the all-important region of Western Europe."[25] Any leftist, people's movements must be put down, since there were antithetical to the glory of U.S. capitalism. Partly to this end, the Bretton Woods system was established.

"The chief features of the Bretton Woods system were the abolition of the gold standard and the introduction of a fixed foreign exchange system that revolved around the U.S. dollar as an international currency."[26] Note that the U.S. dollar was central to this system, and all the signatory countries (a total of 44 Allied nations) were to

---

[21]http://content.cdlib.org/view?docId=kt1000 013q;NAAN=13 030&doc.view=
frames&chunk.id=d0e28 582&toc.depth=1&toc.id=
d0e28 457&brand=calisphere. Accessed on November 1, 2012.

[22]Vatter 1996, p. 46.

[23]Ibid., p. 46.

[24]Please note that it is beyond the scope of this work to discuss the unspeakable horrors of this war.

[25]Cox and Skidmore-Hess 1999, p. 120.

[26]Han-Hee 2009.

follow along. Once again, the United States put itself in the economic driver's seat.

Chapter 10.

Korean War

At the close of World War II, with Japan in ruins due to two atomic bombs dropped by the U.S., there was the potential for a power vacuum in northeast Asia. The world's two super-powers – the U.S. and Russia – didn't want the other to fill that vacuum. The U.S. had hoped that either Japan or China would emerge as a world power, thus creating a balance in the region. But with Japan defeated in the war and China showing signs of a split between Nationalists in the south and Communists in the north, that hope began to fade. A memo from the State Department in the fall of 1943 concluded this:

> Korea may appear to offer a tempting opportunity (for Soviet premier Joseph Stalin) ... to strengthen enormously the economic resources of the Soviet Far East, to acquire ice-free ports, and to occupy a dominating strategic position in relation both to China and to Japan. ... A Soviet occupation of Korea would create an entirely new strategic situation in the Far East, and its repercussions within China and Japan might be far reaching.[1]

Additionally, the U.S. saw Korea as a viable trading partner for Japan and wanted a speedy rehabilitation of Japan from the ravages of World War II. Japan's recovery would, the U.S. believed,

---

[1] "Possible Soviet Attitudes toward Far Eastern Questions" 1943 [October 2].

"safeguard the expansion of U.S. trade throughout the region ...",[2] which is always of paramount importance to the U.S.

Korea was also another strategic tool in the U.S.'s grand design to prevent the spread of communism and maintain power throughout the world. When Russia invaded Japan towards the end of the war and sent troops into the northern part of Korea, the U.S. decided to send troops into the south, to prevent Russia from taking the whole thing. Thus the nation was divided, and has been for over 60 years.

The United States had views for its sudden and unexpected involvement in Korea which may not have been clear to the average American. Within the halls of U.S. government, there was a great fear of 'totalitarian regimes' coming to power in Greece and Turkey, thus destabilizing the Middle East and impacting the countries of Europe, which were in disarray, politically and structurally, due to the war. "To Truman, the proper course was clear: 'It must be the policy of the United States to support free people who are resisting attempted subjection by armed minorities or by outside pressure.'"[3]

As has been the case before and since Korea, the U.S. doesn't seem to be too interested in taking into consideration the wishes of the people it attempts to 'liberate.' A version of right-wing pseudo-democracy seems to be the goal every time.

In order to accomplish its goals of keeping Korea out of the hands of Communists, the U.S. needed a puppet leader in the South, so it installed the aging Syngman Rhee. He was a 70-year-old anti-communist zealot who'd lived for years in the U.S. and was a darling of both the U.S. and the Korean right.

Thirty-three-year-old Kim Il Sun, who had popular support in the north, was a well-known and respected guerilla fighter, who sought land reform that would redistribute the land from the few wealthy landowners who currently owned most of the land, forcing many Koreans to subsist as tenant farmers. The U.S., naturally, opposed

---

[2]McGlothlen 1993, p. 18.
[3]Merrill 2006 [March].

this land reform.

In June of 1950, North Korean troops invaded the south. The U.S. was unprepared for this move, focusing more of its attention on Europe than Asia. President Truman had accused his predecessor, Franklin D. Roosevelt, of being 'soft' on the Soviets, and no president could ever tolerate being 'soft' on whatever bugaboo the nation currently feared and hated. As the 1950s began, that bugaboo was communism. Mr. Truman was further pressured by the investigations of right-wing zealot Senator Joseph McCarthy, who was just beginning his infamous witch hunts. At this time he was chairing a Senate investigation over the 'loss' of China to communists, and had directly accused the Truman administration of being soft on the Chinese Communists. "The intensifying Cold War atmosphere, together with Senator McCarthy's renewed attack on the State Department for giving communism 'a green light to grab whatever it could in China, Korea and Formosa,' placed tremendous pressure upon the Truman administration. Outcries for more resolute American action in the face of Communist aggression prevailed among members of both parties and on major newspapers."[4]

With political pressure being brought to bear, Mr. Truman ordered U.S. forces to launch attacks on the North, and the United Nations condemned North Korea's attack and asked the U.S. president to appoint a commander of United Nations' forces. General Douglas MacArthur was so named.

Because of its unpreparedness, the U.S. had some difficulty, not in selling the war to its citizens – American citizens are always happy to start wars – but, as has been the case before and since the Korean War, in maintaining enthusiasm for it. Throughout the three-year war, several main justifications for it were put forth:

1. Repelling the aggression of the Communist north against the democratic south,

---

[4]Jian 1996, p. 167.

2. Liberating the north from the Communists,

3. Accepting a division of the Korean peninsula, and, of course,

4. Stopping the spread of communism.

While these reasons all tend to resonate with the U.S. citizenry, especially at the dawn of Senator McCarthy's notorious witch hunts, economics also played a large part in U.S. interference in Korea. Secretary of State Dean Acheson learned in 1941, when implementing sanctions against Japan, that Korea was Japan's most important source of food. The U.S. was interested in rebuilding Japan as a profitable source of trade. As of 1947, it was estimated that 1,891,000 tons of food would be needed by the Japanese in order to prevent widespread starvation. For the U.S. to provide that food, it would cost a staggering $330,000,000. Prior to World War II, about two-thirds of Japan's rice imports came from Korea – approximately 1,865,000 tons of rice. About 77% of that was grown in the South. The U.S. now proposed to increase the South's food production capability, some which could be sold to Japan, thus assisting the rebuilding of that nation, while also stimulating the economy of South Korea. The first year cost of this would be $215,000,000, although the eventual cost would exceed the initial $330,000,000 estimate by $210,000,000. However, the expenditure was never approved.[5]

The invasion of the South by the North coincided closely with the rise of Senator Joseph McCarthy, one of the most divisive and disgraceful people ever to serve in the U.S. Senate. With communism on the rise, Senator McCarthy was instrumental in ushering in fear of communism to the U.S. and fanning the flames of the 'cold war.'

Like the Iraq War five decades later, the U.S., this time through the United Nations, assembled a coalition of 16 nations to fight the war. However, also like the Iraq War, approximately 90% of these

---

[5]McGlothlen 1993, pp. 59–60.

'coalition' troops were Americans.[6]

Yet for all its imperial designs and past imperial successes, the U.S. found itself confused and somewhat confounded during the Korean War. Political turmoil at home, caused partly by Mr. McCarthy's outrageous accusations, confused the perceived need for this particular war.

Regardless of the many stated and changing reasons for the war, flagrant and shocking human rights abuses were perpetrated, by both the North and the South. However, the U.S., needing the resources of ROK (Republic of Korea) forces in the south, turned a blind eye to these atrocities. A few examples will suffice.

In 1950 Korean National Police (KNP) in the city of Taejon were 'arresting all Communists and executing them on the outskirts of the city.'[7] A CIA report indicated that the same thing was happening in Suwon. The massacres by the South Koreans in Taejon, estimated by some at 7,000, were more probably between 2,000 and 4,000.

While the U.S. turned an official blind eye to this massacre, it did arrange for U.S. photographers to photograph it. "In 1999, an independent scholar living in New York, Do-young Lee, succeeded in getting the U.S. Archives to declassify many of these photographs, which document the massacre of hundreds of political prisoners in Taejon by South Korean authorities, with the total ranging to at least 2,000; this was the same massacre also witnessed by the CIA [Central Intelligence Agency] agent. ..."[8]

One scholar, Callum MacDonald, "cites available evidence and prior experience to suggest that North Korean claims concerning the massacre of over 170,000 civilians by U.N. Forces during the occupation, and the adoption of a scorched earth policy during retreat, are not unreasonable."[9] It must be remembered that 90% of these

---

[6]http://www.sptimes.com/2003/webspecials03/koreanwar/qanda.shtml. Accessed on October 24, 2012.

[7]"Army Intelligence - Korea".

[8]Carter and Clifton 2002, p. 160.

[9]MacDonald 1991 [April/June].

'U.N. Forces' were U.S. soldiers.

Why, one might ask, would the world's self-proclaimed beacon of peace, freedom and human rights allow such atrocities to occur? These lofty goals, so attractive on paper, are never allowed to interfere with U.S. strategic or corporate interests.

Racism, common in the U.S. then and now, took its toll in the Korean War, as it has throughout U.S. history. Maj. Gen. William Dean, the highest-ranking American officer captured during the Korean War, said that he would "emphasize to our own people the terrific harm done by thoughtlessness. Through all the questioning and my many subsequent conversations with intelligent Koreans who had chosen communism after knowing something about our government in South Korea, ran one refrain: they resented being called 'gooks,' and the slighting references to their race and color more than any of our policies, ill-advised or not. Again and again I was told that this man or that one had come north because he had decided he never could get along with people who called him a 'gook,' or worse, among themselves. ..."[10] While General Dean refers to this behavior as 'thoughtlessness,' that is a rather benign term for rampant, institutionalized racism.

It wasn't, of course, just the military where racism in general, and at this particular time against the Koreans, was strong: "As the Washington correspondent of the *New Republic* (July 10, 1950) put it: 'It is hard for us to face up to the difficulty a capitalistic democracy faces in trying to proselytize a primitive people.' Yes, especially a people barred, on chauvinist grounds, from American citizenship and authoritatively defined in Webster New International Dictionary in this manner: 'Korean' A member of the native race of Korea ... of an adeptly imitative rather than profound intelligence."[11]

On July 26, 1948, President Truman issued Executive Order 9981, directing the U.S. military to remove all discrimination. With the

---

[10]Howes 1993, p. 126.

[11]Aptheker 1962, p. 124.

attitudes quoted above, it isn't difficult to understand why progress was so slow. In September of 1948, Mr. Truman established the Committee on Equality of Treatment and Opportunity in the Armed Services. "At that particular junction the Marine Corps had approximately 1,500 black male Marines on active duty, had no black females, was training black recruits in segregated circumstances ... and was not eager to effect any changes in its policies or practices."[12]

Two months after Mr. Truman's election (he was the incumbent, due to becoming president upon the death of President Roosevelt), the Fahy Committee, named for committee chairman Judge Charles Fahy, began holding hearings.

> The Marine Corps ... had a difficult time explaining why it had failed to follow the Navy's integration policy [note: the Navy is the Marine Corps' 'parent' body]. The Marine representative told the committee that [the Corps'] policy of segregation had been adapted as the best, following an investigation of all the records of the Army on the subject. Questioning by the committee's members revealed that the Marine Corps had only one Negro officer among eighty-two hundred, and that no thought had been given to changing the policy of segregation. When asked what he thought of integration, the Marine representative replied, 'I think you'd be making a problem instead of solving one.'[13]

The Navy wasn't doing much better, despite its stated commitment to integration. At this point, it had five black male officers out of 45,000 on active service. There were six black WAVES among 2,130 total.[14]

Overarching all other concerns was, of course, the profit motive. Foreign policy doesn't always reflect the global needs of the U.S.; domestic considerations are also part of most imperial equations. As

---

[12]Soderbergh 1994, p. 22.
[13]Dalfiume 1969, p. 180.
[14]Soderbergh 1994, p. 23.

tensions increased in Korea, the U.S. business community watched carefully and, perhaps, gleefully.

"The stakes at home are also of great consequence to the American ruling class. First – easy, quick and fabulous profits. Says *Newsweek* on July 10, 1950: 'A localized war, possibly followed by other 'incidents,' would ensure heavy defense spending for a long time. That in turn would put a more or less permanent prop under the present high level of industrial activity. ... Depression jitters should virtually disappear."[15]

The Korean conflict, never formally declared a war by the U.S., lasted for 37 months. The war killed approximately 4,000,000 Koreans, nearly 10% of the entire population. Starting as an internal conflict, it eventually involved forces from sixteen nations, greatly damaged U.S. relations with the People's Republic of China, and "taxed the American armed forces almost beyond the limits of the Pacific War with Japan."[16] By the time of the signing of the armistice on July 27, 1953, 30,000 Americans were dead, and over 100,000 injured. "The total number of U.S. soldiers killed during the Korean conflict represented almost 88% of all deaths for U.N. forces."[17]

---

[15]Aptheker 1962, p. 141.
[16]Carter 1989, pp. 47–48.
[17]Ibid., pp. 47–48.

Chapter 11.

Other Foreign Policy Activities of this Period

The United States emerged from two world wars as a global power and was determined to utilize that power as it had its more limited strength in its earlier years: to arrange the world to its liking, with an eye to maximizing profits everywhere.

> "America's foreign policy has in the twentieth century been determined by the place of the United States in the international system *as it has been understood by American leaders* – meaning how the system and the U.S. place within it were viewed by these leaders is critical to an explanation of how and why foreign policy has taken the form it has. How policy makers see the threats and opportunities confronting the United States, as well as the potential for U.S. action to change the international environment and the ways in which change can and should occur, are variables that cannot safely be discounted. ... [1]

It is certainly reasonable that any nation will establish foreign policy as its leaders understand their nation's place in the international system. What is somewhat unique to the United States is its unwillingness to take a broader view or to see how its own actions may impact the rest of the world in ways the U.S. never anticipated.

---

[1]Schonberg 2003, p. 8.

Any perceived threats were often more to convince the citizenry to support some questionable foreign policy, often a war, but the opportunities have usually been a lot clearer and always involved the opportunity for great power or profits, or both. With this perspective, U.S. foreign policy differs from the foreign policy of other nations in fundamental ways.

> Apart from traditional diplomatic channels, the process of making U.S. foreign policy is remarkably insulated from international perspectives. Although the United States develops its policies partly in response to global events, the U.S. foreign policy community tends to give short shrift to the ideas and opinions of international observers. Foreign attitudes are often overlooked, ignored, or dismissed rather than being integrated into U.S. conversations about the country's global engagement. It is a rarity, for example, for a foreign leader to address Congress. Thanks to weak international coverage by the media – which tends to focus on criticism from European public intellectuals or dramatic denunciations from implacable U.S. foes – the U.S. public has only limited access to the views of non-Americans about the U.S. role in the world.[2]

In the first half of the twentieth century, from a corporate or profit-making perspective, the U.S. most often simply created the conditions necessary for U.S. companies to step in. Companies were then free to enter these countries and start their business, utilizing the cheap labor available and taking advantage of the limited or non-existent safety and environmental regulations of those countries.

But emerging from the ashes of World War II were fears of communism. Several nations were seen to be particularly vulnerable to moving in that direction. In the Middle East, it was Iran. "Iran was the largest oil producer in the Middle East at the conclusion of World War II. It was also a country where the threat of Soviet influence was

---

[2]Malone and Khong 2003, p. ix.

palpable."[3] In 1951, when the Parliamentary Oil Committee sought to nationalize the oil industry, controlled at that time mainly by the British, a diplomatic crisis ensued. "From the outset U.S. leaders were fundamentally concerned with the internal political situation in Iran and the danger of Russian influence. The United States did not act to get additional oil supplies for the western world: Iran's liftings had been replaced by increased production in other countries."[4] Although not concerned with a reduction in Iran's oil output, but knowing that Iran would never agree to an entirely British-owned operation again, the U.S. suggested an international consortium with French, British and American participants. U.S. oil companies were not anxious to be involved, but the U.S. agreed to drop a criminal anti-trust lawsuit, one addressing collusive practices in the world oil market, in exchange for their participation.

But it wasn't just this corporate influence that the Unites States brought to bear. U.S. policy-makers "were decisive in their efforts to change a regime they considered to be tainted with communism. Covert U.S. assistance contributed to the success of the military coup that overthrew [Premier] Mohammed Mossadegh in 1953."[5]

So in an effort to prevent communism from spreading to Iran, the U.S. was willing to allow U.S. oil companies to illegally control the world oil markets and to help overthrow a leader of a sovereign nation.

In 1952, Dwight D. Eisenhower was elected president. "The Eisenhower administration faced the same issues – interventionism, economic nationalism, human rights, extracontinental threats – that have dominated inter-American relations in the twentieth century."[6]

One of President Eisenhower's earliest foreign policy concerns was Guatemala. The end of World War II started the so-called 'Cold War', and Mr. Eisenhower wanted Latin American nations to be

---

[3]Krasner 1978, pp. 119–120.
[4]Ibid., p. 120.
[5]Ibid., p. 120.
[6]Rabe 1993, p. 5.

clear that the Cold War was the overarching framework upon which the foreign policy of all nations should be built. With the supposedly free and democratic U.S. and communist Russia as the two opposing super-powers, the U.S. president wanted the nations of Latin America to defer to the U.S. in all aspects of free-world dealing with Russia.

This concept, although not formalized until after Eisenhower's election, had been threatened with the 1950 election of Colonel Jacobo Arbenz Guzman in Guatemala. A leftist leader, one of Colonel Guzman's central objectives was agrarian reform. The U.S. initially saw in Guatemala a middle-class reform effort, but eventually felt it "had been transformed into a radical political movement that threatened U.S. strategic and commercial interests both in Guatemala and throughout the hemisphere."[7] This was confirmed by an action taken by Guzman in 1952, when "he won approval for a bill that allowed the Guatemalan government to seize uncultivated tracts of land and distribute them to roughly 100,000 Guatemalan families. The initiative quickly encountered fierce resistance from the U.S. government and the U.S.-based United Fruit Company, which owned vast plantations in Guatemala for its banana production."[8]

Fortunately for the United Fruit Company, its representatives had close ties to leading U.S. officials. They argued that the obvious communist tendencies of the Arbenz government represented a threat to U.S. national security. An article by Daniel James in *The New Leader*, said this: "The battle of the Western Hemisphere has begun. We enter upon a new era in our history. We face, for the first time, the prospect of continuous struggle against communism on a hemispheric scale. ... Such is the ultimate meaning of Moscow's first attempt to conquer an American country, Guatemala."[9]

By early 1954, the Eisenhower administration was pushing passage of the Declaration of Caracas at the 10th Inter-American Conference

---

[7]Rabe 1993, p. 42.

[8]Bovier 2002, p. 89.

[9]P. H. Smith 1996, p. 135.

of the OAS (Organization of American States) in Venezuela. This proposal called for direct action in the event of any 'international communist movement' that extended into the American continents. Although opposed by nations that saw it as simply a cover for U.S. intervention in Guatemala, it eventually passed.

> When the OAS rejected U.S. requests for multilateral intervention in Guatemala under the Declaration of Caracas, President Dwight Eisenhower chose to pursue covert, unilateral action. The CIA worked to organize and arm a group of Guatemalan exiles, which it stationed across the Guatemalan border in Honduras, and provided fighter planes for an attack on Guatemala City. President Arbenz resigned in the face of an invasion, and the exile force (led by Carlos Castillo Armas) swept in to seize power. The U.S. government celebrated its victory while massive anti-United States protests erupted in Argentina, Chile, Cuba, Honduras, Mexico, and Panama. The United States had backed a military overthrow of Guatemala's democratically elected president, and the OAS, strongly influenced by U.S. dominance within the organization, had allowed it to do so.[10]

President Eisenhower believed that the key to global peace and prosperity was free trade and investment. In his view, "general world prosperity meant general peace and security – when there was group oppression, mass poverty, or the hunger of children, revolution and social chaos surely followed. And the Communists could be counted on to 'reach out to absorb every area in which can be detected the slightest discontent or other form of weakness.'"[11] He saw economic prosperity, even a very limited prosperity as compared to U.S. standards, as keeping nations from embracing communism. Free trade, he also felt, was necessary for maintaining the United States' freedom. Part of that meant the ability to access raw materials not

---

[10]Bovier 2002, pp. 89–90.
[11]Rabe 1993, p. 64.

available in the U.S., so keeping the nations with those raw materials friendly to the U.S. was obviously within U.S. economic interests. He was not particularly supportive of foreign aid except to those countries he saw as under a direct threat from 'the communist menace.' Other nations, he felt, could earn needed capital by increasing foreign trade and seeking foreign private investment. He operated under a slogan of 'trade, not aid.'

The decade of the fifties also saw the infamous rise and eventual fall of Senator Joseph McCarthy. Elected to the Senate in 1946, he gained instant notoriety in February of 1950, when he charged that Communist Party members, and members of a spy ring, were employed by the State Department. Although never able to prove this charge, his attempts to do so destroyed countless lives and careers, and fostered a fear of communism by U.S. citizens that survived him for decades.

McCarthyism, as the senator's rabid communist-hunting quickly came to be called, impacted U.S. foreign policy. Tom Hayden stated that "domestic McCarthyism drove an aggressive military policy into quagmires first in Korea and ultimately in Vietnam."[12] It would be oversimplifying the case to say that McCarthyism caused U.S. involvement in those wars, but with the terror of communism being raised to a panicked frenzy domestically, the U.S. populace was more than willing to embark on military misadventures to prevent communist 'takeovers' of Korea and South Vietnam. And while that same populace quickly tired of both wars, the U.S. was unwilling or unable to end either of them quickly or satisfactorily.

McCarthyism's impact on the foreign policy of the second half of the twentieth century is demonstrated clearly in the policies that immediately followed the decade of the 1950s. In order to win the election of 1960, Democratic Party leaders

> concluded that they must go beyond negative or defensive anti-Communist strategies. They must take hard-line Cold

---

[12]Hayden 2011 [Summer].

War positions and demand a much-expanded military buildup and weapons program. And above all they must never allow any country to fall to communism. How completely McCarthyism thus triumphed in foreign policy became evident when liberal and Cold War Democrats returned to national power in 1961 ... under John F. Kennedy and consolidated it for most of the decade under Lyndon B. Johnson. Whatever they accomplished domestically was eclipsed by the Vietnam War, more exactly by the assumption that guided their involvement in it – that the public would no more forgive them for losing South Vietnam to the Communists than it forgave the Truman administration for losing China and failing to defeat North Korea.[13]

McCarthy's charges had such impact at least partly because he implied that communists were helping to shape foreign policy, since he claimed that the State Department was overrun with them. He stated that " ... the State Department harbors a nest of Communists and Communist sympathizers who are helping to shape our foreign policy."[14] Like the Tea Party movement half a century later, McCarthy rocketed into the public consciousness, influencing elections and acting with impunity.

Recently revealed documents from the former Soviet bloc illuminate some aspects of U.S. foreign policy during the middle of the twentieth century. "They have suggested, for example, that, whether Washington endeavored to practice 'atomic diplomacy' or not, the overall impact of the bombings of Hiroshima and Nagasaki on Soviet foreign policy was limited. They have shown that the Executive Committee's interpretations of Soviet motives for installing nuclear missiles in Cuba in 1962 were mistaken. They have confirmed that US policy-makers misread the behavior of North Korea in June 1950. ... "[15]

---

[13]Fried 1996, p. 6.
[14]Johnson and Nguyen 2004 [January].
[15]Carter and Clifton 2002, p. 18.

These recent revelations seem to support the idea that U.S. foreign policy has been, and still largely is, established with little global perspective aside from its direct impact to the United States.

Another foreign policy disaster of this time frame concerns Cuba. That nation came under U.S. control as a result of the Spanish–American War (see Chapter 4). Although Cuba ostensibly gained independence in 1898, the Platt Amendment of 1901 severely reduced Cuban autonomy, and established it as a U.S. colony. Although the 1934 Treaty of Relations (part of President Franklin D. Roosevelt's 'Good Neighbor Policy') rejected the Platt Amendment, U.S. control over the island nation was almost total.

By the time of the Cuban revolution, "the U.S controlled 80% of Cuban utilities, 90% of Cuban mines, close to 100% of the country's oil refineries, 90% of its cattle ranches, and 40% of its sugar industry. Cuba also became an investor paradise for U.S. gambling syndicates, real estate operators, hotel owners, and mobsters. The U.S. propped up the repressive and widely hated regime of Fulgencio Batista."[16] Against this imperial backdrop, the people successfully revolted, overthrowing the Batista regime in 1959, and installing Fidel Castro, first as prime minister (1959–1976) and then as president (1976–2008).

The U.S. tried to take back Cuba in 1961. The so-called Bay of Pigs invasion was a disaster. Some background provides additional insight into U.S. foreign policy initiatives and the related decision-making process. President Kennedy has been inaugurated just three months earlier. Upon becoming president, when Mr. Kennedy "dismantled President Dwight D. Eisenhower's national security decision-making structures, a disorganized and collegial system remained; this prevented policy from the rigorous analysis institutionalized by Eisenhower's procedures."[17] This, of course, left the new president at a disadvantage, even if it was one of his own making.

---

[16]http://revcom.us/a/056/cubahist-en.html. Accessed November 12, 2012.
[17]R. R. Friedman 2011 [June].

The secrecy and intrigue that surrounded the Cuban policy, and especially the planning leading up to the catastrophic failure known as the Bay of Pigs invasion, has been mirrored in the early part of the twenty-first century. Shortly afterward, as the world focused on the Cuban crisis, the U.S. Ambassador to the United Nations, Adlai Stevenson, addressed that body. He claimed that the U.S. had no part in the invasion: "the plain fact of the matter is that Stevenson was lied to during the Bay of Pigs controversy in April 1961 and found himself therefore unwittingly lying himself, denying before the UN that America was involved in the invasion. President Kennedy later suggested to him that this had been a 'failure of communications.'"[18]

The disastrous Bay of Pigs invasion, the first major attempt to defeat the Castro regime in Cuba, was defeated by the Cuban people. Since then, the U.S., in an attempt to drive revolutionary leader Fidel Castro from office, has enforced a trade and travel embargo, which, like most of its sanctions around the globe, causes suffering for the people, but is hardly felt by the government the U.S. wishes to topple.

Elsewhere in the world, the French were struggling to hold onto their Vietnamese colony. Ho Chi Minh, who had returned to Vietnam following 30 years in exile, had led a revolution that expelled the Japanese. The French, attempting to counter the popularity of Ho Chi Minh, established what they called an independent Vietnam under Emperor Bao Dai in the South. While Minh never lost his peasant appearance and native identity, his obvious devotion "to the Vietnamese people contrasted with Bao Dai's opulent affectations, philandering and record of collaboration with the French and the Japanese."[19] In May of 1950, the U.S. first authorized economic and military aid to the French.

Vietnam quickly became more than a blip on the U.S.'s radar. In 1952, President Truman's National Security Council said that

---

[18]Beichman 2006 [February–March].
[19]McMaster 1997, p. 34.

"the loss of any countries of Southeast Asia to Communist aggression would have critical psychological, political and economic consequences."[20] Following World War II, communism was the most feared bugaboo in the U.S., and much was done to inflame those fears.

In April of 1954, the French, desperate to hold onto their Vietnamese colony, and needing U.S. military might to do it, asked President Eisenhower for direct military support. He declined, being unwilling to get involved in a war without participation by U.S. allies, and felt, perhaps prophetically, that doing so "would absorb our troops by the division."[21] One month later, the French were handed a decisive defeat at Dien Bien Phu. Following this, a peace agreement was reached in Geneva, Switzerland. The resulting so-called Geneva Accords provided that Vietnam would be divided into a communist north, and a non-communist south. Elections that were scheduled for 1956, which would have been a referendum on reunification, were boycotted by the South, with America's support. The main reason for the refusal to accept an election seemed to be the popularity of Ho Chi Minh. "President Eisenhower wrote later in his memoirs that if in fact the elections had been held, Ho Chi Minh would have gotten 80 percent of the vote."[22]

The 'domino theory,' the belief that if one country 'fell' to communism, others would quickly follow suit, was strongly proclaimed throughout the halls of Congress and from the White House. With the French now expelled, President Eisenhower sent military advisors to train the South Vietnamese Army and authorized the CIA to conduct psychological warfare against the North. The United States' years-long, deadly and disastrous involvement in Vietnam had begun.

---

[20]McMaster 1997, p. 34.

[21]Ibid., p. 35.

[22]Werner 1985 [June].

Part III.

1954–Present: Fighting Invented Enemies

Chapter 12.

Vietnam War

As mentioned in Chapter 11, the U.S. first became involved in the Vietnam War (following giving aid to the French in their quest to maintain it as a colony) in order to prevent an ostensibly free South Vietnam (although run by a U.S. puppet) from reunifying with the Communist North, under the leadership of Ho Chi Minh. The U.S. had no strategic interest in Vietnam, and even lacked any significant commercial interest. Yet fresh off the heels of McCarthyism, when the Soviet 'threat' seemed imminent, no U.S. president wanted to be seen as 'soft' on communism. Senator McCarthy had charged that Harry Truman was, and being a 'commie' or 'pinko' was a devastating insult.

President Truman had first raised the alert; President Eisenhower continued to watch the situation and act accordingly. He was succeeded by President John F. Kennedy, who, during his short administration, sent 400 Green Berets to teach counter-insurgency to the Vietnamese. Like his predecessor, and every president since, he didn't want to be perceived as weak on communism, or whatever other perceived threat the country thought it faced (in the early part of the twenty-first century, the threat of communism has faded, conveniently replaced by a fear of terrorism). President Kennedy may also have wanted to set a tone for his presidency with a show of strength early in his administration.

Under the Geneva Accords, the United States was permitted

to have 685 military advisers in southern Vietnam. Eisenhower secretly sent several thousand. Under Kennedy, the figure rose to sixteen thousand, and some of them began to take part in combat operations. [South Vietnam's President Ngo Dinh] Diem was losing. Most of the South Vietnam countryside was now controlled by local villagers organized by the NLF [National Liberation Front, the Communist army in South Vietnam].[1]

Both President Eisenhower and President Kennedy secretly violated the agreements of the Geneva Accords. This is further evidence of the United States' disdain for international agreements, or the opinions or perspectives of the international community.

As early as President Kennedy's administration, opinions from the Joint Chiefs of Staff on how to proceed in Vietnam ran the gamut from hawk to dove. Marine Corp Commandant David Shoup, the last remaining member from the Eisenhower administration, visited South Vietnam in 1962. This trip "confirmed his abiding conviction that the United States should 'not, under any circumstances, get involved in land warfare in Southeast Asia.'"[2] This was in direct contrast to Air Force Chief of Staff Curtis Lemay, a constant thorn in the side of Mr. Kennedy, who felt that any threat to the security of the U.S. should be responded to with massive retaliation from the air.

When Mr. Kennedy became president, South Vietnam was under the control of Ngo Dinh Diem, first president of the Republic of Vietnam. The U.S. had been a strong supporter of the Diem government, but following the Vietnamese government's response to a May 8, 1963, anti-government demonstration, when crowds were seeking government permission to commemorate Buddha's birthday, that changed. Vietnamese troops fired on unarmed, peaceful demonstrators, killing seven. The following day, 10,000 people demonstrated

---

[1]Zinn 1980, p. 474.
[2]McMaster 1997, p. 43.

against the government, demanding that Buddhists be accorded the same rights as the devoutly Catholic Diem provided the Catholics. The crises spread throughout the country and on June 11, a Buddhist monk named Quang Duc publicly burned himself to death in protest. This was the first in a series of self-immolations that focused world attention on Vietnam.

"The issue of what to do with Diem was perhaps the most contentious foreign policy issue debated within the Kennedy administration. While Kennedy displayed an extraordinary amount of indecision, in the end he decided to stop supporting Diem because he thought his regime was too autocratic to win the popular support necessary to defeat the Viet Cong."[3] Still, as has been the case since World War II, the fear of communism, this time in the form of the North Vietnamese – the Viet Cong – was the motivation for foreign policy initiatives. South Vietnamese President Diem's oppressive government, trampling the basic civil rights of the large Buddhist population, was only incidental.

The Kennedy administration then began to use diplomatic pressure to force Diem to ease up on the oppressive policies of his government, but to no avail. Finally, the U.S. decided on a different course of action. "An August 24, 1963 cable from the State Department authorized the new ambassador, Henry Cabot Lodge, to indicate to Vietnamese military officers that the United States would support a successor regime emerging from a military coup against Diem. From that point, 'We [were] launched on a course of action from which there [was] no longer any respectable turning back, the overthrow of the Diem regime,' argued Lodge."[4]

With the coup d'état not yet occurring, the Kennedy administration, through Ambassador Lodge, demanded that Diem make a series of pro-liberalization changes. Anything regarding the lessening of oppressive restrictions that had been discussed during the previous

---

[3]Perceny 1999, p. 108.
[4]Ibid., p. 102.

three years was now demanded. Diem continued to resist.

It should be noted that, while the U.S. was now actively encouraging the overthrow of the Diem regime, it didn't know what it would be replaced with. No one realistically expected a Western-style democracy to emerge. Yet ousting Diem was deemed of paramount importance.

Finally, Diem seemed ready to make some concessions, but it was too late: "the U.S.-supported coup took place on November 1, 1963. Diem and his brother [who also served as his chief political advisor, Ngo Dinh] Ngu were assassinated. While Kennedy expressed shock and dismay at the assassinations, just three weeks before his own, they were the logical outcome of his administration's support for a coup in South Vietnam."[5]

If the foreign policy of the U.S. in terms of Vietnam wasn't in a shambles already, the assassination of President Kennedy certainly pushed it over the edge. The administration of Mr. Kennedy was sufficiently new, and he himself sufficiently inexperienced, that that policy was vague at best. Having dismantled President Eisenhower's analysis process, and not yet sufficiently establishing his own, his death left the situation in the hands of his equally inexperienced and very insecure vice president, Lyndon Johnson.

President Johnson's entire six years in the White House were colored completely by Vietnam. Initially, there was some doubt about his foreign policy credentials, although there were those who disagreed. "Walt W. Rostow, head of the State Department's Policy Planning Council under JFK and LBJ, believed it was 'palpable nonsense' to think that Johnson 'neither knew nor cared much about foreign policy.' ... As the minority and majority leader of the Senate, he was in the middle of all the great foreign policy decisions of the 1950s. ..."[6]

That Mr. Johnson 'was in the middle of all the great foreign policy

---

[5]Perceny 1999, p. 104.
[6]Dallek 1999, p. 85.

decisions of the 1950s' may explain why the foreign policies of his administration were such a disaster.

The major turning point for U.S. escalation in Vietnam was an incident that supposedly occurred in the Gulf of Tonkin, off the northern coast of Vietnam.

The staging area for the U.S. Seventh Fleet was the Gulf of Tonkin. On August 2, 1964, the U.S. destroyer *Maddox* was on an espionage mission when it was fired on by North Vietnamese torpedo patrol boats. The *Maddox*, with supporting air power, fired back, sinking one North Vietnamese boat.

Two evenings later, the Maddox and another destroyer, the *C. Turner Joy*, were again in the gulf. The *Maddox*'s instruments indicated that the ship was under attack, or had been attacked. The captain began an immediate retaliatory strike. Both ships began firing into the night, with American warplanes supporting them, showcasing American firepower. However, they "later decided they had been shooting at ghost images on their radar. The preponderance of evidence indicates there was no attack."[7]

Regardless of this, the incident was presented to the world, and more importantly, to the U.S. Congress, as an act of aggression against the United States. The Gulf of Tonkin Resolution, empowering the president to take any and all means necessary to repel this 'aggression,' quickly passed Congress. The following is the complete resolution.

> Resolved by the Senate and House of Representatives of the United States of America in Congress assembled,
>
> That the Congress approves and supports the determination of the President, as Commander-in-chief, to take all necessary measures to repel any armed attack against the forces of the United States and to prevent further aggression.
>
> *Section 2*. The United States regards as vital to its national interest and to world peace the maintenance of international

---

[7]Chambers 2000, p. 307.

peace and security in Southeast Asia. Consonant with the Constitution of the United States and the Charter of the United Nations and in accordance with its obligations under the Southeast Asia Collective Defense Treaty, the United States is, therefore, prepared, as the President determines, to take all necessary steps, including the use of armed force, to assist any member or protocol state of the Southeast Asia Collective Defense Treaty requesting assistance in defense of its freedom.

Section 3. This resolution shall expire when the President shall determine that the peace and security of the area is reasonably assured by international conditions created by action of the United Nation or otherwise, except that it may be terminated earlier by concurrent resolution of the Congress."[8]

The U.S. never declared war in Vietnam. But by 1964, the number of U.S. soldiers serving there skyrocketed from 23,000 to 184,300.

President Johnson held steadfastly to his war policies, despite tremendous opposition at home and abroad. While U.S. colleges and universities were sights of huge, sometimes violent, opposition to the war, public opinion polls showed support for it. As he prepared for his first and only presidential election in 1964, against right-wing zealot Senator Barry Goldwater of Arizona, Mr. Johnson did not put country first: "his principle concern was the November election, [and] he was unwilling to tell the Chiefs [Joint Chiefs of Staff] that he was basing his Vietnam decisions on his campaign strategy rather than on military considerations and foreign policy concerns."[9] Running in 1964 against the arch-conservative Mr. Goldwater, who alluded to the possibility of using nuclear weapons in Southeast Asia, Mr. Johnson was elected in a landslide, earning 61% of the vote. Yet the war was taking a toll; young Americans were dying by the thousands; Vietnamese, by the tens of thousands. Desertion rates

---

[8]Westerfield 1996, pp. 53–54.
[9]McMaster 1997, p. 87.

were astronomical, as were the numbers of young men fleeing to Canada to avoid the draft.

Following his landslide election, the Vietnam War continued to consume and plague him throughout his second term. In 1965 he ordered extensive aerial bombing of North Vietnam. Called 'Operation Rolling Thunder,' the bombing escalated over a period of nearly four years, only ending at the time of the next presidential election.

Despite his determination to 'win' in Vietnam and not lose face as a president who 'lost' a country to communism, and despite the belief in some circles that Mr. Johnson was sufficiently knowledgeable about foreign policy to effectively create and implement it, there is evidence that his interest in it was no more than minimal. "'He had no stomach for it,' Mrs. Johnson told me, 'no heart for it; it wasn't the war he wanted. The one he wanted was on poverty and ignorance and disease and that was worth putting your life into. ... And yet every time you took it to the people, every time you said anything in a speech about civil rights your audience would begin to shift their feet and be restive and silent and maybe hostile. But then the moment you said something about defending liberty around the world – bear any burden – everybody would go to cheering.'"[10]

U.S. foreign policy in Vietnam never had a clear purpose under Lyndon Johnson's presidency. U.S. "commitment was a faltering and uncertain one, and once made involved piecemeal deployment as the instinctive reaction to a lost strategic situation."[11] During the Johnson administration, diplomacy and military action were erratic and based more on political considerations than on seeking a peaceful solution or extricating the U.S. from a conflict that it was clear to the president and his cabinet could not be won.

One might wonder, in retrospect, why Mr. Johnson didn't give in to the inevitable, cut U.S. losses and depart from Vietnam, leaving that country to settle its own differences. After all, seven years later,

---

[10]Gibbons 1965 [February 14].

[11]Pimlott 1982, p. 42.

under President Gerald Ford, that's exactly what happened. Yet the specter of McCarthyism cast a long shadow, and this may, in part, explain Mr. Johnson's dogged determination to continue the war. "Johnson committed half a million soldiers to the war even though policy-makers knew all along that the enemy could not be defeated. This we know from the government's own account in the secret Pentagon Papers that came out in 1971 and the public apology that Robert S. McNamara, then Secretary of Defense and one of the chief architects of the war, has recently made. Fear of a backlash, fear of another dark reaction, in a word, fear of McCarthyism redivivus, proved disastrous to liberal Democrats, the consequences of which dog them, and the country, to this day."[12]

This, however, in no way excuses Mr. Johnson's actions, even from only a politically expedient perspective. He seems to have feared a 1950s-style, anti-Communist reaction, which evidence in the mid- to late-1960s didn't support. The nationwide anti-war movement, civil rights, feminism, indeed the creation of a new counter-culture, would seem to have required a review by the Johnson Administration of old assumptions. That this didn't occur was a tragedy for the nation and the world.

On March 31, 1968, with the war continuing to rage without any realistic expectation of victory, or even of conclusion, and with the president's popularity at an all-time low, mainly because of the war and the violence and division at home that it engendered, Mr. Johnson announced that he would neither seek nor accept the Democratic Party's nomination for another term. The party, already seriously divided between 'hawks' and 'doves', now splintered further, opening the door for the election of Republican Richard Nixon and his disastrous presidency.

In some ways, President Nixon was the opposite of his predecessor. Whereas Mr. Johnson seemed detached from foreign affairs, they were President Nixon's main focus; his interest in domestic issues

---

[12]Fried 1996, p. 6.

seemed restricted to how U.S. citizens were gauging his performance on the international stage. Indeed, it appeared at times that that was his major concern.

Mr. Nixon's political machinations began even before he was elected. Seeming to take the high road, he wouldn't speak about specific plans for Vietnam. After his election, speaking of his vagueness as to policy during the campaign, he said: "As a candidate, it would have been foolhardy, and as a prospective President, improper, for me to outline specific plans in detail. I did not have the full range of information or the intelligence resources available to [President] Johnson. And even if I had been able to formulate specific 'plans', it would have been absurd to make them public. In the field of diplomacy, premature disclosure can often doom even the best-laid plans."[13]

Pre-election polls showed the race between Mr. Nixon and the Democratic nominee, Vice President Hubert Humphrey, to be very close. Then, on October 31, just five days before the elections, President Johnson announced that formal peace talks were scheduled to begin in Paris the day after the election. However, in less than 24 hours, South Vietnamese President Nguyen Van Thieu stated that the South would not participate in such talks. The National Liberation Front (NLF), a guerilla army fighting both the South Vietnamese and the U.S. in Vietnam and Cambodia, was to participate in the talks, and Mr. Thieu said that that organization's participation would increase its prestige. "Only later was it generally learned that Anna Chennault, Chinese-born widow of General Claire Chennault, co-chairman of several Nixon supporters' committees, had taken it on herself to contact Saigon and offer them a 'better deal' if they refused to cooperate. Nixon denied all knowledge of the incident. ..."[14]

Unlike President Johnson, Mr. Nixon dabbled in many areas of

---

[13]Pimlott 1982, p. 66.
[14]Ibid., p. 70.

the world; for additional information on this, please see Chapter 17, 'Other Foreign Policy Initiatives of this Time'. But like Mr. Johnson, Mr. Nixon couldn't allow a country to 'fall' to communism on his watch. For any president, especially a Republican, to allow that to happen, would threaten not only his reelection prospects, but his entire legacy as well. So while no better equipped to 'win' the war than any previous president, he was determined to see some kind of conclusion to it that the U.S. could call a win. However, like his predecessors, this goal would escape him.

While Mr. Nixon himself may have been the main problem of his administration, another might have been his selection of Henry Kissinger, first as National Security Adviser, and later as Secretary of State. Mr. Kissinger's thoughts on Vietnam, as stated after the fact, were these: "We could not simply walk away from [Vietnam] as if we were switching a television channel. It seemed to me important for America not to be humiliated, not to be shattered, but to leave Vietnam in a manner that even the protesters might later see as reflecting an American choice made with dignity and self-respect."[15]

How that might be accomplished was anybody's guess; by the time Mr. Nixon became president, the polarization between the dwindling numbers of those who still supported the war and those who opposed it and demanded an immediate and complete withdrawal was firmly established. Mr. Kissinger apparently wanted to please two very disparate groups, and the ultimate conclusion to the war would please no one.

Shortly after his inauguration, Mr. Nixon decided on his plan for Vietnam. Knowing he could neither pull out of Vietnam and leave the South to the mercy of the Communist North, nor continue the disastrous policies of his predecessor that had torn the U.S. apart, he chose a three-pronged approach. He would 1) gradually reduce U.S. fighting forces, 2) attempt to negotiate an agreement with the North, and 3) increase bombing to force the North to negotiate. The

---

[15]Gaddis 2005, p. 288.

reduction of ground forces, he felt, would help to diffuse the growing anti-war movement in the U.S.

Overarching this strategy was what the president called 'Vietnamization,' which would turn responsibility of prosecuting the war to the people of South Vietnam. Mr. Nixon thought that it would be a sign of good faith to the North, to provide a further motivation to negotiate. But, like his predecessors, this president also misread his opponents: "the North read this [Vietnamization] as a sign of weakness, and Nixon's announced troop withdrawal only strengthened the resolve of the North."[16]

Although Vietnamization was doomed from the start, mainly due to the inability of the South to even begin to fight its own war, Mr. Nixon's motivation for it wasn't just to end the war. He hoped that the troop withdrawals would begin to silence, or at least soften, the voices of the anti-war critics. This was not to be. By this time, frustration and anger at the war were too strong to be muted by anything less than a complete and immediate withdrawal. And any credit he might have received from the troop withdrawals was cancelled by the increase in bombing that he ordered.

The bombing extended to Cambodia, but was initially done secretly. Operation Menu was the name given to the bombing campaign. Its purpose was to destroy the sanctuaries of the People's Army of Vietnam (PAVN), which the Viet Cong used for obtaining supplies, training and resting when possible. In May of 1969, William Beecher revealed the secret bombing in a *New York Times* article. The president was furious at the leak, but the news was out. "The secret bombing of Cambodia set in motion a series of events that would lead the administration down a path of illegality and impropriety that culminated in Watergate and the resignation of a president."[17]

Another area where the president erred was in his belief that the North was interested in a negotiated compromise. Unlike the U.S., the

---

[16]Genovese 1990, p. 118.
[17]Ibid., p. 112.

North knew what victory looked like: the reunification of Vietnam under a Communist government. With the U.S.'s announcement of troop withdrawals, the North felt it could outlast Nixon and eventually triumph. Subsequent events proved them correct. As early as 1946, Ho Chi Minh had predicted victory, and the reason for it: "'You can kill ten of my men for every one I kill of yours, but even at those odds, you will lose and I will win.' He was wrong and right. By the time the [Americans] left in 1975, the kill ratio was 54 Vietnamese for every one U.S. soldier who died, but even at those odds Ho won. Over decades, North Vietnamese ability to keep killing U.S. soldiers, despite the Vietminh's own awesome sacrificial losses, fatally undermined the U.S. political/military leadership's will to sustain the war."[18]

With the U.S. efforts on the battlefield and at the negotiation table yielding no results, and with his eye always on reelection, Mr. Nixon decided to act. Anticipating an offensive similar to the Tet Offensive of 1968, the president suggested to President Thieu a combined South Vietnamese and U.S. offensive against the town of Tchepone in Laos. He expected to get great press from this and did not seem to consider the repercussions of extending the war into another country. He was absolutely convinced that this maneuver would be successful, as long as he defined success. "Nixon refused to entertain any concept of loss. 'The operations cannot come out as a defeat,' he said. He wanted to hedge his bets by setting 'very limited goals such as interdicting the trail.' He wanted it 'packaged as a raid on the sanctuaries.' Still, he had every hope that the South Vietnamese could carry it off."[19]

His optimism was not shared by all his advisors. In the State Department, U. Alexis Johnson said that the risks of a failed assault were great. Such an offensive, he said, could cause the Laotian government to collapse, possibly allowing a Communist regime to replace it. Secretary of State William P. Rogers said that the program of

---

[18]Toolis 1996.
[19]Dallek 2007, p. 258.

'Vietnamization' would probably be successful, so the offensive wasn't necessary. A failure of the offensive would be seen as a failure of the Thieu government and the Vietnamization program.

Henry Kissinger wasn't listening. He said the offensive would forestall any major offensive by the North Vietnamese, thus enabling the Vietnamization program to continue that much longer before the U.S. withdrew.

The invasion of Laos, code named Lam Son 719, was a disaster. The North Vietnamese inflicted major casualties on the ARVN (Army of the Republic of Vietnam), also shooting down U.S. helicopters. President Thieu ordered a withdrawal from Tchepone, and panicked South Vietnamese soldiers clung to the skids of U.S. helicopters, providing vivid pictures of the demoralizing defeat for the world to see.

Yet true to his word, Mr. Nixon presented the offense as a success. "The attack deprived the Communists 'of the capacity to launch an offensive against our forces in South Vietnam in 1971.'"[20]

Later, in hindsight, Mr. Kissinger was more thoughtful. "The chief drawback" of the plan, he wrote, "was that it in no way accorded with the Vietnamese realities. South Vietnamese divisions had never conducted major offensive operations against a determined enemy outside Vietnam and only rarely inside." Further: "We allowed ourselves to be carried away by the daring conception, by the unanimity of the responsible planners in both Saigon and Washington, by the memory of the success in Cambodia, and by the prospect of a decisive turn."[21]

Mr. Nixon was acutely aware of the media's attention to the anti-war organization and for a long time was pleased with it, when peace activities were only reported almost as a footnote to the news. "'We've got those liberal bastards on the run, and we're going to keep them on the run.' Attorney General John Mitchell authorized the

---

[20]Ibid., p. 260.
[21]Brewer 2011, p. 214.

FBI to tap the telephones of the organizers and the moratoriums. Six months later Nixon approved a plan to infiltrate, burglarize, wiretap, trick and provoke into violence a variety of anti-war and liberal groups. ... "[22] He justified those actions with the time-honored excuse that the targeted groups were a threat to national security.

It appears, through the long lens of time, that President Nixon was far more concerned with his public image than in ending the war. He knew early on that the U.S. couldn't win the war, and could only hope to leave honorably, with some faint hope that the South Vietnamese would be able to fend off Communist control.

Much has been said about racism in the Vietnam War. "It's common knowledge that when GIs weren't calling the Vietnamese gooks, dinks, slants, and slopes, they could be heard calling them Indians, and their habitat, Indian country. The purpose was clear: perceive the Vietnamese as subhuman (Erick Erickson called this 'pseudo-speciation'), then righteously exterminate them."[23] While racist attitudes remain strong within the United States, and were even stronger during the Vietnam-era, perhaps having faded somewhat since then, U.S. policy at least encouraged, if not mandated, these attitudes. In order to get young U.S. men to kill the Vietnamese, who in no way threatened the United States or its citizens' way of life, the government had to dehumanize both the victim and the perpetrator. One study of the writings of U.S. soldiers who fought in Vietnam comments on this dehumanization, and how it was perpetrated by the U.S. government:

> Once the social order of the military has disestablished pre-
> vious meanings attached to human morality (and given the
> recruit the skills to exploit it and the motive for doing so),
> the military must provide the appropriate object on which to
> train such a world view. And it is this, more than any other

---

[22]Schulzinger 1999, p. 283.
[23]Ringnalda 2008, p. 20.

aspect of military training, that arouses the wrath of the Vietnam narrators. During the dozen years of the Vietnam War, soldiers were taught to focus their murderous impulses not on a faceless 'enemy' as they would during peacetime, but on an entire race: the Oriental. 'We had bayonet training in boot camp every day. We had to scream 'kill' when we stuck the bayonet into the dummy. Then we had to beat the dummy up, hit it with the rifle butt and stick the bayonet into it. And we had to call the dummies a dirty, mother-fucking gook or slant-eye.' It is this central facet of their initiation that the writers find most destructive of their dignity, most corrosive to their morality, and most necessary and powerful for explaining their actions in Vietnam. Soldiers in all branches of the armed services recount receiving essentially the same indoctrination. They learned not only who to kill, but who most richly deserved killing. Whether called gook, slant, slope, dink, Con, Charlie, VC, Red, Commie, or a half-dozen local variations, the message was the same: the enemy is Oriental and inferior.[24]

The training was thorough. In his book *Conversations with Americans*, Mark Lane documented his interviews with over 30 Vietnam soldiers or veterans, asking them about torture and other abuse of the Vietnamese. A few excerpts from these interviews are instructive.

- Interview with Chuck Onan, U.S. Marine Corps (there are unconfirmed reports that Mr. Onan either deserted, or later died in Vietnam):

Q: What were you told to do?

A: To torture prisoners.

Q: How?

A: It was very extensive. Many methods were described and advocated.

---

[24]Lewis 1985, p. 55.

. . .

Q: What other methods were taught. Can you give me one more example?

A: We were told to make use of electrical radio equipment. We were told to attach the electrodes to the genitals.

Q: Did they demonstrate that technique or just talk about it?

A: They had drawings on the board showing exactly how to clap the electrodes onto the testicles of a man or the body of a woman.[25]

● Interview with James Adams, U.S. Marine Corps:

I had a troop handler in ITR (Infantry Training Regiment) who went one step farther and said that they wouldn't have anything at all to do with kids. If they were in the village that they knew was sympathetic to the Vietcong and where the Vietcong were being harbored, whenever the kids did come around they'd give them cookies, waferlike cookies that they made out of C-3 or C-4, which is a plastic explosive that we use. It is also poisonous. They gave them these cookies, and the kids that ate them died. The instructor said something about 'This is of course something that isn't talked about, is it, Lieutenant?' And the lieutenant who was there at the time said, 'Don't talk to me about it. I did it too.'[26]

It wasn't just the Vietnamese that were victimized by these brutal actions. U.S. soldiers, too, in an attempt to dehumanize them to the point where they could actually torture prisoners, underwent extreme hardships at the hands of the U.S. military. Another interview from Mr. Lane provides insight.

---

[25]Lane 1970, p. 27.
[26]Ibid., p. 132.

- Interview with John Zrebiec, U.S. Marine Corps.

Q: What happened there?

A: It was rough from the first day [of boot camp]. The first two weeks actually the roughest. Often the guys would be called into the hut pretty regularly.

Q: What was that about?

A: Usually for messing up on a drill field. Caught smoking or something of this nature.

Q: What happened in the hut?

A: The drill instructors would beat them up.

. . .

Q: How many times were you in the duty hut?

A: I was in the duty hut twice.

Q: Each time you were beaten?

A: Right. One time I was knocked unconscious.[27]

This U.S. attitude of the inferiority of the Vietnamese, and therefore, the ability to treat them as sub-human, was a constant in Vietnam, but was most blatantly manifested during the My Lai Massacre. On March 16, 1968, between 347 and 504 unarmed civilians were killed in South Vietnam under the direction of Second Lieutenant William Calley. The victims, mainly women, children – including infants – and the elderly, were savagely killed and their bodies mutilated. Many of the women were raped. "Prejudice lay at the very heart of the military establishment ... and, in the Vietnam context Calley was originally charged with the premeditated murder of 'Oriental human beings' rather than 'human beings,' and undeniably, men who carried out atrocities had highly prejudicial views about their victims. Calley recalled that on arriving in Vietnam his

---

[27]Ibid., p. 133.

main thought was 'I'm the big American from across the sea. I'll sock it to these people here.'"[28] "Even Michael Bernhard (who refused to take part in the massacre) said of his comrades at My Lai: 'A lot of those people wouldn't think of killing a man. I mean, a white man – a human so to speak.'"[29] Sergeant Scott Camil said that "It wasn't like they were humans. They were a gook or a Commie and it was okay."[30]

These attitudes were learned well by the U.S. soldiers sent to Vietnam. They were "conditioned to idealize killing and devalue normal expressions of fear, helplessness, guilt, and grief, which resulted in a dehumanization of themselves and others. Scott, who had led many search-and-destroy missions, described it this way: 'It was easy killing them gooks. They wasn't even people, they was lower down than animals.'"[31]

It could be argued that the military took steps to not only prevent such extreme atrocities as occurred at My Lai, but also to assure that the Vietnamese people were treated with respect. By the time of the My Lai massacre, 14 directives had been issued by the U.S. regarding the prevention and reporting of war crimes. A pamphlet called *Soldier's Handbook on the Rules of Land Warfare* had been distributed by the thousands. All Army personnel received, upon arrival in Vietnam, information cards entitled: 'The Enemy in Your Hands;' 'Nine Rules;' 'Code of Conduct' and 'Geneva Convention.' Each discussed the requirement of humanitarian treatment of, and respect for, the people of Vietnam. "Although Calley was hazy about what he had learned about the Geneva Conventions, when he was asked whether he had received instructions about the taking of prisoners, his answer was immediate: 'Yes Sir. Treat them with respect, humility. Don't humiliate them. Keep them silent. Keep them

---

[28]Bourke 2000, p. 193.
[29]Camil 1972, p. 14.
[30]Ibid., p. 14.
[31]Brende and Parson 1985, p. 95.

separated and keep them closely guarded, sir."[32] Yet it appears that the repeated drills mentioned above, wherein recruits used bayonets on dummies, stabbing them, hitting them with rifle butts and calling them 'gook' or 'slant-eye' had a greater impact on the new soldiers than information cards presented as they stepped off the plane in Vietnam. The influence and impact of that training must have been extensive, to cause otherwise decent young men to shoot babies and unarmed people who were not resisting them. These soldiers had been taught, by the U.S. government, that the Vietnamese were somehow less than human.

By the time the Vietnam War ended, and the last Americans fled as Viet Cong soldiers triumphantly overran the South, "7 million tons of bombs had been dropped on Vietnam, more than twice the total bombs dropped on Europe and Asia in World War II – almost one 500-pound bomb for every human being in Vietnam."[33] Fifty-five thousand Americans had been killed, and over 2,000,000 Vietnamese had died. In terms of 2011 dollars, the war cost U.S. taxpayers an estimated $738,000,000,000, and that figure only considers the years from 1965–1975. This was the legacy of five presidents, only the last of which faced the inevitable fact that the United States could never win the war against the Vietnamese.

---

[32]Everett, Johnson, and Rosenthal 1971, p. 25.
[33]Zinn 1980, p. 478.

Chapter 13.

The Gulf War

U.S. diplomacy in the Middle East has long been counter-productive. To many in U.S. leadership positions, it is unfathomable that people in Middle Eastern countries despise Americans simply because the U.S. insists on bombing them fairly arbitrarily. The rivalries, alliances, attitudes and beliefs of Middle Eastern people are a mystery to U.S. leaders, one that they are not particularly interested in solving. Why, they seem to ask repeatedly, cannot these nations simply adopt U.S.-style democracy?

The Gulf War, the U.S.'s first invasion of Iraq, is an example of this.

After a massive and very costly military build-up, Iraq found itself in dire economic straits. By 1990, two years after the Iraq-Iran war, Iraq was unable to meet its international debts and other nations stopped issuing credit to Iraq for any additional weaponry. By the middle of that year, inflation in Iraq was at 40%, and cash reserves could only cover the next three months of imports. To complicate matters, Iraq's population grew by 34% between 1980 and 1989. An increased population required increased services, and Iraq had no money to provide them.

Iraqi leader Saddam Hussein also felt that Iraq was isolated in the Arab world and sought a means to end that isolation. Kuwait, an oil-rich country on its border, may have been seen as the answer to many questions. "Combining Kuwait's oil reserves with those of Iraq meant Iraq could become an oil power second only to Saudi Arabia and would give Iraq a decisive edge in 'oil power' over Iran. Seizing Kuwait also meant sending a signal to the Arab world and Iran that Iraq could safely ignore the U.S., other Western states, and other Gulf powers and take decisive unilateral action. It meant exposing the U.S. as a 'paper tiger' and greatly increasing Iraq's strategic leverage over the other southern Gulf and Arab states."[1]

Prior to the Iraqi invasion of Kuwait, Saddam Hussein met with U.S. ambassador to Iraq April Glaspie. "Saddam's man in Washington was probably telling him that the United States had not sent troops when Turkey invaded Cyprus, it did not interfere when China invaded Tibet, nor did it intrude in force when the Soviet Union invaded Afghanistan. So there was no reason to worry; Saddam could stand tough with [U.S. President George] Bush's ambassador."[2]

Ambassador Glaspie tried to placate Hussein, but without success. After trying to explain the importance of Iraq to the U.S., Ms. Glaspie said this: "I admire your extraordinary efforts to rebuild your country. I know you need funds. We understand that, and our opinion is that you should have the opportunity to rebuild your country. But we have no opinion on Arab-Arab conflicts like your border disagreement with Kuwait."[3] On August 2, 1990, Iraq invaded Kuwait, and within days, Kuwait was annexed by Iraq, with Hussein announcing Kuwait as Iraq's nineteenth province.

The U.S. was not pleased by the annexation of Kuwait by Iraq.

The importance of Kuwait to the United States cannot be doubted. In 1947, imports of crude oil to the U.S. were about 0.4 million barrels. "[I]n 1950, U.S. imports from the Middles East jumped to 41.6 million barrels, which was almost one-quarter of total U.S. crude imports. At the same time, U.S. Middle East imports came almost totally from Kuwait, the biggest supplier. . . ."[4]

---

[1]Cordesman and Wagner 1996, p. 37.
[2]Rezun 1992, p. 61.
[3]Simons 2004, p. 349.
[4]Han 1993, p. 18.

This importance continued to grow, and President Jimmy Carter, in his State of the Union Address on January 23, 1980, affirmed that the U.S. was willing to go to war with Russia to protect the Gulf's vast oil supply. The Carter Doctrine indicated "that Soviet Action in Afghanistan was a prelude to further expansion southward into the Persian Gulf, and therefore a threat to the security of Western oil sources in the Arabian Peninsula."[5] It seems interesting that the U.S. would be willing to sacrifice American lives to protect the security of 'oil sources,' but at least, perhaps, Mr. Carter was being more honest than presidents that followed him. This doctrine, along with the Iraqi invasion of Kuwait and the U.S.'s involvement in that war, indicate the importance that the U.S., and other industrialized countries, give to the idea of global 'oil security.'

With strong encouragement from the U.S., the United Nations Security Council issued Resolution 678, which authorized all member states to use 'all necessary means' to restore peace and security in the area.

Five months after Iraq invaded Kuwait, the U.S. entered the war. As has been custom in the late twentieth and early twenty-first century, it was a coalition of nations that went to war to drive Iraq out of Kuwait, but, as has also been typical, the vast majority of those soldiers were from the U.S. The 'coalition' forces (read: U.S. soldiers) drove the Iraqis from Kuwait in just a little over a month. The grateful Kuwaiti leaders, who had fled the country at the first sign of trouble, didn't deign to return to their nation until suitable, luxurious accommodations could be provided.

The U.S.'s decision to invade may have resulted from miscalculations. "Considering the gloom prevailing in the White House as the January 15 deadline approaches, it is obvious that Washington, too, has miscalculated. The United States assumed that assembling a coalition of nations opposed to Iraq's invasion of Kuwait and deploying an armada of men and ships in the area would frighten Saddam

---

[5]Rosenbaum and Ugrinsky 1993, p. 20.

Hussein into submission. Had Washington considered the possibility of an unyielding Saddam, its policies would have been much more conciliatory."[6] The U.S.'s long-used belief in its own might, and a philosophy of 'might makes right', didn't quite succeed in this case. Diplomacy, for the U.S., is never a major consideration when its power or economic interests are threatened.

U.S. attitudes of racism were strong during the war. One soldier, relating contacting another on the field, said this: "I flipped my radio. 'White Four, this is White One, watch for enemy camels attacking our sector.' 'This is White Four Golf – acknowledged. It's just a column of rags at 1600 meters.' ('Rag' was short for raghead, which was soldier-speak for Arabs, the Gulf Theater's equivalent of Korea's and Vietnam's gook.)."[7] This parenthetical remark was not stated with any sense of apology or regret; he was simply discussing contacting someone else and, in this quotation, was sufficiently courteous to explain to his reader what is meant by 'raghead.'

It wasn't just on the battlefield that such terms were used. Young students during this time were also victimized. "Although Aziz ... had been witness to racist attitudes against other groups ... it was not until the first Gulf War in 1990 and 1992 that he had racial and religious epithets hurled at him. Ninth grade was very difficult. It would take forms of like verbal and physical assaults, he said. Aziz was called camel jockey, sand nigger, and other slurs typically associated with Arabs and Muslims."[8]

The use of degrading terms to describe a supposed 'enemy' is a time-honored tradition within the U.S. government. Reducing an entire people to a less-than-human stature is what enables soldiers to kill them. As mentioned above, the 'gooks' from the Korean and Vietnam Wars were replaced by the 'ragheads' of the Gulf War. Terms also used were 'sand niggers' and 'camel jockeys.'

---

[6] Menos 1962, p. 2.
[7] Vernon 1999, p. 43.
[8] K. Y. Joshi 2006, p. 128.

Such attitudes are endemic in the United States.

> The day after the 1991 Gulf War began, a man rang the offices of the American-Arab Anti-Discrimination Committee to say: 'I'm going to be down there in fifteen minutes with a high-powered rifle to shoot you A-tabs ... ' A professor at California State University, Sacramento, declared to his class: 'All you have to know about Arabs is that they lie, cheat and start rumours.' The Anti-Discrimination Committee publishes a 'hate crimes chronology' to record and publicize the numerous incidents of harassment of American-Arabs in the United States: telephone threats, rocks thrown through windows, employment harassment, school harassment (children routinely depicted as 'sand niggers,' 'camel jockeys', etc.) ... [these] were an important element in the cultural climate of the 1991 Gulf War. ... [9]

As terrible as these attitudes are, their results are clearly shown in war, where soldiers are trained to kill and to see the 'enemy' as less than human. Perhaps one of the most shocking atrocities committed by U.S. soldiers in the Gulf War happened early on.

> In the first two days of ground fighting in Operation Desert Storm last February, three brigades of the 1st Mechanized Infantry Division used the grisly innovation to destroy more than 70 miles of Iraqi trenches and bunkers being defended by more than 8,000 Iraqi soldiers, according to division estimates.
>
> About 2,000 soldiers surrendered. But Iraqi dead and wounded, as well as defiant soldiers still firing their weapons, were buried beneath tons of sand, according to participants in the carefully planned and rehearsed assault. [10]

The number of casualties isn't known. "'For all I know, we could have killed thousands,' said Col. Anthony Moreno, commander of

---

[9]Simons 2004, p. 166.
[10]Sloyan 1991 [September 12].

the 2nd Brigade that led the assault on the heaviest defenses. 'I came through right after the lead company. What you saw was a bunch of buried trenches with peoples' arms and things sticking out of them." [11]

U.S. spokesmen defended this action, stating that it was no less humane than blowing up the 'enemy' with hand grenades. "At a news conference here on Thursday, the Pentagon spokesman, Pete Williams, defended the tactic and said it did not violate the Geneva Conventions on the conduct of warfare.' 'I don't mean to be flippant, but there's no nice way to kill somebody in war,' Mr. Williams said." [12]

It must be remembered that this horrific barbarism, along with the cruel taunts that Arab-Americans in the U.S. suffered during this war, were all done in the name of 'oil security.'

The U.S. has always been happy to use its young, usually male, citizens as tools in whatever imperial adventure it wants to embark upon. Convincing its citizens in the righteousness of its own cause, often despite clear evidence to the contrary, enables it to conscript young men sometimes, and, when combined with economic difficulties, get sufficient numbers to enlist. Presidents, members of Congress, distinguished military leaders all laud the efforts of the poor foot soldier, toiling away, we are told, to preserve the freedoms the U.S. holds dear, or to assist another nation in holding on to, or gaining, those same freedoms. The lies inherent in these platitudes have been amply demonstrated in this work. But to compound the tragedy, and add insult to injury, is the government's total disdain for these same soldiers, both when they are on the battlefield, and once they return to civilian life. Examples of this are replete from the Revolutionary War through the Iraq War and are beyond the scope of this work. However, it's interesting to note how the government responded to health-care issues claimed by veterans of the Gulf War.

---

[11] Sloyan 1991 [September 12].
[12] Schmidt 1991 [September 15].

From 1991 to 2003, hundreds of thousands of our bravest men
and women sought help from the Veterans Administration,
from the Defense Department, from the White House, all
to no avail. The official word was that Gulf War Syndrome
did not exist. So they suffered in silence. Tens of thousands
died from these conditions. Many lost their homes because
of the high costs to pay for medical care themselves. Independent investigations, including those conducted by many
of the Gulf War veterans themselves, showed multiple causes
behind Gulf War Syndrome, including experimental vaccines,
exposure to depleted uranium (DU), and toxicity from biological and chemical weapons, oil fires and other environmental
contaminants."[13]

So after being lauded by their country's leaders when they were
in the mortal danger those leaders put them in, in this case for 'oil
security,' they are then tossed aside, made to cope as well as possible
with the physical and emotional problems the U.S. government
gave them. It took years for the government to take seriously what
has come to be called Gulf War Syndrome, which includes such
symptoms as fatigue, memory loss, muscle pain, depression, anxiety
and insomnia. "Approximately 697,000 U.S. veterans served in the
Persian Gulf War, and more than 263,000 have since sought medical
care at the Department of Veterans Affairs. Over 185,000 have filed
claims with the Veterans Administration for service-related medical
disabilities, including significant physical and psychological distress
that they attribute to their participation in the operation."[14]

Once the U.S. leaves behind the mess it made, whether in Vietnam,
Iraq, or anywhere else, the last beneficiaries of its financial largesse
are always the soldiers who did its fighting for it. They are, it seems,

---

[13]http://www.globalresearch.ca/gulf-war-syndrome-ptsd-and-military-suicides-
u-s-government-s-message-to-america-s-vets-drop-dead/20 186. Accessed on
November 21, 2012.

[14]U.S. Department of Veterans' Affairs, http://www.ptsd.va.gov/public/pages/
effects-persian-gulf-war-vets.asp. Accessed on November, 21, 2012.

no more than replaceable pawns in U.S. foreign policy, an unlimited number of tools necessary to further the nation's imperial goals. Like any other tool, once it is used, it is put aside, only used again if, when the time comes, its use is still practical. Some 'tools' are too old to be called back into use, but, luckily for the U.S. government, there is an endless supply of new ones.

Chapter 14.

Afghanistan War

Afghanistan would seem, at first glance, to be an unlikely target for U.S. interference. With no significant natural resources that the U.S. covets, little strategic importance geographically and no military threat, it wouldn't seem that this small nation would draw U.S. attention. Afghanistan has played only a minor role on the world stage. In the nineteenth century, it was caught up in a power struggle between czarist Russia and British India. It declared neutrality during the two world wars and was not sufficiently important enough to be of interest to the Allied or Axis powers. "But then in the mid-twentieth century Afghanistan was transformed into a cockpit for the cold war struggle between the United States and the Soviet Union that reached its climax with the Soviet invasion in 1979 and its withdrawal ten years later. In the subsequent civil war that erupted in the 1990s, Afghanistan became a failed state, ignored by the world. At the beginning of the twenty-first century it burst back onto the world scene when radical Muslim jihadists planned the 9/11 attack against the United States from there and provoked a U.S. invasion in retaliation."[1] Yet the 9/11 attack may have been nothing more than a convenient excuse for the U.S. to invade (see below).

In Afghanistan, the Taliban had slowly come to power. This group arose when the Soviet war against Afghanistan ended in 1989. Following the civil war that followed the Soviet Union's departure, the

---

[1]Barfield 2010, p. 1.

Sunni Muslim state of Pakistan recognized the Taliban, apparently in the hope that it would bring stability to its northern border. Saudi Arabia soon also began supporting the Taliban.

By the end of 1995, the Taliban ruled 12 of Afghanistan's 31 provinces. By the end of the following year, there was no longer any significant opposition in Afghanistan to the Taliban. This was troubling to much of the world. "The Taliban's ideological basis for government is based on a strict and harsh interpretation of the Koran. It differs greatly from all mainstream Muslim regimes, and can only be compared to the Iranian government of the late Ayatollah Khomeni."[2]

The U.S.'s role in the Taliban's rise is not often discussed, but cannot be avoided. In an interview on October 6, 2009, with CBS News Anchor Katie Couric, Secretary of State Hillary Clinton said this:

> And the United States, to some extent, has to acknowledge, being among the creators of the problem we are now dealing with. It seemed like a great idea, back in the '80s to— embolden— and train and equip— Taliban, mujahidin, jihadists against the Soviet Union, which had invaded Afghanistan. And with our help, and with the Pakistani support— this group— including, at that time, Bin Laden, defeated the Soviet Union. Drove them out of Afghanistan, eventually. Saw the fall of the government that they had installed. And the rest we know. They eventually took over. But when we accomplished our primary mission of seeing the Soviet Union thrown out of Afghanistan, we withdrew. And we left the problems of a well-equipped, fundamentalist, ideological and religious group that had been battle hardened to the Afghans and the Pakistanis.[3]

---

[2] Azzi 1999 [Spring].

[3] http://www.cbsnews.com/8301-18 563_162-5367 884.html. Accessed on January 21, 2013.

Following the 9/11 attacks, the U.S. citizenry was frightened far out of proportion to any real threat. Having been attacked with hijacked commercial airliners, the government of the country with the most powerful military in the world, the only nation to have ever used atomic bombs on another country, and the only world power remaining, fanned the flames of fear. People the world over mourned with the U.S., which experienced, for only the third time since the War of 1812, and the first since the attack on Pearl Harbor in 1941, foreign aggression on its own soil, despite the fact that the U.S. had perpetrated countless such attack on other nations throughout its history. Within one month the U.S. invaded Afghanistan for its refusal to surrender suspected key planners in the 9/11 attacks.

The U.S. citizenry, as is its custom whenever the U.S. invents a new enemy and invades a different nation, strongly supported both President George W. Bush, who had been elected the previous year despite garnering fewer votes than his opponent, former Vice President Al Gore, and the new war. Called 'Operation Enduring Freedom' (why the U.S. names its invasions, and who is responsible for coming up with the ridiculous names, are both unknown to this author), this war, like all the U.S.'s more recent military misadventures, was launched by a coalition, consisting of soldiers from the U.S., Britain, France, Australia and some members of the Afghan United Front. As usual, the huge majority of the soldiers were from the U.S.

Yet for all the righteous hand-wringing about the evils of the Taliban, long demonized by the U.S. government with strong support from the U.S. press, the fact that the 9/11 attacks were alleged to be have been planned from Afghanistan may have only been a ruse for the invasion.

> Since the Iran-Iraq wars of the '80s and early '90s, Islam has been demonized as a Satanic terrorist cult that encourages suicide attacks – contrary, it should be noted – to the Islamic religion. Osama [bin Laden] has been portrayed accurately, it would seem, as an Islamic zealot. In order to bring this evil-doer to justice (dead or alive) Afghanistan, the object of the

exercise, was made safe not only for democracy, but for Union Oil of California, whose proposed pipeline, from Turkmenistan to Afghanistan to Pakistan and the Indian Ocean port of Karachi, had been abandoned under the Taliban's chaotic regime. Currently, the pipeline is a go-project thanks to the junta's installation of a Unocal employee as American envoy to the newly born democracy whose president is also a former Unocal employee.[4]

The idea of invading Afghanistan wasn't new; it didn't result simply from the 9/11 attacks. Those attacks merely provided the means for the U.S. to invade, for Congress to approve the invasion, and the U.S. public to support it. As early as 1997, Zbigniew Brzezinski, National Security Advisor to President Jimmy Carter, explained the need for U.S. interference in Afghanistan. "Brzezinski then, reflexively, goes into the standard American rationalization for empire. We want nothing, ever, for ourselves, only to keep bad people from getting good things with which to hurt good people."[5] "It follows that America's primary interest is to help ensure that no single power comes to control this geopolitical space and that the global community has unhindered financial and economic access to it."[6] Note the importance of 'financial and economic' considerations.

President Bush exploited the fears of U.S. citizens in preparing for the invasion of Afghanistan. He accused the Taliban of sheltering and supplying terrorists, and demanded that they surrender all al Qaeda leaders to the U.S. When the Taliban refused, Mr. Bush started the so-called global war on terrorism.

> The United States invaded Afghanistan to hunt down terror-
> ists shortly after 9/11. Then in 2003, the global war enterprise
> extended to Iraq. The United States led a 'coalition of the
> willing' [please see Chapter 15: 'The Iraq War'] to topple

---

[4]Vidal 2002, p. 20.
[5]Ibid., p. 21.
[6]Brzezinski 1998, p. 148.

Saddam Hussein's government, but never found the weapons of mass destruction President Bush had claimed were there. Despite the United States' effort to bring peace and democracy to these countries, Iraq and Afghanistan are still in chaos a decade later.[7]

It seems more than a little ironic that the U.S., the world's largest purveyor of terrorism, launched a war on terrorism. The only nation to have ever used nuclear weapons; a nation that has seldom been at peace with the world for more than twelve consecutive months; a nation that overthrows democratically elected governments if it disagrees with their policies; a government that looks the other way and provides billions of dollars to nations with atrocious human rights violations, proclaims itself as a beacon of peace, human rights and liberty. The facts belie the U.S.'s public relations.

During the Bush administration, Mr. Bush's so-called War on Terror negatively impacted the U.S.'s international reputation, to the point that the president himself was seen, towards the end of his term in office, as the second most dangerous man in the world, after Osama bin Laden. "President Bush's 'you are either with us or against us' foreign policy and disregard for the United Nations Charter and other international laws succeeded only in alienating potential allies."[8]

The foreign policy of the Bush years was more self-destructive and self-defeating than the policies of several of his predecessors. "Animosity toward the United States resulting from military invasions and occupations, use of torture and detention, killing of innocent civilians, bombing villages and homes, and the undercurrent of religious warfare, actually helped terrorist recruiters create more terrorists."[9] Tragically for the world, the U.S. under Mr. Bush didn't recognize any role for international law in the development and implementation

---

[7]Acharya 2011 [Winter].

[8]Ibid.

[9]Ibid.

of its foreign policy.

Prior to the administration of George W. Bush, there was at least a pretense of diplomacy. This changed during the early part of the twenty-first century. "The most important [change] has been the shift from diplomacy to intervention, particularly in the Afghanistan and Iraq invasions. ..."[10]

The diplomacy long-practiced by the U.S. can be described as 'coercive diplomacy': "[C]oercive diplomacy is not meant to entail war, but instead employs military power short of war to bring about a change in a target's policies or in its political makeup."[11]

One of the Afghanistan War's results was the establishment of the U.S.-based prison at Guantanamo Bay in Cuba. "After September 11, The Bush administration was looking for a place to bring prisoners captured during the U.S.-led military invasion of Afghanistan (many of whom were sold to the United States for a bounty), as well as prisoners seized elsewhere in connection with the so-called global 'war on terror.' The administration believed it had captured many dangerous people and wanted to find a place where it could detain and interrogate them without restriction or interference. It also wanted a place that would be beyond the reach of the courts. So it chose the U.S. naval base at Guantanamo Bay, an approximately forty-five-square-mile area at the eastern end of Cuba."[12]

Guantanamo Bay was announced to the U.S. and the world as a safe place to keep extremely dangerous prisoners, with the Bush Administration always at least hinting darkly that the prisoners housed there were somehow involved in the September 11 attacks on the U.S. Yet it wasn't only in Cuba that U.S. political prisoners were being held. The U.S. has used 'extraordinary rendition,' the capturing of perceived enemies and transferring them to nations where they will be tortured. "Backed by Department of Justice legal

---

[10]Thacker-Kumar and Cambpell 2006 [Fall–Winter].

[11]Art and Cronin 2003, p. 5.

[12]Denbeaux and Hafetz 2009, p. 2.

memoranda, Bush administration officials consistently have maintained that foreign nationals detained by the United States outside its sovereign territory are unprotected by federal or international law."[13] Secretary of State Donald Rumsfeld was "a key figure in the Bush administration's campaign to mask from public view the truth about the widespread and systemic torture of prisoners held in U.S. custody overseas in connection with the so-called 'war on terror.'"[14] A few examples will illustrate this unspeakable practice, and its usage during the Bush administration.

- A Canadian citizen, Maher Arar, was arrested in September of 2002 when changing planes at John F. Kennedy International Airport in New York. He was allowed no contact with family or lawyers, and was sent to Syria, where he was confined in an underground cave and tortured for ten months. "After Arar was released by the Syrians and returned home, the Canadian government, which had colluded in his rendition, conducted an exhaustive investigation and concluded that there was no evidence that he had been involved in terrorism."[15]

- In 2005, Hassan Mustafa Osama Nasr, an Islamic cleric living in Milan, was kidnapped by several men, taken to the U.S. Air Force Base in Avian, and transported to Egypt, "where he was imprisoned for more than a year and tortured at the hands of interrogators who have distinguished themselves – even in the Middle East – for their pitiless brutality. Eventually released to house arrest after the questioning yielded nothing of value, the imam was able to make a phone call describing his experience to his wife."[16] In 2009, 23 CIA agents were indicted, with most

---

[13]Kagel 2007 [Winter].

[14]Ibid., p. 246.

[15]Carlston and Weber 2012, p. 28.

[16] "Spy Nation: Does the Vast, Immensely Expensive, and Largely Unaccountable Centralized Intelligence System Created by the Bush Administration Really Make Us Safer?"

convicted in abstentia. The U.S. refused to cooperate with the trials.

- Khaled el-Masri, a German citizen, was vacationing in Macedonia on New Year's Eve in 2003 when he was kidnapped by CIA agents. After being drugged and tortured, he was transferred to Afghanistan, where he spent five months in a notorious secret prison known as the Salt Pit. "[T]he CIA eventually concluded that Masri did not, in fact, have ties to terror organizations. Nearly five months after his kidnapping, Masri's captors returned him to Macedonia and released him on a dark and deserted road near the Albanian border."[17] Marsi was suspected of being involved with the September 11 conspirators. But "authorities now believe it was a case of mistaken identity, a 'stupid mistake.'"[18] Twenty CIA officials and contractors are under investigation for their role in this kidnapping and torture.

While the Bush administration has consistently denied that it used torture, it was more than willing to transfer political prisoners, under CIA auspices, to nations that do torture.

Additionally, the use of waterboarding, defined as torture by the Geneva Conventions, has been used by Americans on prisoners. The Geneva conventions "were dismissed during the [Bush] administration's first term by the then White House counsel Alberto Gonzales for their 'quaint' protections of prisoners and 'obsolete' limitations on interrogations. Donald Rumsfeld publicly announced that the Conventions no longer applied. The Bush administration's basic legal argument, formulated by officials like the Justice Department's John Yoo, was that this was a new kind of war, that the executive branch needed complete freedom and flexibility, with no checks or balances."[19]

---

[17] Abadi 2007 [Spring].

[18] *Newsweek International Periscope*, 2006 [October 2].

[19] Zakaria 2006 [September 25].

With the end of the Bush years, President Obama renamed the 'war on terror', calling it instead the 'war with al Qaeda and its affiliates.' Yet this change in name did little to alter the facts on the ground. The Patriot Act (officially the USA PATRIOT Act, an acronym meaning United and Strengthening America by Providing Appropriate Tools Required to Intercept and Obstruct Terrorism), which gave law enforcement agencies far greater latitude in gathering private information from U.S. citizens, enabled those agencies to more easily detain and deport immigrants, and increased the Treasury Department's ability to regulate financial transactions, has remained the law of the land. Neither did President Obama eliminate the use of rendition – sending political prisoners out of the country for torture. While he finally withdrew U.S. soldiers from Iraq, ending that tragic, costly, imperial misadventure, the "war on al Qaeda has expanded into other states, including Pakistan, Yemen and Somali through the use of unmanned drones."[20]

The Afghanistan War continued through both of President Bush's administrations, and the first term of President Barack Obama. Mr. Obama has planned that U.S. involvement and thus the war, will end in 2014. Since at least 2009, much of the attention given to Afghanistan has been in the context of other regional problems in the Middle East, most notably the U.S.'s opposition to the nuclear ambitions of Iran. In an interview with the Fletcher Forum, R. Nicholas Burns, former Under Secretary of State under President Bush, discussed this situation. Said he: "My strong view is that it would be unwise for us to use military force against Iran. The disadvantages are quite clear: Iran would likely respond and we would risk a wider war in the Middle East, perhaps even a third war to go along with the current wars in Iraq and Afghanistan. A better approach would be to build up our conventional containment of Iran through our efforts in Iraq and Afghanistan. ..."[21] In this

---

[20] Acharya 2011 [Winter].
[21] "Critical Issues of U.S. Foreign Policy: Iran, Afghanistan, and Pakistan" 2012

statement, Afghanistan first gains some strategic importance. Yet Mr. Burns's hopes for the Middle East, at least in this context, have not been fulfilled. The U.S. left Iraq in a shambles, with a weak, puppet government; the Afghanistan War continues; and sanctions against Iran are still apparently not bringing about the desired result. Sanctions the U.S. has imposed against most nations only succeed in hurting the citizenry, not the government. If U.S. foreign policy wonks believe that such hardships will lead the people to revolt against their leaders, they should look to the 50-plus-year-old sanctions against Cuba for an example of the dismal failure that philosophy brings.

[Winter].

Chapter 15.

Iraq War

While the U.S. generally starts wars under what can best be called false pretenses, few of its wars have begun with a foundation of such blatant lies as the Iraq War. President Bush's reasons for invading Afghanistan have been discussed (please see Chapter 14: 'Afghanistan War'). Capitalizing on the fear of the U.S. citizenry following the September 11 attacks, he had a convenient excuse to attempt the overthrow of the Taliban in order to enable the construction of an oil pipeline through that country.

Perhaps seeing Iraq's rich oil fields, Mr. Bush used the same fear-mongering to invade Iraq. The U.S. citizenry in some respects never recovered from McCarthyism, and with the Cold War over and communism no longer seen as a threat, it still needed some 'big bad wolf' to fear. Terrorism, a nebulous, difficult-to-define concept, was effectively used by war-mongering politicians to scare and anger citizens, who now saw any Muslim as a bomb-throwing enemy of the U.S. way of life. The U.S., it was believed, must use its perceived moral and actual military superiority to defeat this new enemy.

Although elected in 2000 with fewer votes than his opponent, Vice President Al Gore, Mr. Bush was in no mood for conciliation to anyone. During his first State of the Union address, he set the tone for the role he would soon adopt, that of 'war president.' In discussing his perceived threats to the United States, he signaled out Iran, Iraq and North Korea as the 'axis of evil.' This may have been meant to inspire the citizenry that had rejected him – he was appointed president by Supreme Court order, despite receiving fewer votes than Mr. Gore – with some measure of confidence in the strength of their new president. However, the remark was, at best, short-sighted, at least from an international perspective. "The term 'axis of evil' is more than an attention-getting line in a speech in South Korea. Many there see it as the label that undid the admittedly tentative rapprochement that had developed in recent years between North and South."[1] Mr. Bush was off to an inauspicious foreign-policy start.

With his three-pronged axis of evil clearly in the crosshairs, Mr. Bush first took aim at Iraq.

On September 12, 2002, a year and a day after the September 11 attacks, Mr. Bush addressed the United Nations. "Today, Iraq continues to withhold important information about its nuclear program – weapons design, procurement logs, experiment data, an accounting of nuclear materials and documentation of foreign assistance. Iraq employs capable nuclear scientists and technicians. It retains physical infrastructure needed to build a nuclear weapon."[2] With the wounds from the September 11 attacks still raw for many U.S. citizens, at least partly because of the administration's continued rhetoric, the idea of Iraq, with a huge Muslim population, building nuclear weapons was indeed frightening.

On February 5 of 2003, U.S. Secretary of State Colin Powell told the U.N. that satellite photos showed the presence of active chemical munitions bunkers disguised from inspectors. He went on to discuss an alleged stockpile of between 100 and 500 tons of chemical weapons.

The United Nations was not idle during this time. As the U.S. continued to seek U.N. approval for direct military action against Iraq, its allies were not supportive. Russia stated categorically that

---

[1] Coday 2003 [February 28].

[2] "We Turn to the Urgent Duty of Protecting Other Lives" 2002 [September 13].

it would veto any such resolution. Germany threatened to remove its weapons-of-mass-destruction units from Kuwait if the U.S. proceeded with an invasion. Canada urged the U.S. not to attack Iraq without U.N. authorization.

At this point, Iraq seemed to provide the U.N. and the rest of the world, with the exception of the United States, what it wanted. "Iraq delivered a letter to the U.N. Secretary General saying Saddam Hussein's government would accept the return of weapons inspectors [without conditions]. The government said it based its decision concerning the return of inspectors on its desire to complete the implementation of the relevant Security Council resolutions and to remove any doubts that Iraq still possesses weapons of mass destruction. The letter also noted that the resolutions called for nations to respect the sovereignty, territorial integrity and political independence of Iraq."[3]

In a CRS [Congressional Research Service] Report for Congress of October 7, 2003, entitled *Iraq: U.N. Inspections for Weapons of Mass Destruction*, the following was reported:

> From late November 2002 to March 2003, U.N. inspectors combed Iraq looking for weapons of mass destruction (WMD). Under the threat of war from the United States and a unanimous Security Council resolution (1441), Iraq was granted a final opportunity to disarm. Many had low expectations for successful inspections. After 6 weeks, inspectors turned up some evidence of undeclared activities, but not enough to convince a majority of the Security Council members that military force was necessary. Nonetheless, on March 19, 2003, U.S. and British forces attacked Iraq to forcibly eliminate its WMD.[4]

Immediately prior to this invasion, President Bush advised the U.N. to remove their inspectors, for their own safety: the U.S. was going

---

[3]Langholtz, Kondoch, and Wells 2005, p. 368.
[4]http://www.fas.org/man/crs/RL31 671.pdf. Accessed on November 28, 2012.

to invade. With this 'shoot first and ask questions later' attitude, the sovereign nation of Iraq was invaded, its leadership overthrown, its infrastructure destroyed, hundreds of thousands of its people killed, while hundreds of thousands more were displaced, some of them fleeing to refugee camps in neighboring countries. Age-old rivalries between the Shias, Sunnis and Kurds, that had simmered below the surface for generations, now erupted. All this in the name of destroying weapons of mass destruction that Iraq didn't have, and/or punishing Iraq for involvement in the September 11 attacks, which it also didn't have. The government's *9/11 Commission Report* stated this:

> Responding to a presidential tasking, [special assistant to the president Richard] Clarke's office sent a memo to [National Security Advisor Condoleezza] Rice on September 18, titled 'Survey of Intelligence Information on Any Iraq Involvement in the September 11 Attacks.' Rice's chief staffer on Afghanistan, Zalmay Khalilzad, concurred in its conclusion that only some anecdotal evidence linked Iraq to al Qaeda. The memo found no 'compelling case' that Iraq had either planned or perpetrated the attacks. It passed along a few foreign intelligence reports, including the Czech report alleging an April 2001 Prague meeting between Atta and an Iraqi intelligence officer ... and a Polish report that personnel at the headquarters of Iraqi intelligence in Baghdad were told before September 11 to go on the streets to gauge crowd reaction to an unspecified event. Arguing that the case for links between Iraq and al Qaeda was weak, the memo pointed out that Bin Ladin resented the secularism of Saddam Hussein's regime. Finally, the memo said, there was no confirmed reporting on Saddam cooperating with Bin Ladin on unconventional weapons.[5]

---

[5]http://www.gpo.gov/fdsys/pkg/GPO-911REPORT/pdf/GPO-911RE-
PORT.pdf. Accessed on November 28, 2012.

One might reasonably ask why, in view of the access the United Nations Weapons Inspectors were receiving from Iraq, and the opinion of U.S. allies that there was certainly insufficient evidence warranting military action, Mr. Bush didn't delay. Perhaps there was something more to his desire to overthrow and occupy Iraq than was stated. Mr. Bush himself was an oil company executive prior to entering political life. This is true of many of his closest advisors. The following is a partial list:

- Vice President Dick Cheney, past chairman and CEO of Haliburton.

- Commerce Secretary Donald Evans, former CEO of Tom Brown, Inc., an oil company.

- Christine Todd Whitman, Environmental Protection Agency. "Whitman owns interests in oil wells in Texas and Colorado valued at between $55,000 and $175,000."[6]

- Donald Rumsfeld, Defense Secretary. "Rumsfeld has between $3,250,000 and $15,500,000 worth of investments in energy-related companies."[7]

- "National Security Adviser-designate Condoleezza Rice is a member of the board of directors of Chevron (which christened an oil tanker the Condoleezza Rice)."[8]

Additionally, according to a study by the Center for Public Integrity, "Of the top 10 lifetime contributors to George W.'s [Bush] war chests, six either come from the oil business, or have ties to it."[9]

---

[6]http://greenyes.grrn.org/2001/02/msg00097.html. Accessed on November 28, 2012.

[7]Ibid.

[8]"The Corporate Conservative Administration Takes Shape" 2001 [January].

[9]http://www.globalresearch.ca/articles/CAV111A.html. Accessed on November 28, 2012.

The U.S. invasion of Iraq caused a rift between the U.S. and many of its closest allies. Russia, Canada, France and Germany all were asked to participate, and all refused. Under Mr. Bush's direction, they are forbidden any of the lucrative contracts anticipated to result from the invasion and subsequent occupation. However, this 'punishment' appears to have been counterproductive.

> But, as the United States seeks international participation in the rebuilding of Iraq, it alienates some of the very countries it tried to woo. President Bush has again angered European allies by restricting the bids for Iraq's reconstruction only to those countries that have embraced the United States' invasion of Iraq, and those that have sent troops to Iraq. This latest outrage came when Deputy Defense Secretary Paul Wolfowitz issued a decree, approved by Mr. Bush, barring any country that did not support the invasion, including France, Germany, Russia and Canada, from competing for the $18.6 billion reconstruction contracts in 2004. Since the Bush administration forbids these ally countries from participating in the reconstruction of Iraq, these countries will most likely no longer be willing to forgive Iraq's debt of the several billion dollars owed to countries like France, Russia and Germany.[10]

The U.S. invaded Iraq on March 20, 2003, and the Iraq military was quickly vanquished by the far superior strength of the U.S. On May 1, 2003, in what was widely criticized as a costly theatrical stunt, Mr. Bush landed by jet on the U.S.S. Abraham Lincoln, an aircraft carrier, and gave a speech in front of a banner reading 'Mission Accomplished,' in which he announced the end of major combat operations and said, "In the battle of Iraq, the United States and our allies have prevailed."[11] So, Mr. Bush seemed to be telling the world, the U.S. war with Iraq had accomplished its goals in just

---

[10]Chantilloupe 2006, p. 314.
[11]Ivins 2006 [May].

six short weeks, with the loss of American lives less than 200, and approximately 1,000 Iraqis dead.

However, the overthrow of the Iraqi government was the easy part; it was the occupation that followed that proved so troublesome for the U.S. As Iraqi freedom fighters, called 'insurgents' by the U.S. media and politicians, refused to surrender the streets to their U.S. conquerors, Mr. Bush had more words of wisdom: "There are some who feel like if they attack us, we may decide to leave prematurely. There are some who feel the conditions are such that they can attack us there. My answer is, bring them on."[12] With this irresponsible, pseudo-macho challenge, Mr. Bush defined his attitude toward Iraqis fighting their imperial, oil-lusting oppressors. Following that challenge, over 3,500 U.S. soldiers were killed, along with an estimated hundreds of thousands of Iraqis.

The war was not going well for the U.S. as the world began looking towards the conclusion of Mr. Bush's eight years in office. In the 2006 mid-term elections, Democrats won control of both the House of Representatives and the Senate, in what was seen largely as a referendum on the Bush policies in Iraq. "In response, President Bush announced changes in the personnel responsible for overseeing the conflict, along with a new strategic approach, dubbed 'The New Way Forward' which involved change in military tactics, new diplomatic and economic initiatives, and, most prominently, an increase in the number of American troops in Iraq. By the summer of 2007, however, authorities in the Pentagon were conceding that little progress had been made, though they emphasized that it was still too early to tell whether the New Way Forward would succeed or fail."[13]

The decision to escalate was made by Mr. Bush, despite the advice and opinions of many experts, including General George Casey, the military leader in Iraq, to withdraw or, barring that, at least the redeployment of U.S. soldiers away from counterinsurgency

---

[12] "Our Troops Won't Be Forced out of Iraq, Pledges Straw" 2003.

[13] Gelphi, Feaver, and Reifler 2009, p. 243.

operations.[14]

As the Iraq war dragged on, with no discernible progress or even a clear definition of what 'progress' or 'victory' would mean, comparisons were often being made to the U.S.'s earlier imperial disaster in Vietnam. Perhaps because of this, the so-called surge, or escalation, was widely unpopular among U.S. citizens. "Echoes of that war moved on Vietnam veteran, Sen. Chuck Hagel, a Nebraska Republican, to challenge Secretary of State Condoleezza Rice in Senate hearings after Bush's speech. When she disputed the use of 'escalation,' Hagel incredulously asked what she would call it, and Rice introduced a new word to our war vocabulary. 'I would call it, Senator, an augmentation,' she said, 'that allows the Iraqis to deal with this very serious problem that they have in Baghdad.'"[15]

As Mr. Bush's term in office drew to a close, the Republican Party nominated Arizona Senator John McCain as its standard bearer. Mr. McCain vowed to continue many of Mr. Bush's foreign policies. The Democrats nominated Illinois Senator Barack Obama, and the contrast between the two men – one a wealthy white man in his 70s, the other an African-American man in his 40s; one a right-leaning Republican, the other a left-leaning Democrat – was striking. Mr. Obama was elected, partly due to his promise to end the war, and partly due to a nation tired of the policies of Mr. Bush, both globally and domestically.

Yet President Obama's fans were unrealistic in their expectations regarding his war policies. Shortly after his inaugural, appearing at Camp Lejeune, Mr. Obama told the Marines assembled to hear him that the U.S. combat role in Iraq would conclude by August 31, 2010. At that time, he said, a contingent of up to 50,000 U.S. troops would remain for training and counter-terrorism activities and to protect U.S. personnel.

However, it wasn't until December of 2011 that U.S. troops de-

---

[14]Duffield and Dombrowski 2009, p. 195.
[15]Page 2007 [January 16].

parted from Iraq, with only about 200 U.S. soldiers remaining, not the 50,000 Mr. Obama anticipated. Although violence in Iraq may have caused the president to delay the U.S. departure, the reason for the complete departure had nothing to do with conditions in Iraq. There was one condition that the Iraqis wouldn't agree to, for a continued U.S. military presence in Iraq. "Talks with the Iraqis broke down, however, over a single issue: the unwillingness of the Iraqi parliament to accept a Status of Forces Agreement (or SOFA) granting U.S. soldiers immunity from prosecution in Iraqi courts."[16]

SOFA agreements are common; they are non-reciprocal and basically put U.S. soldiers above the law in any country with which the U.S. has such an agreement. They cover more than 850 U.S. military bases and installations, and their enactment has not led to civilized behavior. "As East Asia expert and formal naval officer Chalmers Johnson has documented, the history of the U.S. military presence in Korea and in Okinawa has been marked by a long litany spanning more than six decades of unpunished brawls, drug violations, drunk-driving accidents, arsons, and sexual assaults amid the bars and brothels that have sprung up around the sprawling U.S. military installations."[17] And in Iraq, where countless war crimes have been reported, the possibility of those perpetrating them being charged, tried and executed by the Iraqis was more than Mr. Obama was willing to allow.

From a legal standpoint, perhaps, this makes sense, in the context of U.S. wars. As has been shown, racism, cruelty, massacres of civilians, etc., are all part of what happens when the U.S. invades a country to ram down its throat U.S. notions of democracy. Certainly this was no different in Iraq.

Yet in Iraq, the rate of atrocities may have been compounded by President George W. Bush's Attorney General Alberto Gonzales. Mr. Gonzales "advised the president that he should declare that the

---

[16]Osborn 2012 [March 9].
[17]Ibid.

Geneva Conventions do not apply because [i]t is difficult to predict the motives of prosecutors and independent counsels who may in the future decide to pursue unwarranted [war crimes] charges."[18] Mr. Gonzales didn't make any comment about 'warranted' war crime charges, perhaps because he knew that, as he and Mr. Bush redefined torture, U.S. soldiers could be in violation of international law, but not of U.S. law.

While one can argue the legitimacy of any particular war, or even of war itself, it must be acknowledged that, in war, it is expected that the military personnel of each side will attempt to kill their opponents in order to achieve whatever goal is being sought. One might also assume that, in this attempt, some innocent civilians may die. But the targeting of civilians is a war crime, and one that the U.S. refuses to face when perpetrated by its own soldiers. Two examples from Iraq will suffice.

In 2004, the first reports of systemic human rights violations, including physical, psychological and sexual abuse of U.S. prisoners in the Abu Ghraib prison in Iraq, were first released. Shocking pictures were released of U.S. soldiers leading prisoners on leashes like dogs; smiling and giving the 'thumbs up' sign in front of naked prisoners forced to form a human pyramid; smiling and giving the 'thumbs up' sign in front of the bodies of dead Iraqis. A report from the *New York Times* on January 12, 2005, documented these and additional abuses:

- Urinating on detainees;

- Jumping on a wounded limb with such force as to prevent the possibility of future healing;

- Striking a prisoner's wounded leg with a metal baton;

- Pouring the phosphoric acid from chemical lights onto prisoners;

---

[18]Carlston and Weber 2012, p. 21.

- Sodomizing prisoners with a metal baton;

- Attaching ropes to the legs or penis of prisoners and dragging them across the room.

The release of the Taguba report, conducted under the auspices of Major General Antonio Taguba, "found a pattern of 'sadistic, blatant, and wanton criminal abuses' at Abu Ghraib and noted that the detention facility had been effectively put under the control of military intelligence (MI) officers, in violation of military rules."[19] Sadly, the Bush administration, and much of the news media, either viewed this or spun this as a series of isolated incidents.

Time magazine, in March of 2006, published a report of the massacre four months earlier of 24 Iraqi civilians in the town of Haditha. The military had been aware of the incident, but said that 15 of the deaths had been due to an 'insurgent' (read: Iraqi freedom fighter) bomb blast, and the remaining eight deaths resulted from Marines returning fire. "The explosive *Time* account, on the other hand, alleged that according to eye witnesses and local officials, 'the civilians who died in Haditha on November 19 were killed not by a roadside bomb but by the Marines themselves, who went on a rampage in the village after the attack, killing 15 unarmed Iraqis in their homes, including seven women and three children."[20]

Over the years, additional stories of barbaric atrocities committed by U.S. soldiers have been revealed. Yet as reported by many Marines, these are not unusual situations.

> When asked if reports of fifteen or twenty civilians killed by their comrades in a single incident in Haditha sounded excessive to them at the time, the Marines repeatedly testified that it did not. 'This is not unusual,' Colonel John Ledoux said. 'You can see the numbers yourself,' he continued, 'just

---

[19]Bennett, Lawrence, and Livingston 2008, p. 85.
[20]Baum and Groeling 2009, p. 159.

thousands of incidents, thousands of noncombatant deaths as well as, you know, enemy.' According to Ledoux, in the early phase of the war the military made no attempt to investigate civilian deaths. It was only over time that 'things morphed more and more and more into tighter requirements ... because there really were a lot of people getting killed all over, you know, Iraq on escalation of force.' The Pentagon's handling of the Haditha massacre as well as other atrocities in Iraq exposes the military's powerful interest in protecting its own from the demand of justice. It acquitted or dismissed charges against all soldiers involved in the Haditha killing except for one, marine Staff Sergeant Frank Wuterich. ... [21]

The military dropped nine counts of manslaughter against Mr. Wuterich. In exchange, he pleaded guilty to one count of negligent dereliction of duty, and was demoted to the rank of private. "The man who by his own testimony ordered his squad to 'shoot first, ask questions later' in Haditha will not serve a single day behind bars." [22]

Another report stated that over 40 people, including children, were killed when U.S. soldiers opened fire on a wedding party. "A U.S. military spokesman confirmed that the group was killed by U.S. forces at the village of Makr al-Deep near the Syrian border, but denied there was any indication that the victims were part of a wedding party. ... Arab satellite channel Al-Arabiyya reported that the incident occurred after wedding guests in the village starting firing in the air in celebration and the U.S. soldiers mistakenly believed they were being targeted." [23]

While these are shocking incidents, barbaric behavior by U.S. citizens towards the Iraqis was commonplace. The story of Second Lieutenant Dave Hagner is typical of countless U.S. soldiers who served in Iraq.

---

[21]Osborn 2012 [March 9].
[22]Ibid.
[23]Shea 2004 [May 21].

Hagner led his platoon into the ruined, stinking maze of Ramadi. Quietly they slipped by packs of feral dogs, lagoons of sewage. They stepped around the unexploded mortars and crept under open windows, the soft sounds of whispered Arabic falling over them, the speakers unaware of, or unconcerned about, the passage of armed men. When they reached a certain neighborhood, Hagner's Marines would burst into houses and bring the occupants to him as they blinked off sleep. Then the questioning began.

It must have seemed to the Iraqis that they were being hauled before a nightmare judge. They were accustomed to this, to violent noises, interrogations, searches. But still they were cowed by Hagner, by all of it. And even though he was careful to say 'Thank you' and even sometimes 'Things are gonna get better' to those frightened people, the words seemed empty after what had just been done, and Hagner seemed remote and alien. Inhuman.[24]

One wonders just how far a 'thank you' goes after having been dragged from the security of one's home and interrogated by U.S. soldiers. The men in this episode appear to have been lucky; often all males over the age of 15 were dragged away to detention centers, as their hysterical wives, mothers and sisters wept in fear and anguish. There they were held for an indeterminate amount of time, depending on the whim of their jailers.

President Obama finally withdrew the last combat troops from Iraq in December of 2011, thus bringing to a close that U.S. foreign policy disaster. However, while U.S. troops no longer terrorize Iraqi citizens, the nation remains in chaos, with hundreds of thousands of people still in refugee camps, the infrastructure barely functional, and hatred for the U.S. greatly increased.

---

[24]Shea 2008 [Winter].

Chapter 16.

Israeli-Palestine Conflict

Like most of the U.S.'s foreign policy initiatives, a complete study of this issue would take volumes. This work only attempts to portray the conflict in its place in U.S. foreign policy since the founding of the state of Israel, which was accomplished only through the shocking displacement of several hundred thousand Palestinians.

On November 2, 1917, British Foreign Secretary Arthur James Balfour wrote to Lord Rothschild what came to be known as the Balfour Declaration. This officially proclaimed British support for a Jewish homeland in Palestine.

Sadly, this declaration didn't consider the wishes or rights of the millions of Palestinians who were to be driven out of their homes to accommodate this new nation. The U.S. media at the time seldom mentioned the Palestinian people and portrayed their struggle for independence as opposition to the establishment of a Jewish state. In the Balfour Declaration, the Palestinians were only referred to as 'existing non-Jewish communities in Palestine.'

> Despite the fact that there was considerable evidence of the extreme nationalistic drive behind the Zionist movement, which was its motivating force, American journals gave a good press to the Zionists' alleged goal of building a democratic commonwealth in Palestine. How this would be possible when the Arabs constituted two-thirds of the population and were opposed to Zionism, did not seem to be a relevant question

to many of the magazines.[1]

This was only the start of the long-standing, globally perpetrated injustices to the Palestinian people, injustices that the U.S. has been instrumental in fostering.

Zionists had long wanted their own nation and looked to Palestine as its site. The Balfour Declaration came about after years of negotiations with various world leaders.

The unspeakable hypocrisy of the United States is highlighted when looking at the establishment of the nation of Israel in Palestine. The right of peoples to self-determination, recorded as early as the city-states of Mesopatamia, Greece and Rome, was incorporated into the U.S. Declaration of Independence: "That to secure these rights, Governments are instituted among Men, deriving their just powers from the consent of the governed. ..." On May 27, 1916, President Woodrow Wilson said that "Every people has a right to choose the sovereignty under which they shall live."[2]

Mr. Wilson continued his lofty rhetoric, saying on February 11, 1918, that "National aspirations must be respected; peoples may not be dominated and governed only by their own consent."[3] Further: "Self-determination is not a mere phrase. It is an imperative principle of action, which statesmen will henceforth ignore at their peril."[4]

While these principles are continually expressed from the White House, regardless of its occupant, and reiterated from the halls of Congress, they are no more than meaningless platitudes, empty words spoken to foster, at least in the minds of U.S. citizens, the myth of the U.S. as a nation seeking to further the independence and democratic aspirations of people worldwide. However, "The prolongation of conflict in the Middle East is mainly caused by Israel's denial of the right of the Palestinian people to exercise self-

---

[1]Dohshe 1966, p. 240.
[2]U.S. Government Printing Office 1917.
[3]U.S. Government Printing Office 1918.
[4]Shaw and Wilson 1924, p. 475.

determination in their historic homeland. The United States, because of its unconditional political, moral, economic and military support of the Israeli occupation of Palestine, must bear heavy responsibility for the continuing state of unrest in the region."[5]

On January 8, 1918, President Wilson addressed a joint session of Congress and presented 14 points, a statement of basic principles outlining the goals of the post-war global environment. Point 12 reads as follows:

> The Turkish portion of the present Ottoman Empire should be assured a secure sovereignty, but the other nationalities which are now under Turkish rule should be assured an undoubted security of life and an absolutely unmolested opportunity of autonomous development, and the Dardanelles should be permanently opened as a free passage to the ships and commerce of all nations under international guarantees.[6]

These lofty goals, of course, could not be expected to stand in the way of U.S. strategic interests; self-determination and human rights are all well and good, as long as they don't in any way inconvenience the United States. Mr. Wilson's Secretary of State, Robert Lansing, was acutely aware of this. He arrived in France in December of 1918, and the president's use of the term 'self-determination' troubled him greatly. "In his private notes he wrote that it was loaded with dynamite, might breed disorder, discontent and rebellion. His neat, logical mind saw it leading the President into strange contradictions. 'Will not the Mohammedans of Syria and Palestine and possibly of Morocco and Tripoli rely on it? How can it be harmonized with Zionism, to which the President is practically committed?' he asked himself."[7] Heaven forbid the 'Mohammedans' rely on a promise of self-determination. In January of 1919, Wilson's legal counselor,

---

[5]Suleiman 1995, p. 31.
[6]Neiberg 2006, p. 292.
[7]Manual 1949, p. 217.

David Hunter Miller, advised the president that "the rule of self-determination would prevent the establishment of a Jewish state in Palestine."[8] And such a state had the firm backing of the president. On March 2, 1919, Mr. Wilson advised that he was "persuaded that the allied nations, with the fullest concurrence of our own government and people, are agreed that in Palestine shall be laid the foundations of Jewish commonwealth."[9]

This 'foundation of a Jewish commonwealth' would only come at the appalling cost of the displacement of hundreds of thousands of Palestinians and the murders of countless thousands of them. And the numbers of displaced Palestinians would climb into the millions with the passage of time, as their right to self-determination continues to be thwarted by the United States.

> Contrary to Wilson's public utterances contained in his point Twelve ... Palestine was, in fact, handled precisely 'upon the basis of the material interest' and 'advantage' of other nations and was not based upon 'the free acceptance of' consultation with 'the people immediately concerned.' The fate of Palestine was determined in accordance with what the Allies had already planned, in contradiction to Wilson's publicly declared opposition to the implementation of secret treaties arrived at during the war.[10]

The Anglo-American Convention of 3 December 1924 cemented the U.S.'s dominant role in the future of the Palestinian people. It stated that any change to the status of Palestine by the British be approved by the U.S., although any such change could be made without any input from the Palestinians. It further emphasized that the rights of U.S. missionaries in Palestine would be protected, but said nothing about protecting the rights of the Palestinians. "As the political and military status of the United States began to rise to

---

[8]Howard 1963, p. 27.
[9]Walworth 1986, p. 481.
[10]Suleiman 1995, p. 35.

preeminence in the global arena, the American government began to play a more and more substantial role in the denial of Palestinian rights." [11]

Following World War II, the newly formed United Nations, wanting to make some compensation to the international Jewish community for the unspeakable horrors it had suffered during the war, established the United Nations Special Committee for Palestine (UNSCOP), comprised of members with little experience in conflict resolution and almost no knowledge of Palestine's history. On November 29, 1947, General Assembly Resolution 181 was passed, recommending the partitioning of Palestine into two states.

> It is clear that by accepting the Partition Resolution, the UN totally ignored the ethnic composition of the country's population. Had the UN decided to make the territory the Jews had settled on in Palestine correspond with the size of their future state, they would have entitled them to no more than ten per cent of the land. But the UN accepted the nationalist claims the Zionist movement was making for Palestine and, furthermore, sought to compensate the Jews for the Nazi holocaust in Europe.
>
> As a result, the Zionist movement was 'given' a state that stretched over more than half of the country. [12]

In order for the new Jewish settlers to enter, Palestinians had to leave. This was done with the consent of U.S. President Harry Truman.

Mr. Truman formed his opinions and polices on Palestine based on three aspects related far more to U.S. domestic polices than foreign needs.

1. Lobbying by the Zionist movement. There appears to have been "... a concerted effort by American Jews to persuade

---

[11]Ibid., p. 49.
[12]Pappe 2006, pp. 31–32.

Truman to ignore or override the advice of officials in the departments of State and Defense who opposed unequivocal American support for the establishment of a Jewish state in Palestine."[13] And while this probably had a significant impact on the president's policies, he did eventually grow tired of the almost ceaseless lobbying efforts on behalf of partition. "As the pressure mounted, I found it necessary to give instructions that I did not want to be approached by any more spokesmen for the Zionist cause."[14]

2. Financial and electoral support for the election of 1948. The president, who came to office upon the death of President Franklin D. Roosevelt, did not appear in a good position to be elected for a term on his own merits. Democratic Party leaders felt that a supportive U.S. policy towards the establishment of Israel would benefit the president.

3. Conflicts about partition and related issues among top Cabinet officials and senior staff. Mr. Truman seemed to vacillate between one group and the other, depending on domestic policies, global events, or even the strength of the arguments made by his advisors.

In the end, these forces compelled U.S. policy toward support for the creation of the Jewish state, with complete disregard for the rights or interests of the area's majority Arab population. "It is questionable whether Truman thought through the long-term international consequences for American interest of his position on Palestine or if he simply responded to the pressure of the moment. ... [T]he president did not demonstrate any awareness of the humanitarian problems his policies were creating for the indigenous Arab inhabitants of Palestine."[15]

---

[13]Suleiman 1995, p. 59.
[14]Silverberg 1970, p. 372.
[15]Rubenberg 1989, p. 31.

In December of 1947, approximately 75,000 Palestinians were driven from their homes, most of them into refugee camps, all of them without any compensation for lost homes, farmlands, etc. By April of the next year, an additional 250,000 had been forced from their homes, carrying whatever possessions they could with them. During this time, the Deir Yassin massacre took place. "A combined IZP and LHI [Zionist paramilitary groups at the time] unit, supported by Hagana [another Zionist paramilitary group that formed the basis for today's Israeli Defense Forces] mortar fire, attacked and conquered Deir Yassin, an Arab village on the outskirts of Jerusalem, not far from al-Qastal. During the takeover of the village, which up to that moment had remained out of the fighting, the Jewish forces massacred some 120 men, women and children, and the survivors were expelled to East Jerusalem. [David] Shaltiel [military commander of Jerusalem] objected to the operation, as the village was peaceful, and had not been involved in the fighting."[16]

By the end of 1948, at least 750,000 Palestinians had been forcibly displaced from their homes, with thousands killed.

John Foster Dules, later Secretary of State under President Dwight D. Eisenhower, "was no stranger to the intractable problems surrounding the question of Palestine. His sympathetic attitude toward the Jews there was reflected in the active role he played in the adoption of a plank in the Republican convention platform of 1944 calling for the establishment of a Jewish commonwealth in Palestine and the protection of Jewish political rights in the area. He also supported and urged U.S. backing of the UN partition resolution of November, 1947."[17] Not surprisingly, this set the tone for the Eisenhower administration's attitude toward Israel and Palestine.

This support for Israel by Mr. Eisenhower was not always the case. Although providing humanitarian support to Jews after World War II in his role as military governor of Germany, he was not enthusiastic

---

[16]Tal 2003, p. 92.
[17]Alteras 1993, p. 55.

about the establishment of a Jewish state. Later, as president, he spoke to Philip Klutznick, the president of B'nai B'rith. He expressed "his doubts as to whether he would have favored the establishment of Israel. But 'now that it was done,' said Eisenhower, 'we'll have to live with it.'"[18]

Mr. Eisenhower was concerned about the vast oil reserves that the Middle East had, as well as the Soviet 'threat,' as was the case with several predecessors and successors. He wanted ready access to the oil, expressing the need for it for both military and civilian purposes. He also felt that the Palestinian-Israeli conflict provided an opportunity for the Soviets to exploit the situation, and get a strong foothold in the Middle East.

The foreign policy of the Eisenhower administration was rooted in two basic goals: 1) protecting the oil supplies of the Middle East, and 2) minimizing any Soviet (read: communist) involvement in the region. Palestine had no direct control over any oil resources, and was not strong enough militarily to be seen as a target of Soviet interests. This might, one may think, exempt it from unwanted attention by the U.S. However, "Finding a resolution to the Arab-Israeli dispute and the Palestine issue ... was important only insofar as the failure to do so might damage U.S. and Western relations with the Arab world, make Arab states susceptible to Soviet influence, and risk the security of Middle Eastern oil resources. In the 1950s, many in the Foreign Service felt that 'the question of the future status of the Palestinians was one that, unless it were resolved promptly, would pose a far greater threat to the U.S. and Western influence in the area than would any overt moves by the communist bloc.' Yet the polices made in Washington did not reflect this sense of urgency."[19]

Eisenhower wanted to develop strong ties with all anti-communist countries in the Middle East, rather than simply favoring Israel, as President Truman had eventually done. In the spring of 1953,

---

[18]Alteras 1993, p. 30.
[19]Suleiman 1995, p. 87.

Secretary of State Dulles went on a fact-finding trip to the Near East and South Asia. In a radio address following this trip, he addressed the American people:

> Closely huddled around Israel are most of the over 800,000 Arab refugees, who fled from Palestine as the Israelis took over. They exist mostly in makeshift camps, with few facilities either for health, work or recreation. . . .
>
> The United States should seek to allay the deep resentment against it that has resulted from the creation of Israel. In the past we had good relations with the Arab peoples. . . .
>
> Today the Arab peoples are afraid that the United States will back the new state of Israel in aggressive expansionism. They are more fearful of Zionism than of communism, and they fear lest the United States become the backer of expansionist Zionism. . . .
>
> We cannot afford to be distrusted by millions who could be sturdy friends of freedom. . . .
>
> Israel should become part of the Near East community and cease to look upon itself, or be looked upon by others, as alien to this community. To achieve this will require concessions on the part of both sides.[20]

While these sentiments would be proclaimed for years, recognition of Palestine as a national group was never considered.

The administration of President John F. Kennedy ushered in a new epoch in U.S.-Israeli relations, and consequently, in U.S.–Palestinian relations. Mr. Kennedy was concerned about the problem of Palestinian refugees and sought to alleviate it. The basis for his efforts was Paragraph 11 of United Nations General Assembly Resolution of December 11, 1948. It reads as follows:

> Resolves that the refugees wishing to return to their homes and live in peace with their neighbors should be permitted to

---

[20]Ibid., p. 88.

do so at the earliest practicable date, and that compensation should be paid for the property of those choosing not to return and for loss of or damage to property which, under principles of international law or in equity, should be made good by the Government or authorities responsible.[21]

Mr. Kennedy wanted the refugees to decide what they wanted: a return to their homes, or resettlement with compensation.

His efforts were opposed by Israel, which saw the return of the refugees as a threat to their national security. Israeli Prime Minister David Ben-Gurion told the Knesset that "Israel categorically rejects the insidious proposal for freedom of choice for the refugees, for she is convinced that this proposal is designed and calculated only to destroy Israel. There is only one practical and fair solution for the problem of the refugees: to resettle them among their own people in countries having plenty of good land and water and which are in need of additional manpower."[22]

The Palestinians and other Arab states, too, were not impressed with Mr. Kennedy's efforts. They worried that a resolution of the refugee problem would cause their national aspirations to be ignored. Egyptian President Abdul Nasser saw Mr. Kennedy's proposal as a possible trap. "The trap, he warned, was that Arab states were invited to take the initiative in proposing a solution of the refugee problem 'on the assumption that that would lead to the disintegration of the Palestine Question altogether.'"[23]

President Kennedy was also the first U.S. president to praise Israel in emotional terms. In addressing the Zionist Organization of America in August of 1960, shortly before his election, he said that "friendship for Israel is not a partisan matter, it is a national commitment."[24]

---

[21]Wilcox and Kalijavi 1952, pp. 576–577.
[22]Suleiman 1995, p. 117.
[23]Ibid., p. 115.
[24]Ibid., p. 551.

Mr. Kennedy's electoral victory three months later may also have influenced his policies toward Israel, and certainly played a role in his successors' policies. In the November 1960 presidential election, Mr. Kennedy garnered an astounding (at that time) 80% of the Jewish vote. U.S. politicians, always with an eye on the next election, do not want to alienate such a lucrative voting gold mine; again, human rights and the lofty talk of self-determination take a distant back seat to political expediency.

With the November 1963 assassination of President Kennedy, his vice president, Lyndon Johnson, assumed office. President Johnson had no interest in resolving the refugee problem that Mr. Kennedy had worked on; the Democratic Party platform on which Mr. Johnson was elected the following year included a provision to "encourage the resettlement of Arab refugees in lands where there is room and opportunity."[25] Work by the U.S. towards any kind of an equitable resolution for the refugees, such as it was, died with Mr. Kennedy.

Mr. Johnson, kindly disposed to Israel, was surrounded by advisors who had that nation's best interests at heart. These included Arthur Goldberg, the U.S. Representative to the United Nations; Eugene V. Rostow, Undersecretary of State for Political Affairs; and John Roche, a speech writer and close advisor. Additionally, Israeli Ambassador Avraham Harman and Ephraim Evron, Israeli Minister at the Embassy, were personal friends of Mr. Johnson and had easy access to the White House.

Mr. Johnson's biggest investment in the Palestinian-Israel conflict was the June 1967 War. The detailed causes of this war are beyond the scope of this work. Suffice it to say that years of hostility between Israel and its Arab neighbors culminated in deep suspicion and distrust on both sides. From 1965–1967, Israel staged countless provocations along its border with Syria. There was a strong belief by the Syrians and the Soviet Union that Israel was planning to overthrow the government of Syria. In April of 1967, an incident

---

[25]Ibid., p. 126.

in the demilitarized zone between Israel and Syria led to military action on both sides.

The following month, Israel threatened military action against Syria, for that country's alleged support of Palestinian guerillas. At the end of the month, Egypt and Jordan signed a formal defense pact, and the following day, the Iraqi army began deploying troops and armored units within Jordan, at Jordan's invitation. Israel, on June 5, launched an air strike, thus starting what became known as the Six-Day War.

President Johnson did not appear to be in much of a dilemma about how to respond. "The line of least resistance in the Middle East ran to Israel, as always since 1948. Pressure from the pro-Israel lobby encouraged Johnson to approve arms deliveries to Israel. His attempts to arrange third-party suppliers suggest that he might not have approved unpressured, despite his own personal concern for Israel's safety. Pro-Israel pressure made it impossible for him to apply strong sanctions to prevent a preemptive Israeli attack in June 1967. In this instance, Johnson probably did not need the pressure to act as he did, since he sympathized with Israel's predicament." [26]

In 1968, with the Vietnam War raging out of control and U.S. universities and streets burning with opposition to it, the president decided not to seek what would have been his second full term. In November of 1968, Richard M. Nixon was elected president.

President Nixon entered office with less obligation to Israel, and less knowledge about Palestine, than most of his predecessors. He received only about 15% of the Jewish vote and seemed pleased to tell visitors that "the Jewish lobby had no effect on him." [27] In his memoirs, he wrote of his concern about Israel's arrogance, especially as demonstrated following the Six-Day War. He described "an attitude of total intransigence on negotiating any peace agreement that would involve the return of any of the territories they had

---

[26]Brands 1997, p. 262.

[27]Kissinger 2011, p. 564.

occupied."[28]

Mr. Nixon, at least privately, espoused a more balanced approach to the Middle East. "It is apparent that Nixon, as president, was not only acutely aware of the incestuous triangle between Israel, its American supporters, and the White House, but that he was determined to steer his own course."[29] With this in mind, he sent former Pennsylvania Governor William Scranton to the Middle East, ostensibly to study the situation, but actually to gauge the reaction to a change in U.S. policy toward the Middle East and to introduce the idea of such a change. Mr. Scranton publicly stated upon his return that a more 'even-handed' approach was required.

"As predictable as Scranton's conclusion was the uproar the remark incited from Israel and from Jewish Americans who considered such a 'more even-handed' attitude as anti-Israel, even as proof of anti-Semitism."[30]

Unfortunately, this new, 'even-handed' approach was not meant to be. Mr. Nixon had envisioned a figurehead secretary of state and, in appointing William Rogers, he got exactly what he wanted. Mr. Rogers had little ambition and even less experience in foreign affairs, and the president instructed him to tame the agency's "recalcitrant bureaucracy"[31] and leave the running of foreign affairs to Mr. Nixon and his national security advisor, Henry Kissinger.

Mr. Nixon had his hands full with Vietnam, but he was also concerned about Russia and China, and Japan's growing influence. The Middle East wasn't much of a concern, and that is the only area of the world that he assigned to Secretary of State Rogers. Mr. Rogers's efforts were mainly to counter "the intransigence of Israel, a country of only 3 million or so people, a country, moreover, that was totally dependent on the good will and economic support of the United States. Finally, Rogers had much to bring to the problem:

---

[28]Nixon 1994, p. 283.
[29]Suleiman 1995, p. 134.
[30]Ibid., p. 134.
[31]Nixon 1994, p. 339.

honesty, integrity, objectivity, and experience in government, if not in the Middle East. But he was lacking two essentials: the trust of the Israelis and the respect of Nixon's new National Security Adviser, Henry Kissinger."[32]

Mr. Kissinger had little knowledge of the issues of the Middle East. However, his parents had fled Germany shortly before the Holocaust, and his bias was plainly towards Israel. He had never visited an Arab country, and had been to Israel only three times. This bias was plainly manifested in his dealings with Secretary Rogers. He encouraged U.S. and foreign ambassadors to go directly to him, completely bypassing the State Department.

It must be remembered that President Nixon was a hard-line anti-communist, who saw all world events in this context. Every conflict on the globe was somehow related, in his mind, to the struggle between the U.S.'s rather loosely defined version of freedom and democracy, and communist encroachment and aggression. Mr. Kissinger shared this skewed belief. Both believed that the Soviets wanted a strong presence in the Middle East only for oil, land and power, rather than any sympathy to Arab nationalism.

Also, reference to Palestinians only appears three times in Mr. Nixon's memoirs. Focused on the perceived aggression of the Soviets in 'Arab' lands, he had little interest in the finer points of the conflicts.

In order to counter what he saw as Soviet advances in the Middle East, President Nixon wanted to improve relations with Arab nations, relations that had been tenuous at best prior to the 1967 War, but were shattered at that time. It was on this point that he and Mr. Kissinger differed.

The U.S. at this time only had relations with Israel, and that suited Mr. Kissinger. "Rather than make any effort toward the Arab states, much less the Palestinians, Kissinger felt the United States should let them stew until they came begging to Washington."[33]

---

[32]Suleiman 1995, pp. 138–139.
[33]Ibid., p. 143.

He later wrote: "I thought delay was on the whole in our interests because it enabled us to demonstrate even to radical Arabs that we were indispensable to any progress."[34]

Those knowledgeable about the Middle East didn't agree with this analysis. Global issues of communism versus capitalism were, if anything at all, a very minor part of conflicts caused by issues about local control of land and water. Middle East experts saw the dispossession of the Palestinian people and the expansion of Israeli settlements as a major source of conflict in the region.

Mr. Nixon wanted to encourage greater cooperation and diplomacy with the Middle East; Mr. Kissinger preferred to keep things the way they were, with Israel the U.S.'s only ally in the region.

In September 1970, so called 'Black September,' civil war erupted in Jordan. Palestinian guerrillas in Jordan, many of them refugees from the dispossession of 1947–1948 as well as the 1967 War, sought to take power. Syria, siding with the Palestinians, eventually sent tanks into Jordan to support them. The Palestinian population of Jordan at that time exceeded that of Jordanians. President Nixon, characteristically, saw this conflict through the lens of communist aggression, although there was no evidence at the time, nor has any come forth since, to indicate that the Soviet Union anticipated this conflict any more than the U.S. did. It was this conflict, perhaps, that was a turning point in U.S.-Israel relations. Mr. Kissinger requested Israeli assistance in the war to include a reconnaissance mission and the possibility of air and land strikes against Syria.

Israel was hesitant to do so, without some very specific assurances from the U.S. Israel demanded, and received, U.S. promises that the U.S. would protect Israel from any Soviet or Egyptian aggression. They also wanted additional weapons, and this, too, was granted. Israel did deploy forces along its borders with Jordan and Syria, but no other action was needed by that nation. Before Israel was asked to make land or air strikes, Jordanian troops pushed Syrian troops

---

[34]Kissinger 2011, p. 354.

back into their own country, hundreds of thousands of Palestinians were driven out of Jordan, going mostly to Lebanon, and the conflict ended.

For Mr. Nixon, this was a clear victory in the U.S.–Soviet conflict that consumed him. Said he: "We could not allow Hussein to be overthrown by a Soviet-inspired insurrection. If it succeeded, the entire Middle East might erupt in war … the possibility of a direct U.S.–Soviet confrontation was uncomfortably high. It was a ghastly game of dominoes, with nuclear war waiting at the end."[35]

Messrs. Nixon and Kissinger publically proclaimed this a global crisis that was resolved by the U.S., with assistance from Israel, and one that thwarted the efforts of the Soviet Union. "This distorted beyond recognition Moscow's role, which most analysts now agree was limited to cautioning Syria, and greatly exaggerated Israel's contribution."[36]

Despite Israel's very limited contribution to the war, Mr. Kissinger was effusive in his thanks to Israeli Ambassador Yitzhak Rabin. "The President will never forget Israel's role in preventing the deterioration in Jordan and in blocking the attempt to overturn the regime there. He said that the United States is fortunate in having an ally like Israel in the Middle East. These events will be taken into account in all future developments."[37]

Those events, or at least Mr. Kissinger's interpretation of them, were indeed taken into account. "During 1971, U.S. aid to Israel was dramatically increased to nearly five times the largest amount and close to fifty times the smallest amount given in any previous year."[38]

After President Nixon's resignation, his successor, Gerald Ford, was too busy with trying to keep the country together, and overseeing the end of the Vietnam War, to spend much time on the Middle East.

---

[35] A. R. Taylor 1991, p. 84.
[36] Suleiman 1995, p. 149.
[37] A. R. Taylor 1991, p. 84.
[38] Ibid., p. 84.

His short administration ended when he was defeated for election by Georgia Governor Jimmy Carter.

Mr. Carter campaigned on a pro-Israel, anti-Palestine platform that had gained so much popularity in the U.S. Yet as president, he demonstrated, in the eyes of some, more openness toward the Palestinians than his campaign rhetoric may have intimated. "Indications that the administration might be moving away from a completely pro-Israeli stance and toward consideration of Palestinian rights elicited a predictable reaction from the Zionist lobby. Most Zionists viewed the struggle as a zero sum game in which recognition of the Palestinians – on any level – was a loss for Israel; recognition of, or negotiation with, the Palestinians was therefore totally unacceptable."[39] Yet their concerns were unfounded; as president, Mr. Carter never seemed to consider the feasibility of a separate Palestinian nation.

This attitude was not uniform among the Carter Administration. National Security Advisor Zbigniew Brzezinski certainly supported the president's view, but in a letter to Mr. Brzezinski from the U.S. Ambassador to Saudi Arabia, James E. Atkins, Mr. Atkins said this: "there could be no peace in the Middle East unless the rights of the Palestinians are recognized; that this includes the right of self-determination; and that everyone knows the Palestinians want a state of their own."[40]

A Harris poll administered in 1979 asked the U.S. public to agree or disagree with this statement: "As the most powerful force among Palestinian Arabs, the PLO should be in on negotiations about Gaza or the West Bank, even if the PLO are terrorists."[41] The bias in this statement is apparent, but it serves to highlight the general attitude toward the Palestinians during this timeframe. Fifty-seven percent of respondents disagreed with the statement, while 34% agreed.

---

[39]Suleiman 1995, p. 164.

[40]Ibid., p. 169.

[41]Ibid., p. 171.

Mr. Carter presided over the Camp David Accords, a two-framework agreement that was supposed to bring peace to the Middle East. The first of the two dealt with Palestine, and nothing in it was ever achieved. The second led to a peace treaty between Israel and Egypt.

With multiple problems plaguing him both domestically and internationally, Mr. Carter was defeated in his bid for re-election in 1980, and former actor and governor of California Ronald Reagan became president.

Reagan, like President Nixon before him, saw any global conflicts as somehow a manifestation of the Soviet 'threat'. One way he felt that that threat could be countered was by strengthening U.S. ties with Israel, thereby preventing the Soviet Union from gaining a strong foothold in the Middle East. As a result, his policies were often conflicting. He declared early in his administration that Israeli settlements in the occupied territories were not illegal, despite years of global condemnation of those settlements, including by the United Nations. In 1982, "He sought to reassure Israel by declaring that the United States would 'not support the establishment of an independent Palestinian state in the west Bank and Gaza,' and would endorse Israel's request for changes in the 1967 territorial lines so as to ensure its security. But he also tried to reassure the Palestinians by declaring that 'we will not support annexation of permanent control by Israel,' and by calling for 'the immediate adoption of a settlement freeze by Israel.'"[42]

The first sustained diplomatic efforts to resolve Mid-East problems during the eight years of the Reagan Administration resulted from the intifada of 1987. The U.S. recognized that the long-stalled peace process had led to the uprisings in the West Bank and Gaza Strip.

Secretary of State George Shultz created a plan to hopefully resolve the underlying issues. He called for 1) the convening of an international conference; 2) a six-month negotiating period that

---

[42]Suleiman 1995, p. 179.

would bring about an interim phase for Palestinian self-determination for the West Bank and Gaza Strip; 3) a date of December 1988 for the start of talks between Israel and Palestine for the final resolution of the conflict.

Israeli Prime Minister Yitzhak Shamir immediately rejected this plan, claiming that it did nothing to forward the cause of peace. In response, the U.S. issued a new memorandum, emphasizing economic and security agreements with Israel, and accelerating the delivery of 75 F-16 fighter jets. This, ostensibly, was to encourage Israel to accept the peace plan proposals. Yet Israel did not yield. "Instead, as an Israeli journalist commented, the message received was: 'One may say no to America and still get a bonus.'"[43]

During this time, support for U.S. policies toward the Israel-Palestine conflict began to shift. A Gallup survey in 1988 showed that 30% of Americans viewed Israel less favorably than had done so prior to the intifada. Also, as contrasted to the Harris survey of 1979, respondents in a February–March 1988 Gallup survey indicated that 53% favored direct U.S. talks with the PLO, with only 26% supporting official U.S. policies.[44]

President Reagan was succeeded in the White House by his vice president, George H.W. Bush. President Bush's administration saw the strengthening of U.S.–Israel ties, and further marginalization of the Palestinians. This was done in a variety of ways:

- Blocking the PLO from membership in multiple international organizations;

- Complete disregard for unspeakable human rights violations committed by Israel against Palestinians living in the occupied territories;

- A vision of peace based solely on Israel's terms;

---

[43]Ibid., p. 185.
[44]Farsoun and Zacharia 1997, pp. 242–243.

- Opposition to U.N. resolutions addressing Israel's violations of international law in crimes committed against the Palestinians;

- Support for massive Jewish immigration to the occupied territories; and

- Increasing financial assistance to Israel, despite that country's pursuit of policies that contradicted U.S. principles.

Thomas Friedman of the *New York Times* commented on the state of relations between the U.S. and Israel during the Bush Administration: "Although the Bush Administration's whole approach to peacemaking is almost entirely based on terms dictated by Prime Minister Yitzhak Shamir, the Israelis nevertheless see the Bush Administration as hostile."[45] The 'bonuses' provided by the Reagan administration, given for Israel's refusal to support U.S. policies, continued unabated.

Mr. Bush's administration is perhaps best remembered for the Gulf War, the invasion to 'liberate' Kuwait after the Iraqi invasion. "The Provisional Government of the State of Palestine refused to join the so-called Coalition put together by President Bush Sr. to attack Iraq, but instead did its levelheaded best, working in conjunction with Libya and Jordan, to produce a peaceful resolution of this inter-Arab dispute. For their policy of principle and peace, the Palestinian leadership and people were and still are unjustly but predictably vilified by the United States government and Western news media sources."[46]

President Bush served one term and was defeated by Arkansas governor Bill Clinton. President Clinton appointed people to high-level cabinet positions who had definite pro-Israel biases. CIA Director James Woolsey and Pentagon chief Les Aspin had long served both

---

[45]T. Friedman 1991 [September 19].

[46]http://globalresearch.ca/articles/BOY204A.html. Accessed on January 16, 2013.

the Washington Institute for Near East Policy, and the Jewish Institute for National Security Affairs. National Security Advisor Anthony Lake had served in the Carter administration, but his deputy, Sandy Berger, had some association with American Friends of Peace Now, thus raising red flags in Israel. This represented a breach in the wall of Zionist organizations that stridently purported to represent Jewish voices in the U.S. In referring to these organizations that did not reflect the Zionist view, the *New York Times*' Thomas Friedman said that "their monopoly on representing Jewish positions is being broken."[47]

In March of 1993, following clashes between Palestinians and Israelis in both Israel and the occupied Palestine territories, Yitzhak Rabin closed the borders between Israel and Palestine. This had a drastic detrimental effect on lives and basic subsistence for at least tens of thousands of Palestinians. The Clinton Administration chose to look the other way, as Israel perpetrated this unspeakable act of collective punishment.

The U.S. press during this time toed the U.S. party line. Said the *New York Times*: "So far in the quid pro quo that is part of negotiations, the concessions have come from Israel. Next week, Israeli and American officials say, it is time for a significant gesture from the Palestinians."[48] These concessions from Israel included allowing a prominent Palestinian to join the Palestinian delegation and allowing several Palestinians expelled from Palestine to return. No one seemed to ask why Israel was in a position to allow either of these 'concessions,' since both seem to be issues for which the Palestinians alone should decide. Additionally, one might consider that the Palestinians had already made sufficient concessions by surrendering, at gunpoint, a large section of their country.

Following President Clinton's two terms as president, George W. Bush was appointed by the Supreme Court, after losing the popular

---

[47]T. Friedman 1993 [January 5].
[48]Holmes 1993 [May 2].

vote to Vice President Al Gore. Irregularities in polling in Florida caused the election to be brought before the highest court in the land, and Mr. Bush became president.

Like his predecessors, Mr. Bush was beholden to the Israeli lobby, and paid proper homage to it. Also like previous occupants of the White House, he saw human rights through the skewed lens of the U.S.'s definition of democracy. When Hamas was elected to power in the Gaza Strip in 2006, Congress approved a near-total ban on aid to Palestine. Outside observers generally saw this as a relatively free election, not encumbered by vote-count fraud as experienced in the U.S. in 2000, in the election that brought Mr. Bush to power. "Noam Chomsky commented on this situation: 'You are not allowed to vote the wrong way in a free election. That's our concept of democracy. Democracy is fine as long as you do what we (the United States) says. ... ' An exchange between Hearst White House correspondent Helen Thomas and then White House spokesman Tony Snow is also enlightening. Ms. Thomas asked about the foreign aid ban.

> 'Well,' Mr. Snow replied, 'the U.S. role is one of working with Israel and, when possible, with the Palestinians to try to generate a peace, the same it has always been, Helen.'
>
> 'Then why is it bankrupting the Palestinians?' she interrupted.
>
> 'The Palestinians are not being bankrupted, Helen. What's happening, as you know, is that Hamas is a terrorist organization. We do not give money to terrorist organizations. What has happened is that this government has tried in a number of ways to make humanitarian aid available to the Palestinian people. We draw a distinction between Hamas, which is ... '
>
> 'And they were democratically elected,' she interjected.
>
> 'They were democratically elected, and they're still a terrorist organization,' Mr. Snow persisted.[49]

---

[49]http://www.stateofnature.org/israelPalestineAndTerror.html. Accessed on January 16, 2013.

The election of Barack Obama in 2008 didn't bring about the promised 'hope and change' on which he'd campaigned, and nowhere is that more apparent than in U.S. relations with Israel and Palestine. Although the U.N. has passed numerous resolutions over the years condemning Israel's treatment of the Palestinians, the U.S., under President Obama, has chosen to veto them. On February 18, 2011, a Security Council resolution came up for a vote. This resolution condemned all Israeli settlements built in occupied Palestine since 1967, saying that such settlements are illegal under international law. The resolution was co-sponsored by more than 120 of the U.N.'s 192 member states and was voted affirmatively by 14 of the 15 members of the Security Council. Only the U.S. voted against it, effectively vetoing the resolution. U.S. Ambassador to the U.N. Susan Rice said after the vote that, while the U.S. agrees the settlements are illegal, the resolution harmed chances for peace talks. Incongruously, she emphasized that the U.S. opposes the settlements: "On the contrary, we reject in the strongest terms the legitimacy of continued Israeli settlement activity. Continued settlement activity violates Israel's international commitments, devastates trust between the parties, and threatens the prospects for peace ..."[50] The inherent contradiction within her statements is evident.

In October of 2011, the United Nations voted to accept Palestine as a member of UNESCO (United Nations Educational, Scientific and Cultural Organization) with 107 member nations voting in favor, 14 voting against and 52 abstaining from voting. This was despite the U.S. threat to stop all its funding to the organization (22% of UNESCO funding). "The U.S. government is legally required to cut funds to any U.N. agency that recognizes a Palestinian state."[51] As of October of 2012, this left UNESCO with a shortfall of $152,000,000.

On November 29, 2012, the United Nations again defied the United

---

[50]Knickerbocker 2011 [February 18].

[51]http://www.voanews.com/content/us-funding-for-unesco-cut-over-palestine-agency-struggles/1524 934.html. Accessed on January 21, 2013.

States, when it voted overwhelmingly to recognize Palestine. This time the vote was 138 in favor, 9 opposed and 41 abstaining. The U.S., naturally, condemned this vote and threatened to cut aid to Palestine as a result.

Again, human rights are a distant second to the political interests of the U.S. government.

Chapter 17.

Other Foreign Policy Initiatives of this Time

It is difficult to look at U.S. foreign policy during the period of the 1960s and 1970s without focusing completely on Vietnam. That war was the focus of national and international attention during much of those decades, but presidents during this time, especially President Richard Nixon, were not entirely negligent of the rest of the world.

Mr. Nixon differed from his predecessor in that he wanted to be known for his foreign policy expertise and to have his presidency defined by dramatic global political advances that he would initiate. Having served as vice president during the rise and fall of Senator Joseph McCarthy, he was a strong opponent of communism and saw his role on the world stage as containing it wherever and whenever possible. Part of his strategy was to neutralize what he saw as the Soviet threat, partly by exploiting hostilities between Russia and China. Referred to as 'Triangular Diplomacy,' noting the major players of the U.S., China and Russia, this, in part, led to what is commonly seen as one of the greatest achievements of his damaged, flawed and tainted presidency, the official recognition by the United States of the People's Republic of China. Although this was Mr. Nixon's brainchild, implementation was mainly the responsibility of Henry Kissinger.

Since 1949, when Mao Tse Tung came to power, the U.S. had

steadfastly refused to recognize the country, opting instead to recognize Taiwan and approve its admittance to the United Nations. Mr. Kissinger first visited China secretly in 1972, to prepare the way for the eventual visit by the president. Mr. Nixon surprised the world shortly thereafter by announcing plans to visit the People's Republic of China in February of the following year. Understandably, this caused no end of consternation in the Soviet Union, to see its two main enemies cozying up to each other.

Mr. Nixon's scheduled summit with the Soviets, just three months later, happened as planned, although as the time drew near, there was some thought that it might be cancelled. The North Vietnamese launched an intense offensive against the South and the U.S., and the president responded by mining North Vietnamese harbors and bombing its transportation, storage and air defense systems. He believed, correctly as it turned out, that Russia would tolerate this U.S. aggression against its ally, North Vietnam, in exchange for better relations with the U.S. "As the Soviets went ahead with the May summit despite the Americans' massive bombing campaign against their allies in North Vietnam, triangular diplomacy was seemingly vindicated. The Soviets, or so the conventional wisdom would later have it, were so concerned about the opening to China that they were willing to ignore the events in Vietnam in order to safeguard détente."[1]

But, as always, there was another motivation involved. While these diplomatic overtures to China and Russia certainly weren't entirely related to the Vietnam War, it was clear that Mr. Nixon hoped to get some benefit from them in terms of that war: "in the midst of the May summit, Kissinger was also busily selling the idea of a 'decent interval' in Vietnam to the Soviets and the Chinese. ... the Americans, he would effectively explain to the Soviet foreign minister Andrei Gromyko and to the Chinese premier Zhou Enlai, simply wished to withdraw their troops without witnessing an immediate

---

[1]Hanhimaki 2004, p. 186.

takeover of the South by North Vietnamese forces. But, if a period of time elapsed after the American withdrawal, the United States would not reintervene in Vietnam."[2] There was, however, no indication that either the Chinese or the Soviets would use their influence to encourage the North Vietnamese to end their offensive in the south.

There was, of course, a broader goal of the summit with the Soviets. "On May 21, 1971, President Nixon announced a breakthrough in talks with the Soviets: the two sides would seek an ABM [Anti-Ballistic Missile] agreement and constraints on offensive weapons."[3]

This goal was not quickly or easily reached, partly because of the challenges Mr. Kissinger, then the National Security Advisor, encountered from Secretary of State William P. Rogers, Defense Secretary Melvin Laird and Gerard C. Smith of the Arms Control and Disarmament Agency (ACDA), who served as chief U.S. delegate to the Strategic Arms Limitation Talks (SALT) in 1969. "In depth study demonstrates, however, that the national security advisor employed numerous influence strategies, at times even hiding bureaucratic conflicts from the public. Kissinger's famed use of the 'backchannel' to block the State Department's influence while he conducted secret arms control negotiations with the Soviets, Vietnam peace talks in Paris, and talks with China, provides three notable examples."[4]

The topic of détente is worthy of several volumes, but will be included here to show shifting attitudes in foreign policy. This is not meant to imply any change from the pursuit of power and wealth, but how the manifestations of those lusts evolved.

Détente, the focused, intentional easing of the cold-war tensions between the U.S. and the Soviet Union, was the brainchild of President Nixon, who saw it as "a political, military and economic strategy to stabilize relations. It was to be embedded in a new and more stable international structure."[5] The signing of Strategic Arms Limitations

---

[2]Ibid., p. 186.
[3]Garrison 1999, p. 53.
[4]Ibid., p. 16.
[5]Hyland 1987, p. 8.

and Anti-Ballistic Missile treaties gave the U.S. a much better impression of the Soviet Union. In 1954, 5% of U.S. citizens had a favorable view of Russia; in 1973, that rose to 34%. "Nixon changed the course of U.S. foreign policy radically, and Americans, by and large, approved."[6]

However, private, separate interpretations of détente appeared to be operational in both Russia and the U.S., although the U.S. was only pointing an accusing finger at the Soviets. But the U.S. was certainly taking its own international road, one that did not appear to follow the map of détente. Returning from the Moscow Summit of 1972, Mr. Nixon, along with Secretary of State Kissinger, visited Tehran and offered his support to the Shah in his efforts to destabilize Iraq, a Moscow ally. The following year, economic sanctions were used against the government of Salvadore Allende in Chile, in support of attempts to overthrow it.

By the mid-'70s, with Mr. Nixon out of power and Gerald Ford now president, things were not going well for the U.S. in terms of foreign policy. In March of 1975, the last U.S. soldiers fled Vietnam, as the Communist North declared victory over the South and the United States. The U.S.-backed government of Cambodia came under attack from the Khmer Rouge. The Russian-supported, leftist government of Portugal survived a coup attempt. In all of these, the Soviet Union was viewed by the U.S. with great suspicion. The Russians, it was felt, were either not respecting détente, or interpreting it far differently than the U.S. There was little or no public discussion of the U.S.'s interpretation, only of how the U.S. wanted Russia to understand it.

Partly because of this, not everyone was pleased with détente. Influential conservatives outside of the Nixon administration had been concerned from the start about what it might be doing to the U.S.'s leading position in the world. They felt that the U.S. was deceived by the 'myth of overestimation,' the belief that in an arms race, each side overestimates the strength of their opponent. These

---

[6]Cahn 2006, p. 7.

conservatives felt, in fact, that the U.S. was underestimating Russian strength.

Although significant strides were made towards accommodation with the Soviet Union under Mr. Nixon, the policy proved to be unsustainable. During the last half of President Carter's administration, "the Soviets drove the final nail into the coffin of 'détente' when they took Kabul. Jimmy Carter responded with further defense spending increases, the removal of SALT II from Senate consideration, the grain embargo, the Olympic boycott, and the 'Carter Doctrine.'"[7] (Please see Chapter 12 for information on the Carter Doctrine.)

El Salvador

Like many Central American nations, poverty, socioeconomic inequality and general political instability have long characterized El Salvador. As such, the U.S. looked with concern upon this small nation, fearing the 'domino effect,' and not wanting to risk El Salvador having a successful revolution in the Cuban model.

In October of 1979, El Salvador's leader, General Humberto Romero, was overthrown, and it was widely believed that the U.S. was behind this coup d'tat. "Although the State Department hotly denied U.S. involvement in Romero's overthrow, observers in Washington and San Salvador noted that little happened within the American-trained Salvadorean military without the United States knowing and approving in advance."[8]

Yes, the U.S. had its interfering finger in the Salvadorean pie. While President Carter's involvement in that nation will be discussed, it was Mr. Reagan who, perhaps best, described U.S. interest in El Salvador. In an address at the March 10, 1983, meeting of the National Association of Manufacturers, Mr. Reagan discussed Central America as a whole, but singled out a few nations, including El Salvador. In

---

[7]Busch 1997 [Summer].

[8]*Washington Post*, 1981 [March 8].

that context, he first mentioned Panama, pointing out that "half of all the foreign trade of the United States passes through either the canal ... or other Caribbean Sea lanes on its way to or from our ports."[9] He further stated that "The problem is that an aggressive minority has thrown in its lot with the Communists, looking to the Soviets and their own Cuban henchmen to help them pursue political change through violence."[10] Their first target, he warned darkly, was El Salvador.

That nation was, at that time, already suffering from political chaos with thousands dying at the hands of the U.S.-supported military. Mr. Reagan warned that "The killing will increase and so will the threat to Panama. ..."[11] Panama, through which so much profitable trade flows, must not be jeopardized in any way.

During the Carter Administration, U.S. foreign policy in reference to El Salvador tried "to promote a centrist government, agrarian reform, more democracy, and human rights in that country. The unfolding of the situation in and around El Salvador during 1980 proved that none of these objectives was achieved. On the contrary, it has become clear that precisely the opposite actually happened in El Salvador during 1980."[12]

One wonders how this might have happened. Couldn't one of the world's super-powers correctly read and intervene in a small, Third World country to shape it in whatever way it chose? The answer, of course, is that the U.S. could and, indeed, did, shape El Salvador as it wanted to. During Mr. Carter's presidency, various human rights abuses caused a cessation, or at least a diminution, of U.S. military aid. U.S. aid to El Salvador was $102,000,000 in 1977; it decreased to $303,000 in 1978 and grew only slightly in the next few years.

Yet these reductions were only symbolic. During those years, El

---

[9]http://www.reagan.utexas.edu/archives/speeches/1983/31 083a.htm. Accessed on December 12, 2012.

[10]Ibid.

[11]Ibid.

[12]Ibid.

Salvador received massive military aid from Israel, France and Brazil, most of it originating in the U.S. So the Carter Administration was able to continue to fund the repressive, right-wing government of El Salvador, while professing to the U.S. and the world that, due to that country's human-rights abuses, it was decreasing or suspending such aid.

One incident is instructive regarding the U.S.'s meaningless lip-service to human rights.

In February of 1977, Oscar Romero was named Catholic Archbishop of El Salvador. Although initially quite conservative, Archbishop Romero was the close friend of a Jesuit priest named Rutilio Grande, who was prominent in organizing the campesinos (peasants), to assist them in bettering their lives. This, of course, was opposed by the military and political leaders of the country, who had a general hostility toward the clergy. Mr. Grande's assassination a month after Mr. Romero's elevation to archbishop is said to have profoundly changed him. It is suggested "that the assassination of Grande radicalized Romero, and it certainly drew the archbishop fully into an unholy war that would over the next three years kill hundreds of people, mostly farmers but also ten priests. Romero's thinking, his growing anger, can be seen in retrospect in his public statements, his homilies and pastoral letters. ... less than a month after Father Grande and his two companions were killed and as the country was convulsed by civil unrest [he wrote]: 'the church cannot be defined simply in political or socio-economic terms. But neither can it be defined from a point of view that would make it indifferent to the temporal problems of the world.'"[13]

Increasingly, as his rhetoric and actions reflected support for the campesinos and opposition to the right-wing, repressive government, Mr. Romero himself became a target of criticism from the government. He also began getting international notice, receiving an honorary doctorate from Georgetown University in 1978 and being nominated

---

[13]Adams 1991, pp. 269–270.

for the Nobel Peace Prize that same year. He criticized the low wages of coffee, sugar cane and cotton farm workers, and called 'national security' a 'new kind of idolatry.'

"This frail, introspective man, against all predictions, had turned into the conscience of Latin America. Vilified in slanderous publications, he had even received death threats, he told his parishioners. Yet he kept up his attacks, knowing they were against men whose predilection for the most obscene forms of violence was well documented."[14] Perhaps most damning, he said: "The full liberation of the Salvadoran people, not to mention personal conversions, demands a thorough change in the social, political and economic system. . . ."[15]

In February of 1980 he wrote President Carter, asking that he cease sending military supplies to the government. He received a reply from Secretary of State Cyrus Vance, saying, "We share a repugnance for the violence provoked by both extremes."[16] Nothing changed.

By March of 1980, every statement the archbishop made was a major event. He charged the army with genocide and encouraged soldiers to disobey orders that violated God's law.

On the evening of March 23, when saying Mass, a hired sniper entered the church and shot him. His last recorded words, prior to being shot, were these: "We know that every effort to better society, especially when injustice and sin are so ingrained, is an effort that God blesses, that God wants, that God demands of us."[17]

His funeral a week later was a major international event, but one that was marred by extreme violence. "The fifty thousand people with the courage to attend Romero's funeral were sprayed with pesticide from crop dusting aircraft during the procession. Later, in the plaza in front of the Cathedral, between 26 and 40 of them died when bombs exploded and gunfire erupted between armed members of the

---

[14]Adams 1991, p. 273.
[15]Ibid., p. 273.
[16]Ibid., p. 274.
[17]Ibid., p. 275.

Revolutionary Coordinator of Masses and security force personnel."[18]
The U.S. was complicit in Mr. Romero's assassination, and possibly
in the violence at his funeral: "The Honduran intelligence unit,
trained by the CIA ... killed at least 184 people. One of those was
the former secretary to Archbishop Oscar Romero of El Salvador,
himself a victim of a CIA-funded death squad in 1980."[19]

Ronald Reagan came into power, facing immediate crises that his
predecessor, President Jimmy Carter, had been unable to resolve.
The Afghanistan situation was one of three that Mr. Reagan in-
herited when he came into office. The other two were the planned
construction of a pipeline for natural gas from Siberia to Western
Europe. The third was unrest in Poland. Overarching all this was
the rapid deterioration of détente. The first three are all intertwined,
as the following discussion will indicate.

The beginning of a Soviet quagmire in Afghanistan would be
mirrored decades later by the U.S. In April of 1978, a bloody coup resulted in the installation of a revolutionary president in Afghanistan.
This new government soon signed a twenty-year agreement of 'friendship and cooperation' with the Soviet Union. By the following summer, government forces and rebels were fighting, and the death
toll was mounting. In December of 1979, Soviet troops entered
Afghanistan, and President Carter issued a warning to the Soviets, calling their action "a callous violation of international law and
the United Nations Charter."[20] He further announced that the U.S.
would resume providing military equipment to Pakistan, recalled
the U.S. Ambassador to Moscow and cancelled a series of meetings
scheduled with Russia on agriculture, business, civil aviation and
health. He also placed embargoes on exports to Russia of grains and
high-technology products, with the grain embargo being potentially
the most serious for the Soviets. However, other nations didn't honor

---

[18]Stanley 1996, p. 198.
[19]Rothschild 2005 [April].
[20]Vasquez 1986, p. 101.

the embargo, so it had no impact on the Russian government.

In Poland, the first non-communist-controlled labor union, known as Solidarity, was gaining power and influence. By September of 1981, approximately one-third of all Poland's labor force were members.

Using civil resistance to force concessions from the government, Solidarity continued to grow in popularity to the point that martial law was declared. The U.S. responded by suspending economic assistance to Poland, consisting mainly of $100,000,000 in grain. "In the two weeks following, other sanctions were spelled out. Again, economic penalties were the primary ingredients. Furthermore, the sanctions were expanded to apply not only to Poland but also to the Soviets for their presumed complicity in the martial law decision."[21]

Meanwhile, discussions were underway for a massive natural gas pipeline from Russia: "estimates indicate that West Germany's gas consumption, then 15% reliant on the Soviet Union, would become 30% dependent on that source. French consumption, also 15%, would jump at least to 35% from the Eastern bloc leader."[22] By the middle of 1981, President Reagan was warning Europe of the dangers of becoming energy dependent on Russia. However, this was to little avail. While the initial talks were between the Soviet Union and West Germany, companies from France, Italy and Japan soon joined the project. Exxon, Texaco, British Petroleum, Mobil and Royal Dutch/Shell soon announced their participation. "In short, by November 1981, President Reagan's doubts seemed to be overwhelmed by the momentum of business deals."[23]

The president was still unhappy about the Soviet invasion of Afghanistan and Russia's influence over the government of Poland, especially in the context of that nation's imposition of martial law. He saw the pipeline as a 'gift' from the U.S. to a belligerent adversary. He then issued an embargo extending to foreign companies that produced

---

[21]Vasquez 1986, p. 104.

[22]Ibid., p. 103.

[23]Ibid., p. 104.

pipeline equipment under any U.S.-issued licensed patent. This move, however, was not well-received in the international community, with many nations either challenging it, or simply ignoring it. In November of 1982, Mr. Reagan lifted the sanctions, announcing at the time that an agreement had been reached with U.S. allies on a broader trade strategy in reference to the Soviet Union, although no details were provided. Allied leaders, off the record, stated that they had not made any significant concessions to the U.S. Pipeline-related sanctions had done nothing to influence Soviet actions in either Afghanistan or Poland.

Mr. Reagan was succeeded by his vice president, the patrician George H.W. Bush. His one term, except for the Gulf War (please see Chapter 13) was mainly uneventful in the context of foreign policy, but one area is worth noting.

On May 12, 1992, U.N. Secretary Boutros Boutros-Ghali advised Mr. Bush that the U.S. response to the unfolding disaster in Somalia was negatively impacting the U.S. reputation in the Middle East. "Somalia [was] in a state of anarchy, ruled (if that's the right word) by gangs of bandits and clan leaders styled 'warlords' in the press. It literally [had] no government, and the rival clans [had] prevented the distribution of food by the United Nations."[24] There appeared to be a perception that the U.S. wasn't paying much attention, since most of the victims there were Muslim. Mr. Bush had committed over $240,000,000 in food aid to the ravaged nation, but it was apparent that little food was reaching the starving people.

In early November, pictures of starving children in Somalia reached U.S. television audiences for the first time. That same month, Mr. Bush was defeated in his bid for reelection by Arkansas governor Bill Clinton, yet he was determined to act on the Somalia situation before leaving office.

A few weeks later, just before Thanksgiving, Mr. Bush approved an operation called 'Operation Restore Hope,' which involved the use

---

[24]Francis 1993 [January 4].

of ground troops to assure that the starving Somalis were obtaining food. He envisioned a quick and very short-term operation. "Brent Scowcroft [National Security Advisor] looked uneasy. 'Sure we can get in,' he said. 'But how do we get out?' 'We'll do it, and try to be out by January 19,' the President concluded. 'I don't want to stick Clinton with an ongoing military operation.'"[25]

U.S. marines arrived in Mogadishu, Somalia's beleaguered capital, on December 9, 1992. Eventually, 24,000 troops from the U.S. arrived in Somalia, soon joined by an additional 20,000 from other nations. The operation was successful in providing humanitarian relief, but Mr. Bush's hope of completing the operation, so as not to leave it as unfinished business for President-elect Clinton, was not realized.

Even before Mr. Bush first sent troops, expecting them to be finished and back home by the time Mr. Clinton was inaugurated, there were disagreements and doubts among members of his Cabinet about the time frame of the operation. "High-level Administration officials exuded confidence (at least on a 'not for attribution' basis) that American forces would be able to complete their mission and return to the U.S. in time for the inauguration of Bill Clinton on Jan. 20, 1993. Secretary of Defense Richard B. Cheney and military leaders were more circumspect, indicating that it probably would be three months before the bulk of U.S. troops could be withdrawn. Colin Powell, chairman of the Joint Chiefs of Staff, compared the U.S. mission to having the cavalry ride to the rescue and then transferring responsibility to the 'marshals' (i.e. U.N. peace-keepers) once the situation stabilized."[26] Yet it wasn't until March of 1994 that Mr. Clinton finally removed all U.S. military presence from Somalia. This was in response to the deaths of 18 marines during an uprising by Mogadishu warlords.

The U.S. had no strategic interest in Somalia. Prior to the U.N. Secretary General's advice to Mr. Bush that the U.S. reputation

---

[25]Bose and Perotti 2002, pp. 265–266.
[26]Carpenter 1993 [May].

was suffering because of U.S. non-involvement, the nation and its problems were not on the U.S. radar. Mr. Boutros-Ghali's comments, along with the now-famous CNN photographs, triggered minimal U.S. interest in Somaila.

Overall, U.S. involvement in Somalia was deemed a failure. Although it is estimated that 100,000 people were kept from starving as a result of U.S., and then U.N., intervention, from a policy standpoint, it left the U.S. is some disarray as to when it is appropriate to intervene for humanitarian causes. It was also deemed a failure due to 'mission creep.' The U.S. sent ground forces to Somalia for the sole purpose of assuring that starving people were receiving the food provided by the international community. The U.N., however, hoped that the United States would help establish conditions for a more enduring solution for Somalia. For example, it wanted the U.S.-led coalition to disarm the Somali militias at the outset of its operation."[27] This was far outside of what either Presidents Bush or Clinton intended. By the time the U.S. left Somalia in March of 1994, more than 14 months after Mr. Bush anticipated their departure, this goal had not been accomplished.

Another early challenge for Mr. Clinton concerned the island nation of Haiti.

Despite two generations of Duvalier dictatorships (Francois, known as Papa Doc, and his equally corrupt and incompetent son Jean-Claude, known as Baby Doc), the U.S. never bothered much with that country. Both dictators seemed impervious to any leftist movements, which always caused the U.S. concern, so occasional foreign aid, usually given with a meaningless lecture about freedom and democracy, was about all the attention the U.S. paid to Haiti. In the mid-'90s, Baby Doc, perhaps not a total fool, decided to leave the country, and did so on a plane provided by the Reagan administration. Following a short reign by a military junta, elections were held and a Catholic priest, Jean-Bertrand Aristide, was elected president

---

[27]Clarke and Herbst 1997, p. 175.

in December of 1990. Within a year, he was overthrown.

Prior to Mr. Clinton's election, so-called 'boat people' were fleeing Haiti to Florida, where the Bush administration turned them back, forbidding them from applying for political asylum. Mr. Clinton pledged to accept these refugees until democracy, such as it was, could be restored in Haiti, under President Aristide, whom Mr. Clinton vowed to return to power.

Once in office, Mr. Clinton continued the policy of his predecessor in refusing asylum to Haitian refugees. The new administration did, however, establish an international embargo of trade, along with a freeze of Haitian assets.

At the U.N., the 'Governors Island Accord' was approved, calling for the gradual return of Mr. Aristide to power. This agreement was accepted by the military leader, General Raul Cedras. Parts of the trade embargo were lifted. Yet the assassination of a chief financial officer, and the shooting of the designated justice minister, soon showed that the Haitian military was still in complete control and was only manipulating policies to see the embargo lifted. On October 11 of 1993, just three weeks before Aristide's scheduled return, several U.S. and Canadian engineers, wearing U.N. helmets, were prevented from going ashore. The following day, another U.S. ship was turned away, and Haitians sang and cheered as it departed. For the U.S., this was a major humiliation, and effectively ended the Governors Island Accord.

Mr. Clinton, not wanting a defeat halfway to his next election day, decided to act. "Rather than confront the military regime, Clinton turned to the United Nations. The U.N. Security council passed a resolution ordering a tightening of the embargo and naval blockade of Haiti."[28] U.S. ambassador to the U.N. Madeline Albright said that the U.S. was willing to do whatever was necessary, up to but not including an armed intervention. Yet on September 15, Mr. Clinton told the Haitian military regime that their time was

---

[28]Hyland 1999, p. 61.

up; he was willing to use force to restore Mr. Aristide to power. "Even as he spoke, however, Clinton was preparing to authorize a last-minute maneuver proposed by former president Jimmy Carter, who urged that he be allowed to go to Haiti and talk with Cedras. ... Clinton finally agreed, but insisted that his deadline for the invasion was nonnegotiable. With this leverage, Carter, accompanied by Senator Sam Nunn and General Colin Powell, negotiated an agreement in which Cedras and his entourage agreed to transfer power and leave. American troops landed unopposed, Cedras left, and Aristide returned triumphantly."[29] "Haiti was no longer on the 'A-list' of crises, a White House aide callously remarked at the end of November."[30]

"Arguably, the catalyst for U.S. failure to persevere in Somalia was the death of 18 American soldiers. The failure to persevere in Haiti might be attributed to a government and its institutions being so corrupted and the country's infrastructure so destroyed that both exceeded America's capacity to help. While Somaila and Haiti demonstrate U.S. failure to persevere, U.S. operations in Egypt (the Multinational Force and Observer [MFO] mission), air operations over Iraq, and ongoing NATO collation operations in Bosnia and Kosovo demonstrate perseverance at the extreme."[31]

As the new millennium began, George W. Bush's foreign policy initiatives were not all focused on, and hampered by, the Iraq War (please see Chapter 15), although many of them were. Yet it is suggested that there has been a guiding philosophy of U.S. foreign policy that has been more or less followed by every president since Woodrow Wilson. This philosophy, summarized, is "that to create a peaceful, prosperous, and safe world, the United States would have to commit itself not simply to ad hoc coalitions, but to enduring

---

[29]Ibid., p. 63.
[30]Ibid., p. 62.
[31]Phelps 2004 [May–June].

international organizations and treaties."[32] President Bush didn't seem to see things this way. In his first year as president, he repudiated the following agreements arranged by his predecessor, President Bill Clinton.

1. The Kyoto Protocol (without even consenting to trying to renegotiate its terms);

2. The nuclear test ban treaty;

3. A new protocol to the biological weapons treaty;

4. A pact to control the illicit trade in small arms;

5. The authority of the International Criminal Court.[33]

A look at each of these in detail is instructive.

The Kyoto Protocol

The Kyoto Protocol is an international agreement under the auspices of the United Nations Framework Convention on Climate Change. It set binding obligations on the world's industrialized countries relating to the reduction of greenhouse gases.

As early as 1992, President George H. W. Bush signed an agreement on the subject of global warming, thus indicating the U.S. government's acceptance of it as a legitimate issue and recognizing the U.S.'s role within the international community. "In December 1997, the negotiations, after Vice President [Al] Gore managed to break several stalemates, produced the Kyoto Protocol, intended to control greenhouse gases and thereby forestall catastrophic climatic change."[34]

---

[32]Judis 2006, p. 165.
[33]Ibid., p. 165.
[34]Tiefer 2004, p. 164.

During the 2000 presidential campaign, Candidate Bush vaguely criticized the Kyoto Protocol, but mainly kept silent about it. The public was hearing increasingly troublesome reports from the scientific community, so a too-vocal opposition to Kyoto was not in Mr. Bush's interest. Mr. Bush also had some problems with voters due to his strong anti-environmentalism record as governor of Texas. So throwing a bone to environmentalists, he promised to cap carbon dioxide as a power plant pollutant and said on national television that "global warming needs to be taken very seriously."[35]

The following month, Mr. Bush lost the popular vote, but was soon appointed president through a Supreme Court decision. The following March, in an open letter, he formally declared his opposition to the Kyoto Protocol, despite his recently stated feelings about global warming, saying this: "I do not believe, however, that the government should impose on power plants mandatory emissions reductions for carbon dioxide."[36] This decision produced intense international criticism, which continued almost unabated through Mr. Bush's two terms as president.

It should be noted that Kyoto had long been opposed by conservative Republicans, and Mr. Bush was ever beholden to this group.

The Nuclear Test Ban Treaty

"The Comprehensive Test Ban Treaty was signed by 146 countries in New York City on September 24, 1996, and it culminated nearly 40 years of efforts to ban nuclear testing. This treaty prohibits all nuclear weapons testing and any other nuclear explosions without exception and in every environment."[37] President Clinton was the first world leader to sign the treaty, and it was submitted to the U.S. Senate for approval a year later.

---

[35] Hill 2000 [October 12].
[36] Tiefer 2004, p. 165.
[37] Atkins 2000, p. 97.

The treaty was never ratified by the U.S. Senate; that august body was too busy examining Mr. Clinton's sex life to bother about such things as nuclear weapons. With the Supreme Court appointment of Mr. Bush as president in 2000, any hope of ratification vanished. Mr. Bush was not interested. "The Bush administration apparently does not wish to recognize any international obligation and prefers to act at its own discretion. At the same time, the United States is inclined to demand from others observance of those international rules that the United States itself is not prepared to respect."[38]

Biological Weapons Convention

This agreement, a supplement to the 1925 Geneva Protocol that banned the use of such weapons, but not their possession or production, was several years in the making, and ratified on March 26, 1975, by the United Nations. It was reported in 2005 that the Bush Administration opposed any verification protocol for the Biological Weapons Convention. Earlier, "In 2001 and 2002, the LCNP [Lawyers Committee on Nuclear Policy] and the Institute for Energy and Environment Research produced a report analyzing how the United States is undermining or rejecting treaty regimes on nuclear, chemical and biological weapons, landmines, global warming and international justice."[39]

Illicit Trade in Small Arms Pact

'The United Nations Conference on the Illicit Trade in Small Arms and Light Weapons in All Its Aspects' was a two-week conference held from July 9–20, 2001, in New York. It resulted in the 'Programme of Action to Prevent, Combat and Eradicate the Illicit Trade in Small

---

[38] Gurtov and Van Ness 2005, p. 140.

[39] "The Disarmament Debate: The Fate of the Nuclear Non-Proliferation Treaty" 2005 [Summer].

Arms and Light Weapons in All Its Aspects.' This is commonly referred to as the PoA (Program of Action).

The United Nations Office for Disarmament Affairs (UNODA), on its website, summarizes the problems of small arms, as follows:

> Insurgents, armed gang members, pirates, terrorists – they can all multiply their force through the use of unlawfully acquired firepower. The illicit circulation of small arms, light weapons and their ammunition destabilizes communities, and impacts security and development in all regions of the world.
>
> The illicit trade in small arms, light weapons and ammunition wreaks havoc everywhere. Mobs terrorizing a neighbourhood. Rebels attacking civilians or peacekeepers. Drug lords randomly killing law enforcers or anyone else interfering with their illegal businesses. Bandits hijacking humanitarian aid convoys. In all continents, uncontrolled small arms form a persisting problem.
>
> Small arms are cheap, light, and easy to handle, transport and conceal. A build-up of small arms alone may not create the conflicts in which they are used, but their excessive accumulation and wide availability aggravates the tension. The violence becomes more lethal and lasts longer, and a sense of insecurity grows, which in turn leads to a greater demand for weapons. Most present-day conflicts are fought mainly with small arms, which are broadly used in inter-State conflict. They are the weapons of choice in civil wars and for terrorism, organized crime and gang warfare.[40]

Bush spokesman John Bolton, then Under Secretary of State for Arms Control and International Security, and later U.S. Ambassador to the United Nations, said this when addressing the U.N. on July 9, 2001: "The United States will not join consensus on a final document that contains measures contrary to our constitutional right to keep

---

[40]http://www.un.org/disarmament/convarms/SALW/. Accessed on November 29, 2012.

and bear arms ... "[41] The following day, the Bush Administration announced its formal opposition to the agreement.

The International Criminal Court

The International Criminal Court, established as of July 1, 2002, has the authority to prosecute individuals for genocide, war crimes, and crimes against humanity. One hundred twenty-one nations have signed onto the Statute of the Court, with three notable exceptions: the United States, Israel and Sudan. By the time of the establishment of the court, President Bush had already advised the U.N. Secretary General that the U.S. would accept no obligations arising from the court, nullifying any previous U.S. signatures to the agreement. However, Mr. Bush opposed the International Criminal Court (ICC) with a firestorm of international and domestic activity. "Its campaign against the ICC began in earnest in May 2002, after it repudiated the Clinton Administration's prior signing of the Rome Statute. As noted by the current U.S. Ambassador-at-Large for War Crimes issues, with this gesture the United States 'essentially filed for divorce from the court.' After announcing its intent to leave the ICC, the Bush Administration sought, in the United Nations Security Council and in capitals around the world, to limit the court's jurisdiction, particularly over U.S. nationals. In late 2002, Congress enacted legislation threatening a variety of measures against countries that cooperate with the ICC. Many observers believe that the United States seeks nothing less than the total collapse of the court."[42]

The following quotation seems to summarize Mr. Bush's presidency very well:

> George W. Bush may be the most satirized president since Abraham Lincoln, yet as with Lincoln, the satire rarely seems

---

[41]Robinson 2001 [July 16].
[42]Danner 2003 [May].

to affect its intended victim. It is all too easy to ridicule Bush's shifty eyes and stumbling tongue, while his history of alcoholism and draft avoidance are a satirist's dream. The dim-witted zealots in his cabinet are even more preposterous than he is. Yet Bush strides on unscathed, cutting taxes for the rich, trampling on civil liberties, despoiling the environment, leading us into one foreign misadventure after another, while his approval ratings remain tolerable. In any other democracy the 9/11 disasters and the Iraqi debacle would have swept Bush from office, but in the United States they have become sources of strength. Perhaps he is so outrageous as to be beyond criticism, and certainly beyond satire.[43]

Riding in on a white charger to rescue a nation long tired of the Bush misadventures, President Barack Obama's foreign policy expectations promised the dawning of a new day. Two unwinnable wars, the world was told, would be ended; the decades-old problems between Israel and Palestine would be resolved and the U.S. would extend the hand of friendship to any currently hostile nation that, in the words of Mr. Obama during his inaugural address, would unclench its fist. Perhaps because Mr. Obama needed to focus on the worst economic downturn since the Great Depression, many of the miraculous changes his most ardent supporters expected failed to come to pass.

---

[43]Hornby 2005 [Winter].

Part IV.

Conclusion

Chapter 18.

Summary and Analysis

The United States of America was born of a revolution by the 13 distant colonies of an imperial nation. Great Britain was not interested in allowing the colonies any rights that might have jeopardized its lucrative businesses, or slowed the natural resources North America had aplenty. So believing that God was on their side, they declared their independence and successfully waged war against England, and thus was born a new imperial nation.

The previous chapters in this book have amply demonstrated the fact that the U.S. has sought power, land and riches, and has not hesitated to grab them wherever and whenever the opportunity arose. It was also not averse to creating opportunities for exploitation, when those opportunities didn't spontaneously present themselves. From overthrowing left-leaning, democratically elected governments, such as Guatemala in 1954 or Venezuela in 2002, to misinterpreting information for its own benefit, as in the Gulf of Tonkin non-attack in 1964, to falsifying information, making it up, as in Iraq's non-existent weapons of mass destruction, the United States seeks to protect its empire and financial interests at any cost.

It has been said that the first victim of war is truth. That is probably true, and the second victim may be human rights. The U.S. has clearly demonstrated its lack of concern about both. The Iraq War was waged due to the lies that President George W. Bush, Vice President Dick Cheney, Secretary of State Colin Powel and National

Security Advisor Condoleezza Rice told the U.S., the United Nations and the world about the threat that Iraq posed to the world. Mr. Bush then ordered the bombing of population centers in a nation where more than 50% of the population was under the age of 15. After the fall of the Baghdad government, when the cities of Iraq were in chaos, and universities and museums were being looted, Mr. Bush assured that U.S. and 'coalition' soldiers secured the Oil Ministry and other aspects of the oil industry.

How has the U.S. managed to convince its citizens of a fantasy that the rest of the world has long since rejected? Why do U.S. citizens, despite compelling, even overwhelming, evidence to the contrary, continue to believe the myth of U.S. exceptionalism, the bastard spawn of Manifest Destiny?

The answers to these questions boil down to the U.S. government's skillful acquisition of power over two centuries. For example, the U.S. has a permanent seat on the U.N. Security Council, able to veto any resolutions it doesn't like, for any reason. This is most clearly demonstrated when the U.N. seeks to sanction Israel for its many horrific human rights abuses against the Palestinians. In 2012, when Palestine was officially recognized by the United Nations General Assembly, 138 member nations voted in favor, with only 9 voting against. The U.S. was joined by Canada (much to its disgrace) and Israel, as expected. Also voting against the resolution were the Czech Republic, Panama, the Marshall Islands, Micronesia, Nauru and Palau. This was a resounding diplomatic defeat for the U.S.

Yet the U.S. was not about to take this lying down. As the voting day approached, with passage assured, three U.S. senators proposed severe punitive measures against Palestine, should that country proceed with its request for U.N. recognition. When one recognizes the power of lobbies within U.S. politics, this isn't surprising.

The U.S., in its arrogance, portrays an attitude of being above the law and demanding of the world what it, itself, refuses to give. In September of 2008, five and a half years after the invasion and occupation of Iraq, Vice President Dick Cheney said this: "Recent occurrences in Georgia, beginning with the military invasion by Russia, have been flatly contrary to some of our most deeply held beliefs. Russian forces crossed an internationally recognized border into a sovereign state; fueled and fomented an internal conflict; conducted acts of war without regard for innocent life, killing civilians and causing the displacement of tens of thousands."[1] Mr. Cheney himself was a chief architect of the U.S. invasion of Iraq which was '. . . flatly contrary' to some of the U.S.'s most vocally expressed, if not deeply held, beliefs. The U.S. 'crossed an internationally recognized border into a sovereign state; fueled and fomented an internal conflict; conducted acts of war without regard for innocent life, killing civilians and causing the displacement of tens of thousands.' For some reason, these atrocities were perfectly acceptable when perpetrated by the U.S., but are shocking when perpetrated by any other nation.

As has been shown throughout this book, the U.S. demands that other nations adhere to a lofty standard of human rights. The only exceptions are those for which those human rights may interfere with U.S. strategic, political and/or economic interests. And the U.S. itself need not follow them. Waterboarding, an ancient method of torture forbidden by the Geneva Conventions and other international laws, including laws and treaties signed by the U.S., is acceptable if performed under the direction of the U.S., upon its self-defined enemies. Somehow, it is not torture if the U.S. does it.

The U.S. prides itself as the world's brightest beacon of democracy, although one with a definite capitalistic bias. It proclaims to support the democratic aspirations of all the peoples of the world. However, that isn't necessarily the case if the brand of democracy practiced by those peoples somehow interferes, or may potentially interfere, with U.S. interests.

Chile is a prime example of this. In 1970, Salvador Allende was elected president of that nation in elections largely felt to be fair and

---

[1]http://newsgroups.derkeiler.com/Archive/Alt/alt.gathering.rainbow/2008-09/msg00644.html. Accessed on January 18, 2013.

democratic. Mr. Allende, unfortunately, had the temerity to be a Marxist, which U.S. President Richard Nixon could not countenance. After first trying to influence the Chilean congress not to confirm him as president – it had been a close race – the U.S., through the CIA, caused workers' strikes and funded his opponents. With direct U.S. funding, the conservative Chilean periodical *El Mercurio* continually criticized Mr. Allende. Three years later, Mr. Nixon's campaign succeeded, after plunging Chile into a sustained period of social, political and economic unrest. General August Pinochet overthrew the government. "The experience was particularly tragic because no other Latin American country could equal Chile's experience with constitutional government and with the institutional elements essential to civil society: an accountable executive, a capable bureaucracy, laudatory experience with civil and political rights, the rule of law, and transparency in political decision making."[2] General Pinochet declined to return the government to civilian rule. Upon seizing power, he immediately banned the left-leaning parties that had supported President Allende, and all other parties were eventually banned. 'The National Commission for Truth and Reconciliation Report' in 1991, generally referred to as the Rettig Report, said the following, in reviewing General Pinochet's 17 years in power: "The Rettig Report found that 3,000 Chileans were 'disappeared' or murdered by the security forces during the regime. Beyond that, a report compiled last year (2004) by a special commission documented the torture suffered by more than 27,000 former political prisoners."[3] At least General Pinochet wasn't a Marxist.

The following is a partial list of countries whose governments suffered the displeasure of the U.S. since the start of the Cold War. For each of these nations, the U.S. actively overthrew their government during a military invasion, such as Iraq in 2003, was

---

[2]Johnston 2003, p. 145.

[3]"Chile: Former Intelligence Director provides List of Political Murders after Going Back to Prison" 2005 [June 3].

covertly involved in their overthrow, or is currently attempting their overthrow.

- Syria: 1949

- Iran: 1953

- Guatemala: 1954

- Tibet: 1955

- Indonesia: 1958

- Cuba: 1959

- Democratic Republic of the Congo: 1960–1965

- South Vietnam: 1963

- Brazil: 1964

- Ghana: 1966

- Chile: 1970–1973

- Afghanistan: 1979–1989

- Turkey: 1980

- Poland: 1980–1981

- Nicaragua: 1981–1990

- Cambodia: 1980

- Angola: 1980s

- Philippines: 1986

- Iraq: 1992–1996

- Venezuela: 2002

- Palestinian Authority: 2006–Present

- Somalia: 2006–2007

- Iran: 2005–Present

- Libya: 2011

- Syria: 2012

This is an extensive list, and a comprehensive study of each of these crimes by the U.S. is beyond the scope of this study. However, it is clear that the U.S., the most powerful military nation in the world, has used its power to destabilize entire countries, often causing unspeakable suffering to those nations' citizens.

Meanwhile, as the U.S. spends trillions of dollars on wars and covert operations globally, the U.S. economy teeters on the brink of disaster. The nation's infrastructure is falling apart, and the public school system is turning out millions of students unprepared to compete in the global economy.

As soldiers deploy to do America's dirty work, their families are often left destitute. "It has been reported that families of American soldiers working abroad, mostly in Iraq, have been left in poverty. According to American news channel CBS News, the majority of families are living below the poverty line, living off welfare benefits and charity."[4] One author who studied this situation said this: "To my astonishment, I found that hunger exists among enlisted personnel in every branch of the United States military. I learned that not only do our soldiers stand on our front lines, they and their wives and their children also stand on our food stamp lines and our free bread

---

[4]http://www.todayszaman.com/newsDetail_getNews-
ById.action?load=detay&link=13 176.

lines."[5] So while the U.S. enriches its corporations, those called upon to enable them to do so live in poverty.

The U.S. holds the opinions of other nations in disdain. This ignoring of the opinions of the international community was seen strongly in the buildup to the invasion of Iraq in 2003 and played out in the presidential campaign of 2004, when incumbent President George W. Bush, who lost the popular vote four years earlier, debated the Democratic Party candidate, Massachusetts Senator John Kerry.

> Kerry: But if and when you do it [launch military action against another country], Jim [Lehrer; debate moderator] you have to do it in a way that passes the test, that passes the global test where your countrymen, your people understand fully why you're doing what you're doing and you can prove to the world that you did it for legitimate reasons.
>
> Bush: I'm not exactly sure what you mean, 'passes the global test,' you take preemptive action if you pass a global test.
>
> My attitude is you take preemptive action in order to protect the American people, that you act in order to make this country secure."[6]

President Bush ignored the counsel of many of the U.S.'s strongest allies.

Prior to the War of 1812, the U.S. believed that the British in Canada were in league with Native Americans to destroy the United States. Centuries later, the U.S. believed that Iraq had weapons of mass destruction and intended to use them to destroy the United States. Both rationales were at least a partial justification for each war, and both served to rally the citizenry around the war.

The expansionist philosophy that motivated different administrations to steal land from Native Americans, Mexicans, the Spanish

---

[5]Schwartz-Nobel 2002, p. 29.

[6]http://www.washingtonpost.com/wp-srv/politics/debatereferee/debate_-0930.html. Accessed on November 6, 2012.

and so many others translates today into exceptionalism, the widely held belief that the U.S. is somehow superior to all other nations. This arrogance enables successive U.S. administrations to lumber recklessly across the globe, wreaking havoc as it attempts to order the world to its own liking.

Long before becoming president, Abraham Lincoln recognized that, given the power to wage war, presidents would use it (please see Chapter 3: 'Mexican–American War'). President George W. Bush wasted no time in invading Iraq once Congress provided him with support do to so. While United Nations weapons inspectors were searching the country for evidence of chemical or biological weapons, and gaining free access, Mr. Bush advised them to leave, for their own protection, due to his coming war.

When one considers the war on 'terror', it's helpful to define what the terms means. Noam Chomsky began writing about terror in the 1980s. "So I started to write about it, and I used the official definitions: the ones in the US Code, the army manuals, the British government definition. They're all pretty much the same, but essentially it [terrorism] is the calculated use of violence or threat of violence against civilians for the purpose of intimidation or coercion or changing government policy."[7] Based on this, Mr. Chomsky reaches a logical conclusion: "It immediately follows that the United States is one of the leading terrorist states in the world, if not *the* leading terrorist state."[8]

Why, then, does the U.S. perpetrate terrorism, while at the same time condemning it? Ismael Hossein-zadeh gives a plausible explanation:

> Official reasons such as 'global terrorism' or 'Islamic fundamentalism' for US military interventions abroad can easily be dispensed with as flimsy, hare-brained pretexts for war and militarism. US beneficiaries of war dividends have proven

---

[7] Aksan and Bailes 2013, p. 32.
[8] Ibid., 32. Emphasis in original.

quite resourceful in frequently inventing (or manufacturing, if necessary) new 'external threats to our national interests', or 'the interests of our allies', in order to justify their imperial wars of choice."[9] Further, "This helps explain why since the Second World War powerful beneficiaries of war dividends have almost always reacted negatively to discussions of international cooperation and tension reduction, or détente.[10]

Based on information provided in earlier chapters, Mr. Hosseinzadeh's opinion seems to be strongly supported by two centuries of evidence.

Additional information is provided. At the start of the Cold War, the world, in some regards, could be seen as divided between two contending camps, the United States and the Soviet Union. Latin America was, at least loosely, in the U.S. camp. "Desperate to attract capital investment, domestic elites, many of them committed reformers, offered little resistance to or dissent from the twin goals of the US Cold War foreign policy: to halt the spread of communism and not only advance capitalism but ensure US dominance within that system."[11]

On September 21, 2001, President Bush said this in a major address: "They hate our freedoms: our freedom of religion, our freedom of speech, our freedom to vote and assemble and disagree with each other."[12] This simplistic, myopic view of the U.S.'s role on the world stage has been repeated countless times by other conservative politicians and pundits, in explaining the hostility of other peoples, often Muslims, toward the United States. The terrorism that the U.S. inflicts almost daily on many of the nations of these people is not

---

[9]Ibid., p. 151.

[10]Ibid., p. 151.

[11]Ibid., p. 206.

[12]http://articles.cnn.com/2001-09-20/us/gen.bush.transcript_1_joint-session-national-anthem-citizens/4?_s=PM:US. Accessed on January 23, 2013.

considered. Bombs dropping on their children, economic sanctions that cause unspeakable hardships for the residents of those targeted countries, and continued aid to other nations not nearly as impoverished are not seen as reasons for this hostility.

For over two centuries, human rights and every basic facet of human dignity has been subservient to the almighty U.S. dollar; the facts, going back to even before the nation was established, all support this belief. A fundamental shift is required to change it, but there is no indication that such a shift will occur anytime soon, if ever.

Bibliography

Abadi, Cameron (2007 [Spring]). "'Disappeared' but Not Silenced". In: *Amnesty International.*

Acharya, Upendra D. (2011 [Winter]). "International Lawlessness, International Politics and the Problem of Terrorism: A conundrum of International Law and U.S. Foreign Policy". In: *Denver journal of International Law and Policy.*

Acuña, Rodolfo F. (2010). *Occupied America: A History of Chicanos.* Pearson.

Adams, Jerome R. (1991). *Liberators and Patriots of Latin America: Biographies of 23 Leaders from Dona Marina (1505-1530) to Bishop Romero (1917-1980).* MacFarlane and Company.

Aksan, Cihan and Jon Bailes (2013). *Weapon of the Strong: Conversations on US State Terrorism.* Pluto Press.

Allen, Devere (1972). *The Fight for Peace.* Jerome S. Ozer.

Alteras, Isaac (1993). *Eisenhower and Israel: U.S.-Israeli Relations, 1953-1960.* University Press of Florida.

Aptheker, Herbert (1962). *American Foreign Policy and the Cold War.* U.S. Kraus International.

Art, Robert J. and Patrick M. Cronin, eds. (2003). *The United States and Coercive Diplomacy.* United States Institute of Peace.

Atkins, Stephen E. (2000). *Historical Encyclopedia of Atomic Energy.* Greenwood Press.

Azzi, Pierre (1999 [Spring]). "Harsh Rule: Recognizing the Taliban". In: *Harvard International Review.*

Bagby, Wesley M. (1999). *America's International Relations since World War I.* Oxford University Press.

Barfield, Thomas (2010). *Afghanistan: A Cultural and Political History*. Princeton University Press.

Barkan, Elliot R., ed. (2007). *From Arrival to Incorporation: Migrants to the U.S. in a Global Era*. NYU Press.

Basler, R., ed. (1946). *Abraham Lincoln: His Speeches and Writings*. Cleveland World Publishing.

Batkar, Carol J. (2000). *Reforming Fictions: Native, African, and Jewish American Women's Literature and Journalism in the Progressive Era*. Columbia University Press.

Baum, Matthew A. and Tim J. Groeling (2009). *War Stories: The Causes and Consequences of Public Views of War*. Princeton University Press.

Bautista, Veltisezar (2002). *The Filipino Americans: From 1763 to the Present*. Bookhaus.

Beichman, Arnold (2006 [February–March]). "The Politics of Self-Destruction: Stevenson and McCarthy as Anti-Leaders". In: *Policy Review*.

Benn, Carl (2003). *Essential Histories: the War of 1812*. Routledge Press.

Bennett, W. Lance, Regina G. Lawrence, and Steven Livingston (2008). *When the Press Fails: Political Power and the News Media from Iraq to Katrina*. University of Chicago Press.

Bose, Meena and Rosanna Perotti (2002). *From Cold War to New World Order: The Foreign Policy of George Bush*. Greenwood Press.

Bourke, Joanna (2000). *An Intimate History of Killing: Face-To-Face Killing in Twentieth-Century Warfare*. Basic Books.

Bovier, Virginia M. (2002). *The Globalization of U.S.-Latin American Relations: Democracy, Intervention, and Human Rights*. Praeger.

Boxer, Andrew (2009). "Native Americans and the Federal Government: Andrew Boxer Traces the Origins of an Issue Still Current Today". In: *History Review 64*.

Braeman, John, Robert H. Bremner, and David Brody (1971). *Twentieth Century American Foreign Policy*. Ohio State University.

Brands, H. W. (1997). *The Wages of Globalism: Lyndon Johnson and the Limits of American Power*. Oxford University Press.

Brende, Joel Osler and Erwin Randolph Parson (1985). *Vietnam Veterans: The Road to Recovery*. Plenum.

Brewer, Susan A. (2011). *Why America Fights: Patriotism and War Propaganda from the Philippines to Iraq*. Oxford University Press.

Brzezinski, Zbigniew (1998). *The Grand Chessboard: American Primacy and its Geostrategic Imperatives*. Basic Books.

Busch, Andrew E. (1997 [Summer]). "Ronald Reagan and the Defeat of the Soviet Empire". In: *Presidential Studies Quarterly*.

Cahn, Anne Hessing (2006). *Killing Detente: the Right Attacks the CIA*. Pennsylvania State University Press.

Camil, Sergeant Scott (1972). *The Winter Soldier Investigation: An Inquiry into American War Crimes*. Beacon Press.

Carlston, Julie A. and Elisabeth Weber (2012). *Speaking About Torture*. Fordham University Press.

Carpenter, Ted Galen (1993 [May]). "Foreign Policy Perils: Somalia Set a Dangerous Precedent". In: *USA Today*.

Carter, Dale and Robin Clifton (2002). *War and Cold War in American Foreign Policy, 1942-1962*. Palgrave Macmillan.

Carter, K. Holly Maze (1989). *The Asian Dilemma in U.S. Foreign Policy: National Interest Versus Strategic Planning*. M.E. Sharpe.

Chambers, John Whiteclay, ed. (2000). *The Oxford Companion to American Military History*. Oxford University Press.

Chantilloupe, M. M. (2006). *Iraq: The War that Shouldn't Be - You Decide*. Infinity Publishing.

Chevalier, Tracy (1997). *Encyclopedia of the Essay*. Fitzroy Dearborn.

"Chile: Former Intelligence Director provides List of Political Murders after Going Back to Prison" (2005 [June 3]). In: *NotiSur - South American Political and Economic Affairs*.

Christensen, Carol and Thomas Christensen (1998). *The U.S.-Mexican War*. Bay Books.

Clarke, Walter M. and Jeffrey M. Herbst (1997). *Learning from Somalia: The Lessons of Armed Humanitarian Intervention*. Westview Press.

Coday, Dennis (2003 [February 28]). "U.S. Angers Koreans as Reunification Stalls: 'Axis Evil' Rhetoric, Bush's Pro-War Policies Blamed for Chill in Talks". In: *National Catholic Reporter*.

Cooper, John Milton (1990). *Pivotal Decades: The United States, 1900-1920*. W.W. Norton.

Cordesman, Anthony H. and Abraham R. Wagner (1996). *The Gulf War*. Westview Press.

Cox, Ronald W. and Daniel Skidmore-Hess (1999). *U.S. Politics and the Global Economy: Corporate Power, Conservative Shift*. Lynne Rienner.

"Critical Issues of U.S. Foreign Policy: Iran, Afghanistan, and Pakistan" (2012 [Winter]). In: *The Fletcher Forum of World Affairs*.

Curtis, George Ticknor (2012). *Life of Daniel Webster Vol. 2*. Forgotten Books.

Dalfiume, Richard M. (1969). *Desegregation of the U.S. Armed Forces: Fighting on Two Fronts, 1939-1953*. University of Missouri Press.

Dallek, Robert (1999). *Flawed Giant: Lyndon Johnson and His Times, 1961-1973*. Oxford University Press.

— (2007). *Nixon and Kissinger*. Harper Collins.

Dangerfield, George (2008). *The Era of Good Feelings*. ACLS Humanities E-Book.

Danner, Allison Marston (2003 [May]). "Navigating Law and Politics: The Prosecutor of the International Criminal Court and the Independent Counsel". In: *Stanford Law Review*.

Denbeaux, Mark P. and Jonathan Hafetz, eds. (2009). *The Guantanamo Lawyers: Inside a Prison outside the Law*. New York University Press.

Dohshe, Michael A. (1966). *American Periodicals and the Palestine Triangle, April, 1936 to February, 1947*. Ph.D Diss., Mississippi State University.

Ducat, Craig R. (2009). *Constitutional Interpretation: Powers of Government*. Cengage Learning.

Duffield, John S. and Peter J. Dombrowski (2009). *Balance Sheet: The Iraq War and U.S. National Security*. Stanford Security Studies.

Early, Frances H. (1997). *A World without War: How U.S. Feminists and Pacifists Resisted World War I*. Syracuse University Press.

Everett, Arthur, Kathryn Johnson, and Harry F. Rosenthal (1971). *Calley*. Dell.

Farsoun, Samih K. and Christina E. Zacharia (1997). *Palestine and the Palestinians*. Westview Press.

Feuer, A. B. (1993). *The Santiago Campaign of 1898: A Soldier's View of the Spanish-American War*. Praeger.

Finding, John E. (1987). *Close Neighbors, Distant Friends: United States-Central American Relations*. Greenwood Press.

Fisher, Louis (2010). "When Wars Begin: Misleading Statements by Presidents". In: *Presidential Studies Quarterly 40*. 1.

Foos, Paul (2002). *A Short, Off-Hand, Killing Affair*. University of North Carolina Press.

Francis, Samuel (1993 [January 4]). "Bush's Legacy: A 'Lunatic' Trip into Somalia". In: *Insight on the News*.

Fried, Albert (1996). *McCarthyism: The Great American Red Scare: A Documentary History*. Oxford University Press.

Friedman, Rebecca R. (2011 [June]). "Crisis Management at the Dead Center: The 1960-1962 Presidential Transition and the Bay of Pigs Fiasco". In: *Presidential Studies Quarterly*.

Friedman, Thomas (1991 [September 19]). "A Window on Deep Israel-U.S. Tensions". In: *New York Times*.

— (1993 [January 5]). "Clinton Nominees Disturb Some Jews". In: *New York Times*.

Gaddis, John Lewis (2005). *Strategies of Containment: A Critical Appraisal of Postwar American National Security Policy*. Oxford University Press.

Gambone, Michael D. (2002). *Documents of American Diplomacy: From the American Revolution to the Present*. Greenwood Press.

Garrison, Jean A. (1999). *Games Advisors Plan: Foreign Policy in the Nixon and Carter Administrations*. Texas AM University Press.

Gelphi, Christopher, Peter D. Feaver, and Jason Reifler (2009). *Paying the Human Costs of War: American Public Opinion and Casualties in Military Conflicts*. Princeton University Press.

Genovese, Michael A. (1990). *The Nixon Presidency: Power and Politics in Turbulent Times*. Praeger.

Gibbons (1965 [February 14]). "U.S. Government and Vietnam, III". In: *New York Times*.

Gilderhus, Mark T. (2006 [March]). "The Monroe Doctrine: Meanings and Implications". In: *Presidential Studies Quarterly*.

Greenspan, Alan (2008). *The Age of Turbulence: Adventures in a New World*. Penguin.

Greer, Thomas H. (1999). *What Roosevelt Thought: The Social and Political Ideas of Franklin D. Roosevelt*. Michigan State University Press.

Grigg, William Norman. "Spy Nation: Does the Vast, Immensely Expensive, and Largely Unaccountable Centralized Intelligence System Created by the Bush Administration Really Make Us Safer?" In: *The New American 22*. 15.

Gurtov, Mel and Peter Van Ness (2005). *Confronting the Bush Doctrine: Critical Views from the Asia-Pacific*. Routledge.

Han-Hee, Lee (2009). "North Korea and Shifting Global Balance of Power". In: *SERI Quarterly 2*. 2.

Han, Vo Xuan (1993). *Oil,The Persian Gulf States, and the United States*. Praeger.

Hanhimaki, Jussi (2004). *The Flawed Architect: Henry Kissinger and American Foreign Policy*. Oxford University Press.

Harry S. Truman Presidential Library (HST), Presidential Secretary's File (PSF). "Army Intelligence - Korea". In: *box 262, joint daily sitrep no. 6, 2-3 July 1950*.

Hayden, Tom (2011 [Summer]). "Left, Right, Left, Right; Populism and Foreign Policy". In: *Harvard International Review*.

Hickey, Donald R. (1990). *The War of 1812: A Forgotten Conflict.* University of Illinois Press.

Hill, Patrice (2000 [October 12]). "Second Presidential Debate between Gov. Bush and Vice President Gore". In: *New York Times*.

Hingham, Charles (2007). *Trading with the Enemy: The Nazi-American Money Plot 1933-1949.* iUniverse.

Holmes, Steven A. (1993 [May 2]). "Israeli Concessions Said to Revive Peace Talks". In: *New York Times*.

Hornby, Richard (2005 [Winter]). "War Fever". In: *The Hudson Review 57*. 4.

Horsman, Reginald (1962). *The Causes of the War of 1812.* University of Pennsylvania Press.

Howard, Harry N. (1963). *The King-Crane Commission: an American Inquiry in the Middle East.* Beirut: Khayats.

Howes, Craig (1993). *Voices of the Vietnam POWs: Witnesses to their Fight.* Oxford University Press.

Humphreys, R. A. (1961). *The Diplomatic History of British Honduras.* Oxford University Press.

Hyland, William G. (1987). *Mortal Rivals: Superpower Relations from Nixon to Reagan.* Random House.

— (1999). *Clinton's World: Remaking American Foreign Policy.* Praeger.

Ivins, Molly (2006 [May]). "Emerging Democracies". In: *The Progressive*.

Jaher, Frederic Cople (1974). *Doubters and Dissenters: Cataclysmic Thought in America, 1885-1918.* Free Press of Glencoe.

Jennings, Walter W. (1926). *A History of Economic Progress in the United States.* Thomas Y. Crowell Company.

Jian, Chen (1996). *China's Road to the Korean War: The Making of the Sino-American Confrontation.* Columbia University Press.

Johansen, Bruce Elliott, ed. (1998). *The Encyclopedia of Native American Legal Tradition.* Greenwood Press.

Johnson, Dewey E. and Huy Nguyen (2004 [January]). "The Changing Face of a Constant Issue: Emerging Privacy Issues Post War Privacy Issues". In: *Journal of Applied Management and Entrepreneurship.*

Johnston, Donald H. (2003). *Encyclopedia of International Media and Communications - Vol. 2.* Academic Press.

Jones, Wilbur Devereux (1974). *The American Problem in British Diplomacy, 1841-1861.* University of Georgia Press.

Joshi, Khyati Y. (2006). *New roots in America's Sacred Ground: Religion, Race, and ethnicity in Indian America.* Rutgers University Press.

Joshi, S. T. (1999). *Documents of American Prejudice: An Anthology of Writings on Race from Thomas Jefferson to David Duke.* Basic Books.

Judis, John B. (2006). *The Folly of Empire: What George W. Bush Could Learn from Theodore Roosevelt and Woodrow Wilson.* Oxford University Press.

Kagel, Laura Tate (2007 [Winter]). "Germany's Involvement in Extraordinary Renditions and its Responsibility under International Law". In: *German Politics and Society.*

Keegan, John (2000). *The First World War.* Vintage.

Keenan, Jerry (2001). *Encyclopedia of the Spanish American and Philippine American Wars.* ABC-CLIO.

Kissinger, Henry (2011). *The White House Years.* Simon and Schuster.

Knickerbocker, Brad (2011 [February 18]). "If Obama Opposes Israeli Settlement Activity, Why Did US Veto UN Vote?" In: *The Christian Science Monitor.*

Konkle, Maureen (2004). *Writing Indian Nations Native Intellectuals and the Politics of Historiography, 1827-1863.* University of North Carolina Press.

Kovalio, Jacob (2006 [Spring]). "The Dominion and the Rising Sun". In: *International Journal.*

Kramer, Paul A. (2006). *The Blood of Government: Race, Empire, the United States, and the Philippines.* University of North Carolina Press.

Krasner, Stephen D. (1978). *Defending the National Interest.* Princeton University Press.

LaFeber, Walter (1994). *The American Age: United States Foreign Policy at Home and Abroad.* W.W. Norton.

Lane, Mark (1970). *Conversations with Americans.* Simon and Schuster.

Langholtz, Harvey, Boris Kondoch, and Alan Wells (2005). *International Peacekeeping: The Yearbook of International Peace Operations - Vol. 9.* Martinus Nijhoff.

Lewis, Lloyd B. (1985). *The Tainted War: Culture and Identity in Vietnam War Narratives.* Praeger.

Lilly, J. Robert (2007). *Taken by Force: Rape and American GIs in Europe in World War II.* Palgrave Macmillan.

Livermore, Abiel Abbot (2011). *The War with Mexico Reviewed.* University of Toronto Libraries.

Longley, K. L. (2002). *In The Eagle's Shadow: The United States and Latin America.* Harlan Davidson.

Luzyiminda, Francisco (1973). "The First Vietnam: The US-Philippine War of 1899". In: *Bulletin of Concerned Asian Scholars 5,* p. 15.

MacDonald, Callum (1991 [April/June]). "'So Terrible a Liberation.' The UN Occupation of North Korea". In: *Bulletin of Concerned Asian Scholars.*

Malone, David M. and Yuen Foong Khong (2003). *Unilateralism and U.S. Foreign Policy: International Perspectives.* Lynne Reinner.

Manual, Frank E. (1949). *The Realities of American-Palestine Relations.* Public Affairs Press.

McGlothlen, Ronald L. (1993). *Controlling the Waves: Dean Acheson and U.S. Foreign Policy in Asia.* W.W. Norton.

McMaster, H. R. (1997). *Dereliction of Duty.* Harper Perennial.

Mead, Gary (2000). *The Doughboys: America and the First World War.* Overlook Hardcover.

Menos, Dennis (1962). *Arms Over Diplomacy: Reflections on the Persian Gulf War.* Praeger.

Merrill, Dennis (2006 [March]). "The Truman Doctrine: Containing Communism and Modernity". In: *Presidential Studies Quarterly 36.* 1.

Meyer, Karl E. (2004 [April 12]). "The Perils of Interventionism: It was Once a Matter of Course for Washington to Intervene Forcible to Change Regimes, Collect Debts, Restore Order and Preach Democracy". In: *Newsweek International.*

Morris, Richard B., William Greenleaf, and Robert H. Ferrell (1971). *America: A History of the People. Vol. 2.* Rand McNally and Co.

Neiberg, Michael S. (2006). *The World War I Reader.* NYU Press.

Nixon, Richard M. (1994). *Memoirs of Richard Nixon.* Buccaneer Books.

O'Brien, Kenneth Paul and Lynn Hudson Parsons, eds. (1995). *The Home-Front War: World War II and American Society.* Praeger.

Oplinger, Carls S. and J. Robert Halma (2006). *The Poconos.* Rutgers University Press.

Osborn, Ronald (2012 [March 9]). "Immunity, Impunity the End of War". In: *Commonweal.*

"Our Troops Won't Be Forced out of Iraq, Pledges Straw" (2003). In: *London Daily Mail.*

Oyos, Matthew M. (2000 [June]). "Theodore Roosevelt, Congress, and the Military: U.S. Civil-Military Relations in the Early Twentieth Century". In: *Presidential Studies Quarterly 30.* 2.

Page, Clarence (2007 [January 16]). "Semantics of 'Surge': Administration Has a Strange Way of Honoring Troops". In: *Columbia Daily Tribune.*

Pappe, Ilan (2006). *The Ethnic Cleansing of Palestine.* One World Publications.

Perceny, Mark (1999). *Democracy at the Point of Bayonets*. Pennsylvania State University Press.

Phelps, William G. Jr. (2004 [May–June]). "Training for War While Keeping the Peace". In: *Military Review*.

Pimlott, John, ed. (1982). *Vietnam: The History and the Tactics*. Crescent Books.

"Possible Soviet Attitudes toward Far Eastern Questions" (1943 [October 2]). In: *Records of Harley A. Notter, 1939-45 Box 119, RG59, NAII*.

Prucha, Francis Paul, ed. (1975). *Documents of United States Indian Policy*. University of Nebraska Press.

— (1986). *The Great Father: The United States Government and the American Indians*. University of Nebraska Press.

Quint, Howard H. and Milton Cantor (1975). *Men, Women, and Issues in American History - Vol. 2*. Wadsworth Publishing.

Rabe, Stephen J. (1993). *Eisenhower and Latin America: The Foreign Policy of Anticommunism*. University Press of Florida.

Reimers, David (1999). *Unwelcome Strangers: American Identity and the Turn Against Immigration*. Columbia University Press.

Rezun, Miron (1992). *Saddam Hussein's Gulf Wars: Ambivalent Stakes in the Middle East*. Praeger.

Richardson, Dick, Slyn A. Stone, and Glyn Stone (1994). *Decisions and Diplomacy: Essays in Twentieth Century International History*. W.W. Norton.

Rickover, Hyman George (1976). *How the Battleship Maine was Destroyed*. University of Michigan Library.

Ringnalda, Don (2008). *Fighting and Writing the Vietnam War*. University Press of Mississippi.

Robinson, Matthew (2001 [July 16]). "Bolton Defends 2nd Amendment at UN". In: *Human Events*.

Roosevelt, Nicholas (1926). *The Philippines: A Treasure and a Problem*. J.H. Sears Co.

Rosenbaum, Herbert D. and Alexej Ugrinsky (1993). *Jimmy Carter: Foreign Policy and Post-Presidential Years*. Praeger.

Rosenfeld, Harvey (2000). *Diary of a Dirty Little War: The Spanish-American War of 1898*. Praeger.

Rothschild, Matthew (2005 [April]). "A Servant of Empire". In: *The Progressive*.

Rubenberg, Cheryl A. (1989). *Israel and the American National Interest*. University of Illinois Press.

Russell, Charles Edward (2001). *A-Rafting on the Mississip'*. University of Minnesota Press.

Schirmer, Daniel B. et al. (1999). *The Philippines Reader: A History of Colonialism, Neocolonialism, Dictatorship, and Resistance*. South End Press.

Schmidt, Eric (1991 [September 15]). "U.S. Army Buried Iraqi Soldiers Alive in Gulf War". In: *The New York Times*.

Schonberg, Karl K. (2003). *Pursuing the National Interest: Moments of Transition in Twentieth-Century American Foreign Policy*. Praeger.

Schulzinger, Robert D. (1999). *A Time for War: The United States and Vietnam, 1941-1975*. Oxford University Press.

Schwartz-Nobel, Loretta (2002). *Growing Up Empty: The Hunger Epidemic in America*. Harper.

Shaw, Albert and Woodrow Wilson (1924). *The Messages and Papers of Woodrow Wilson - Vol. 1*. Review of Reviews Corporation.

Shea, Neil (2004 [May 21]). "On the Brink of Failure?" In: *MEED Middle East Economic Digest*.

— (2008 [Winter]). "Ramadi Nights". In: *The Virginia Quarterly Review*.

Silverberg, Robert (1970). *If I Forget Thee, O Jerusalem: American Jews and the State of Israel*. William Morrow.

Simons, Geoff (2004). *Iraq: From Sumer to Saddam*. Palgrave Macmillan.

Sloyan, Patrick J. (1991 [September 12]). "Iraqis Buried Alive - U.S. Attacked with Bulldozers during Gulf War Ground Attack". In: *The Seattle Times*.

Smith, Jeffrey Alan (1999). *War Press Freedom: The Problem of Prerogative Power*. Oxford University Press.

Smith, Neil (2004). *American Empire: Roosevelt's Geographer and the Prelude to Globalization*. University of California Press.

Smith, Peter H. (1996). *Talons of the Eagle: Dynamics of U.S.-Latin American Relations*. Oxford University Press.

Smith, S. Compton (2012). *Chile Con Carne, or The Camp and the Field*. Gale Sabin Americana.

Soderbergh, Peter A. (1994). *Women Marines in the Korean War Era*. Praeger.

Spanier, John and Steven W. Hook (2009). *Twentieth-Century American Foreign Policy*. CQ Press.

Spickard, Paul R. (2007). *Almost All Aliens: Immigration, Race, and Colonialism in American History*. Routledge.

Stanley, William Deane (1996). *The Protection Racket State: Elite Politics, Military Extortion, and Civil War in El Salvador*. Temple University Press.

Stueck, William (2004). *Rethinking the Korean War: A New Diplomatic and Strategic History*. Princeton University Press.

Suleiman, Michael W., ed. (1995). *U.S. Policy on Palestine from Wilson to Clinton*. Association of Arab-American University Graduates.

Tal, David (2003). *War in Palestine, 1948: Strategy and Diplomacy*. Routledge.

Taylor, Alan R. (1991). *The Superpowers and the Middle East*. Syracuse University Press.

Taylor, George Rogers, ed. (1963). *The War of 1812: Past Justifications and Present Interpretations*. D.C. Heath Co.

Thacker-Kumar, Leena and Joel R. Cambpell (2006 [Fall–Winter]). "U.S. Foreign Policy in Asia since 9/11: Temporary Alliances or Permanent Changes?" In: *International Social Science Review*.

Thayer, Bradley A. (2009). *Darwin and International Relations: On the Evolutionary Origins of War and Ethnic Conflict*. University Press of Kentucky.

"The Corporate Conservative Administration Takes Shape" (2001 [January]). In: *Multinational Monitor*.

"The Disarmament Debate: The Fate of the Nuclear Non-Proliferation Treaty" (2005 [Summer]). In: *Harvard International Review 27*. 2.

The Republican National Committee (1884). *Republican campaign text book for Republican Congressional Committee*. Republican National Committee.

Tiefer, Charles (2004). *Veering Right: How the Bush Administration Subverts the Law for Conservative Causes*. University of California Press.

Toolis, Kevin (1996). "The Rules of Successful Rebellion: By Historical Standards, the Palestinians Have Waged an Ineffective Terrorists Campaign, but he Costs to Israel are Still Too High". In: *New Statesman 133*. 4713.

U.S. Government Printing Office (1917). "64th Congress, 1st Session". In: *Congressional Record 54*. 2, p. 1742.

— (1918). "65th Congress, 2nd Session". In: *Congressional Record 56*. 2, pp. 1952–53.

— (1942). "Papers Relating to the Foreign Relations of the United States, 1928". In: *1*, pp. 153–155.

"Unfulfilled Hope: The Joint Board and the Panama Canal, 1903-1919" (2006 [July]). In: *Joint Force Quarterly*. 42.

Valone, Stephen (1995). *Two Centuries of U. S. Foreign Policy: The Documentary Record*. Praeger.

Vasquez, John A. (1986). *Evaluating U.S. Foreign Policy*. Praeger.

Vatter, Harold G. (1996). *The U.S. Economy in World War II*. M.E. Sharpe.

Vernon, Alex (1999). *The Eyes of Orion: Five Tank Lieutenants in the Persian Gulf War*. Kent State University Press.

Vidal, Gore (2002). *Dreaming War: Blood for Oil and the Cheney-Bush Junta*. Thunder's Mouth Press.

Waldrep, Christopher and Michael Bellesiles (2006). *Documenting American Violence: A Sourcebook*. Oxford University Press.

Walworth, Arthur (1986). *Wilson and His Peacemakers: American Diplomacy at the Paris Peace Conference*. W.W. Norton.

Warde, William F. (1949 [January]). "A Suppressed Chapter in History of American Capitalism: The Conquest of the Indians". In: *Fourth International 10*. 1.

"We Turn to the Urgent Duty of Protecting Other Lives" (2002 [September 13]). In: *The Washington Times*.

Welch, Richard E. Jr. (1987). *Response to Imperialism*. University of North Carolina Press.

Werner, Jayne (1985 [June]). "A Short History of the War in Vietnam". In: *Monthly Review 37*.

Westerfield, Donald L. (1996). *War Powers: The President, the Congress and the Question of War*. Praeger.

Wilcox, Francis O. and Thorsten V. Kalijavi (1952). *Recent American Foreign Policy: Basic Documents 1941-1951*. Appleton-Century-Crofts.

Wilson, Sandra (2001). *The Manchurian Crisis and Japanese Society, 1931-33*. Routledge.

"Winds of Change" (1998 [Summer]). In: *Native American Magazine 13*. 3.

Wrobel, David M. (2006 [Fall]). "Exceptionalism and Globalism: Travel Writers and the Nineteenth-Century American West". In: *The Historian*.

Zakaria, Fareed (2006 [September 25]). "Questions for the Interrogators: No other Nation has Sought to Narrow the Geneva Conventions' Scope by 'Clarifying' Them". In: *Newsweek*.

Zinn, Howard (1980). *A People's History of the United States*. Harper Collins.

About the Author

Robert Fantina is an author and activist for peace and international human rights. A U.S. citizen, he moved to Canada following the 2004 presidential election. He has written about military desertion from the United States in his book *Desertion and the American Soldier*, and has also written about the impact that war has on individuals, in his novel, *Look Not Unto the Morrow*, a Vietnam-era, anti-war story. His writing appears regularly on Counterpunch.org, Warisacrime.org, and other sites. Mr. Fantina resides near Toronto, Ontario.

CPSIA information can be obtained at www.ICGtesting.com
Printed in the USA
LVOW04s2124081015

457571LV00012B/164/P